HONEST DOGS

A Story of Triumph and Regret
from the
World's Toughest Sled Dog Race

BY

BRIAN PATRICK O'DONOGHUE

E P I C E N T E R   P R E S S

Epicenter Press, Inc. is a regional press founded in Alaska whose interests include but are not limited to the arts, history, environment, and diverse cultures and lifestyles of the North Pacific and high latitudes. We seek both the traditional and innovative in publishing nonfiction tradebooks, contemporary art and photography giftbooks, and destination travel guides emphasizing Alaska, Washington, Oregon, and California.

Editor: Tricia Brown
Mapmaker: Gail Niebrugge
Proofreader: Sherrill Carlson
Cover/text design, typesetting: Elizabeth Watson

Library of Congress Catalog Card Number: 99 075719

ISBN 0-945397-78-x

Cover photo: Leaving Circle City on the Yukon River. Inset: Martin, a member of Brian O'Donoghue's Yukon Quest team. (Photos by Brian O'Donoghue)

To order single, trade paperback copies of *Honest Dogs*, mail $16.95 (Washington residents add $1.46 sales tax) plus $5 for first-class mailing to: Epicenter Press, Box 82368, Kenmore, WA 98028.

Booksellers: Retail discounts are available from our distributor, Graphic Arts Center Publishing, Box 10306, Portland, OR 97210. Phone 800-452-3032.

Printed in Canada

First printing September 1999

10 9 8 7 6 5 4 3 2 1

PHOTOGRAPHS : Cover and page 1: Martin; Page 3: Gwen sets the pace on a tame section of the Yukon.; Pages 4-5: The Dalton Gang rolls down the Yukon outside Circle.; Page 6: Scrimshaw; Pages 326-327: Shadow dogs join the procession.; Page 332: The Fortymile's deep snow provides a cozy bed for weary travelers.; Page 336: Kahn, being an old dog, knew to save his energy for the trail.

*I've been over Eagle Summit six times,
and I never know if my team is ready for it.
Shoot, there's no way to know until you get there,
and by then it's too late.*

—Veteran Quest musher Tim "The Mowth" Mowry,
on the mountain passage that brings exhaltation,
or crushing defeat.

CONTENTS

AUTHOR'S NOTE

This book is dedicated to Rory Patrick, who entertained us all; Robin James, who was along for the ride and didn't even know it; and the prettiest gal on the trail, my wonderful wife Kate.

I couldn't have attempted the Quest without huge financial and personal support from a legion of friends and family. In particular, I'd like to thank Mark Freshwaters, Dave Arlan, and Eric Troyer for helping put miles on the dogs prior to the race. I am also indebted to sportswriter Chris Talbott for his assistance in recruiting Hobbes and Danger, whose exploits await readers.

This story herein owes much to the many mushers and handlers who generously participated in taped debriefings following the race. I know that reliving the experience brought back a lot of memories, including those that were painful and embarrassing. If something is missed in the retelling, blame it on me.

Every musher enjoys a different vantage. Traveling five minutes behind a driver experiencing the run of his life, on a fast trail graced by a magnificent aurora, comes the musher lost in despair, wondering if his or her nightmarish, injury-plagued trek will ever end. I've made use of literary chicanery to convey that, incorporating thoughts running through the minds of participants as they allegedly occurred.

Obviously, this strays into fiction, for who can truly say they know anyone's mind, including his own? I don't and wouldn't dream of taking such liberties in my day job at the *Fairbanks Daily News-Miner*. In the context of this book, however, asking mushers what they were thinking at a given time, then working those recollections into the story, usually verbatim, provides rare insights into an adventure as wild as the Yukon itself.

—Brian O'Donoghue
Two Rivers, Alaska, 1999

INTRODUCING THE ATHLETES

CINDER

Sturdy, stubborn blackie out of former Iditarod champion Gerald Riley's kennel. Touchy around other males. Generally runs in wheel.

CYCLONE

Strutting little Napoleon from the village of Tanana, where he mastered the art of dodging open eater and bad ice. At seven years old, the team's fastest, reasonably dependable lead dog.

DANGER

Stupendous athlete capable of blistering performance in lead and a three-time Quest finisher for Doc May, who vowed to never use him in another race after his psychotic antics cost his former team a chance to win the previous Quest.

FEETS

Veteran Iditarod team dog from Dave Sawatzky. Long-backed, somewhat skittish. No aptitude for leading, but the hardest puller in any team. Lives for belly rubs.

HOBBES

Raised on former Quest champ John Schandelmeier's trapline, the burly girl made it 700 miles as a pup in his third-place 1997 team. Will lead on occasion, but shies from the slightest surprise. Thick coat makes her rebellious in warm weather.

KHAN

Sixty-eight pounds of howling fury, a tireless born leader trained by Iditarod musher Lynda Plettner. Stupendous sled dog, but undeniably past his prime ... though the Savage One will launch a bloodbath before bowing to younger rivals.

LUTHER

Barely two and a half years old, painfully shy, but impressive in harness, one of several pups on loan from Quest veteran Dave Dalton, who wants them groomed for a more competitive fun with in his 1999 team.

MARTIN

Freshwaters pegged this friendly mournful-eyed Dalton pup as the team's best candidate for a speed leader. But his failure to finish the Two Rivers 200 makes Martin a question mark entering the 1,000-mile Quest.

N.C.

Veteran team dog on loan from Minto villager Lloyd Charlie. Coal black and wide eyed, barrel-chested and brutish, N.C., a seeming Quest natural, was the team's last addition, displacing shy old Beast.

PICARD

Big shouldered, snaggle-tooth fool out of Iditarod musher Ramey Smyth's kennel. His sheer power and energy inspires high hopes, along with fears concerning his snarling provocation of other young males.

RICK

Hard working personable young male from the Smyth kennel, came on strong the final months of training, showing signs of possessing what it

takes to become a rock-solid leader. A past scrap with Khan and his persistent dislike of Picard are Rick's only drawbacks.

SEARCHLIGHT

Sweet, long-legged gal out of Bill MacKee's kennel making her long-distance racing debut. Her mental toughness and stamina are suspect from the start.

SCRIMSHAW

Flyweight 41-pound female out of Doc May's Kennel, slightly over the hill as she pushes eight years old, but a speedster none the less. Though she ran lead a few times in training, she tends to quit eating under pressure, casting doubt on her Quest prospects.

TOPHER

At 78 pounds, one of the largest dogs in the 1998 Quest, tall and ungainly, a happy galoot, but untested and prone to pace instead of pulling.

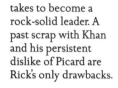

YUKON QUEST INTERNATIONAL

Between Fairbanks, Alaska, and Whitehorse,

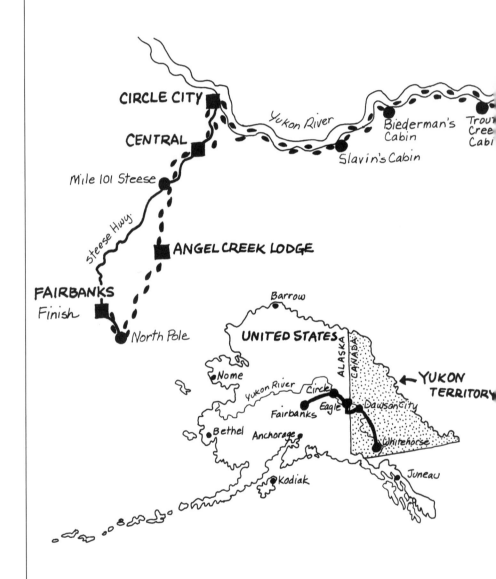

CIRCLE CITY

CENTRAL

Yukon River

Biederman's Cabin

Trou Cree Cabi

Slavin's Cabin

Mile 101 Steese

Steese Hwy.

ANGEL CREEK LODGE

FAIRBANKS

Finish

North Pole

Barrow

UNITED STATES

Nome

Yukon River

Circle

Eagle

Dawson City

Fairbanks

Bethel

Anchorage

Kodiak

ALASKA

CANADA

YUKON TERRITORY

Whitehorse

Juneau

SLED DOG RACE

Yukon Territory

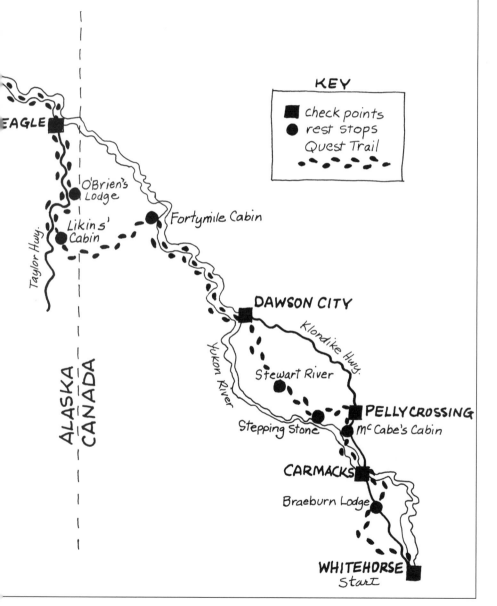

EAGLE

O'Brien's Lodge

Likins' Cabin

Fortymile Cabin

Taylor Hwy.

KEY

■ check points
● rest stops
  Quest Trail

DAWSON CITY

Klondike Hwy.

Stewart River

Yukon River

PELLY CROSSING

Stepping Stone

Mc Cabe's Cabin

ALASKA | CANADA

CARMACKS

Braeburn Lodge

WHITEHORSE
Start

PLAYERS ASSEMBLE

PICARD

The radio in the old F-250 Ford pickup was shot. Not that it mattered. Few broadcasters aimed their signals at the Alaska Highway and those that did were, for the most part, Holy Roller outfits, first and foremost of them being KJNP-FM. A heathen like Bill McKee needed more than the Christian chatter of King Jesus North Pole to hold sleep at bay on his solitary six hundred-mile drive.

McKee found his preferred brand of salvation in the little boom box, powered off his cigarette lighter, blaring bootleg tapes of vintage Grateful Dead shows the Colorado native hadn't heard in years.

Trucking in company with the familiar riffs, McKee tooled down the two-lane rural blacktop in a merry, contemplative state, oblivious to the attempted breakaway in progress.

Back in Fairbanks, the red-and-white 1970 pickup was generally reserved for snowplow duty and short forays into town. Tonight McKee and the old Ford were holding down the caboose position in a short convoy of Alaska pickups bound for Whitehorse, Yukon Territory, and the starting line of the fifteenth annual Yukon Quest International Sled Dog Race.

The first of the two spiffy pickups traveling ahead of McKee was emblazoned with a name well-known across the sled dog racing circuit: Rick Mackey, a past Iditarod winner and defending champ in the thousand-mile Quest. The custom lettering heralding the team aboard the second truck was every bit as bold. Brenda Mackey, nineteen, couldn't match the accomplishments of her dad, or her granddad for that matter, but her turn was coming. Spread between the two vehicles were Patti Mackey, wife to the one musher and mother to the other, Roland, the family's belated toddler, assorted team handlers, including McKee's wife Sandy, and dogs, more than two dozen of the world's finest racing sled dogs.

Each of those furry athletes rested upon straw inside an individual compartment of the tall, double-, sometimes triple-tiered structure, topped by sleds, that distinguishes a lowly pickup from what mushers proudly term a dog truck.

The weathered brown, oft-patched dog box bolted to the rear of McKee's rusty pickup didn't really measure up to the Mackeys' grand fleet. But there was no reason to expect it would. Both Brenda and her dad made their living off the family kennel. McKee was taking off a few days from his work as a Fairbanks schoolteacher to haul the last six dogs from my own team to the starting line.

I'm Brian O'Donoghue, a Fairbanks reporter best known for proposing to fellow reporter Kate Ripley on the floor of the Alaska House. I also hold a record of sorts, being the only musher to lead the Iditarod field out of Anchorage and finish dead last 1,150 miles later. The feat earned me the shiny Red Lantern sitting on our bookshelf at home.

That's right. *Our* bookshelf. Kate said yes to my rather public proposal, though she vows to kill me if I ever put her on the spot like that again.

The McKees reside across the street from Rip O'Roaring Kennel, our three-acre estate in mushing-mad Two Rivers, Alaska. Bill's assistance was more than a neighborly gesture. My Quest team boasted three McKee dogs—Cyclone, Searchlight, and Topher—giving him a rooting interest in getting us off to a good start.

From the driver's seat, McKee occasionally heard, or more accurately, felt some of the dogs stirring within their compartments. Nothing appeared amiss during the convoy's first pit stop in Delta Junction, one hundred and twenty miles down the road. It wasn't until he stepped from the cab at a gas station in Tok, some five hours into the trip, that McKee heard the gnawing.

A dog was in the final stages of consuming his compartment's rickety door. The critter had bored through the heavy chicken wire and was chewing on the plywood front panel, expanding on what already was a ten-inch diameter hole.

The snout withdrew at McKee's approach. Peering into the dark chamber, Bill saw the culprit was a big dog with crazy eyes: one sky blue, the other too dark to attach a color. *Who is that? Eyes are wrong for Topher. Dog's too big for Cyclone.*

A snaggletooth jutted from the dog's lower lip. "Picard," McKee cried, recognizing that trademark. "And what am I supposed to do with you now?"

The schoolteacher knew he was probably imagining it, or to be more accurate, anthropomorphizing, by attributing human emotions to an instinctive, feral, expression, but it sure looked like a grin spreading across Picard's smug mug.

There was nothing to prevent the dog from jumping out. The one free compartment left in the dog truck already sported a hole only slightly smaller than Picard's current project. McKee cursed his own failure to bring more tools.

Opening what was left of the mangled door, McKee unloaded the squirming seventy-pound sled dog and chained him to the side of the truck. Maybe his convoy partners had room.

Patti Mackey pulled out an assortment of spare bolts and screws. McKee took the best parts from two worn compartment doors and fashioned a replacement, boasting a double layer of wire on the inside panel.

"Well, that ought to hold you," he said, casually lifting Picard. McKee was used to his own dogs, even the largest of whom looked forward to riding in the truck. He didn't appreciate how much my snaggle-toothed sled dog abhorred the box. Superbly muscled from more than eleven hundred miles of conditioning, Picard placed his wide paws on the sides of the chamber and quietly but effectively foiled McKee's best effort to thrust him inside.

He summoned Sandy, who pried Picard's paws loose. Pushing together they finally squeezed the big dog back inside his box. McKee raised no objection when Rick Mackey suggested that the group skip its planned overnight stop and push straight through.

"The sooner we get there, the better," said McKee, who figured it was only a matter of time before one of my unruly dogs was running down the side of the road.

Picard, momentarily thwarted, hadn't given up. Not for a second. Inside the cab of the old Ford's cab, the twanging sound of Picard's furious assault on the feeble wire intruded upon Jerry Garcia's guitar work. The combination kept McKee on edge for the remaining four hundred miles to Whitehorse.

I was parked outside the River View Hotel in Whitehorse, tearing apart the dashboard of my Chevy S-10, which had been blowing fuses at an alarming rate.

"I see this is a real Quest truck," announced John Schandelmeier, grinning under his black mustache. The lean fisherman from Paxson told me about his own scare the previous night, when his truck engine appeared to seize following a highway dinner stop. Like most Alaska mushers, we felt triumphant having made it to town for the mandatory pre-race meetings, set to start inside this hotel in a few minutes.

"So how's Hobbes?" Schandelmeier asked, referring to a shy female he'd raised from a pup and taken on last year's Quest. I'd heard that

Hobbes, then just two years old, made it about seven hundred miles before her master, a two-time Quest champion, dropped her on the way to his third-place finish. Afterward, figuring to take off a year or two from racing, Schandelmeier gave her away, along with most of his other dogs.

A friend loaned Hobbes to me early in training season. She quickly became one of my favorites. When Schandelmeier got the old itch and belatedly entered this year's race, I'd worried he might ask for her back. Not wanting to open that door, I never sought his advice about handling her, though I often considered doing so. For Hobbes, my sweet, burly girl, was full of quirks.

"She's one of my main dogs," I said fondly. "I use her in lead a lot, but only when we aren't likely to meet anybody. She'll ball the whole team up if we meet another team, or a snowmachine."

Schandelmeier laughed. "That because where she grew up, we never meet anybody."

Nineteen mushers faced each other across a ring of tables in the hotel's conference room. Most of us were long-time Alaskans. Some were local Yukoners. Others hailed from as far away as Germany and Japan. Our racing experience ranged from first-time entrants in a long-distance sled dog race, like Rusty Hagan, the grinning musher seated on my left, to the savvy dog driver on my right, Dave Olesen, an eight-time Iditarod finisher.

My own qualifications fell somewhere between. I've seen the trail as a reporter covering three Quests, including Schandelmeier's first victory in 1992. Of course, I also landed that booby prize in that Other Race. So while no one would call me a contender, I've been the distance. That counts for a lot, driving dogs.

What brought us together was our status as Quest rookies. Introductions were made. Race Marshal Dave Rich handed the opening pitch to Marina Alpeza, chief veterinarian for the Yukon side of the race. She warned of a disease outbreak in Yukon kennels that hadn't vaccinated for Corona virus.

And that's good news for us, I figured, because my dogs had had their shots for Corona and a half-dozen other common illnesses. *If other drivers were foolish enough to cut corners, so be it.*

The briefing on snow conditions sounded more worrisome. As Rich noted, it was "no secret" that snow was in short supply this year. We faced a trail stripped of its usual thick cushion, a hard trail likely to subject sleds, dogs, and mushers to miles and miles of jarring impacts.

My knees and back were in good shape. My dogs would be pulling a Ray Mackler sled, a Quest-tested, guaranteed unbreakable design. It was the description of the Yukon River that gave me pause: Fields of jumbled ice had developed near virtually every curve in the river's serpentine channel, creating what local residents described as the worst ice conditions seen in twenty years.

"You've got twenty-foot-high chunks of ice," Rich, the race marshal, said. "It's pretty hard to bend a fourteen-dog dog team around some of those things."

Don't worry, we were told, volunteers were using chain saws to open a path through the worst sections of ice.

Chain saws? Now that's a comforting image.

I remembered a similar trail briefing before embarking on the Iditarod. With one big difference: Most of the race to Nome follows a well-traveled—thus hard-packed and fast—network of village trails. The Quest Trail retraces routes blazed by various waves of gold seekers, starting with trickle of prospectors probing the Fortymile River and its tributaries in the 1880s, swelling to the flood of humanity that spilled across the Yukon after the Klondike strike of 1898. At the peak of the rush, boomtowns sprouted overlooking the Yukon River near the mouth of nearly every gold-bearing creek. Most of those settlements faded as quickly as they arose. Today, except for a brief period surrounding the race itself, large sections of the Quest Trail see scant use, magnifying potential natural hazards.

Mel Beshara, a race judge from Dawson, said there was no reason to get discouraged.

"It's rough, but there's starting to be some traffic. There is snow. So I think it's going to be OK."

He thinks so.

Turning to the race rules, the race marshal and the other officials warned against accepting any unauthorized help, particularly from team handlers. Planned assistance, we were reminded, is only allowed in Dawson City. Rich interpreted that rule as prohibiting not just physical help, such as awakening a musher resting at a checkpoint, but any verbal assistance wives, handlers, or friends might be tempted to share.

"If your handler has a propensity for being a pain in the ass," Rich added, "you're going to be penalized."

With his wife's help as translator, Andre Nadeau, a square-jawed newcomer from Quebec, asked if it would be all right to turn dogs loose should necessity arise, say, maneuvering his sled in a tight spot. The question sent officials into a huddle.

"It would be dangerous for him," Race Judge Joe May replied at last.

"We would like to know if he could do it," Nadeau's wife persisted.

Another huddle by the officials. This time the rules were pulled out.

The Frenchman's question struck Amy Wright as proof of the fellow's inexperience.

Wright, a stocky, thirty-seven-year-old woman with a strong face and wavy black hair, shared Nadeau's status as a Quest rookie. But she was no newcomer to sled-dog racing. She was a Wright and thus blood kin to an extended family of sprint circuit and mid-distance champions. She grew up on a dogsled and dreamed of running the Quest long before she ever laid eyes on her husband Peter Butteri, whose recent top five finish certified his emergence as a major contender. This year Peter was driving the family's dog truck, while Amy checked out the trail with their puppy team, seasoning the incoming class for a competitive run pulling Peter's sled.

Turning dogs loose in any race, Amy knew, was a huge risk, because dogs are dogs and might just decide to play around, creating havoc, possibly even subjecting a musher to disqualification if a dog ran off.

My own reaction was similar, and I silently added the Frenchman to the growing list of mushers I expected to beat: Obviously, he didn't know diddly about long-distance sled-dog racing.

Seated around the tables, I counted at least a half-dozen drivers likely to flame out or fall behind my team before the finish line. Some, including Rusty, were too easygoing to grasp what was waiting. Take his approach to training: Rather than run dogs on real trails, Rusty had relied upon on a custom-built carousel for the bulk of his team's mileage.

"Rusty will be easy to see from the air," one of the judges quipped. "His team will be the one running in circles out there."

I figured guys like Rusty were about to taste reality through a body slam from Hulk Hogan. I also put Gwen Holdman in that group. The shy, soft-spoken blonde had great dogs. Her boyfriend Ken proved that much—winning $5,000 with this team in a stage race down in Skagway. More telling, I believed, was Gwen's history of scratching, at least twice that I was aware of, in mid-distance races.

Gwen's recent trouble in the Henry Hahn 200 was damning. She simply hadn't taken seriously a rule requiring teams to depart the turn-around checkpoint by noon. When a race judge had called her attention to the time, ten minutes ahead of the deadline, Gwen continued leisurely packing. She was shocked when that same judge, at two minutes past the hour, informed her that she was disqualified.

Later, when I bumped into Gwen at Grubstake, the feed store where she worked, she was still seething about picky officials. *She just doesn't get it,* I thought, listening to her rant.

As an Iditarod finisher, acceptance of my Quest entry was automatic. I had entered the same two-hundred-miler as a sort of canine qualification trial, narrowing my selections for the Quest team. From that standpoint the race couldn't have worked out better. Rick, running in lead for only the second time in his life, had set the pace for an astonishing hundred and fifty miles. He was the team's rising star. On the down side, young Martin developed a mild limp, and I dropped him sixty miles from the finish line, casting doubt on his Quest fitness.

My team placed eleventh out of twenty-five entrants in the Hahn 200, a decent showing. Best of all, we finished in style, coming from behind to pass John Nash's team in "no man's land," where the musher in front has no obligation to yield to an oncoming team. It took three tries, but Rick and the mighty Khan, my main leader, finally charged past Nash's team.

Nash, a thirty-four-year-old barge fuel manager, was a fellow rookie here today. He and I joked that Quest amounted to a rematch; his name was high on my list.

Glancing around the conference room, there were several other notable rookies whose successes in shorter races might actually hurt them.

Topping that category was Brenda Mackey. I'd heard through the McKees that Brenda was aiming to run with her father, Rick, the Quest's defending champ. Brenda apparently wasn't satisfied with her fourth-place finish in the Hahn. Word had it she continued shopping for better lead dogs until the day she loaded her dog truck for Whitehorse.

Her ambitions were understandable. Both her dad and her grandfather, Dick Mackey, were past Iditarod champions. Brenda, at nineteen, probably knew as much, or more, about sled dogs as anyone in the room today. But those high expectations had to magnify the thousand-mile load.

The cover girl smile captured in Brenda's publicity photos looked weak today. She'd mentioned to me in the lobby that she hadn't been sleeping. The admission tipped the scales, and I mentally added her name to my list.

The race marshal found the answer to the Frenchman's question in Quest Rule No. 19.

"No, he can't do it," Rich concluded. "The rule says dogs must be on the tow line or in the basket at all times."

After about an hour, Quest veterans joined us for the official driver's meeting. Voices seemed to get louder, the laughter more giddy, smiles more strained with the entrance of Brenda's dad and Whitehorse favorite Frank Turner, the 1995 champion. The presence of hungry contenders such as Cor Guimond of Dawson; Brian MacDougall and one-legged William Kleedehn of Whitehorse; as well as Dave Dalton, Keizo Funatsu, and Jerry Louden, whom I knew from Fairbanks, added to the tension. Schandelmeier was the last to arrive and slouched on the wall by the door. The fisherman's casual posture was offset by a wolfish grin.

Captain Sylvan of the Canadian Rangers unfurled a set of maps and briefed us on the trail, this time with considerable more detail. Yukon musher Ned Cathers shared what he knew about the plans of respective cabin owners. Guimond, in a similar spirit, offered his own trail tips and invited us all take a break at his Yukon River cabin, thirty miles north of Dawson.

"So Cor," shouted Tim Mowry, a Fairbanks musher, "promise me you're going to be there when I arrive?"

Guimond, who's known for charging ahead of the field, chuckled heartily, a predator sharing a very good joke with his prey. "*Oh, sure,* Mowry," he said. "I'll be there *waiting* for you."

The leader of the military's trail-breaking party repeated the grim warnings about ice conditions on the Yukon. Other aspects of the trail looked very good compared with years past, Captain Sylvan said, citing a relative lack of overflow and glaciers. The best news concerned the marking of the trail we were to follow.

"No way you guys are going to get confused between 'ere and Carmacks," the French Canadian ranger said. "No way. No way. No way."

Now that mushers were all assembled, the race marshal addressed the race rules with the solemnity of a nun teaching catechism. He took them one at a time, assigning a different musher to read each rule aloud, while the rest of us followed along.

"The rules we're running under are the ones you just read," Rich concluded. "Break them and you're going to be penalized, and it's going to be a monetary penalty too."

The discussion shifted to the "mushers' support program" sponsored by Fulda, a German tire company returning for the second straight year as the Quest's biggest financial backer. Fulda was providing all of us who agreed to participate with custom Arctic parkas and a full set of dog coats. We were also supposed to get fifteen hundred booties to protect our dogs' feet. Orders for those booties had been submitted months earlier, specifying the quantities desired in each of three sizes, cut from either thin cloth or fluffy fleece material.

All sorts of problems had arisen over the Fulda freebies. The parkas were ready only weeks before the race, too late for most of us to test the crucial cold-weather armor under race conditions.

The booty situation was worse. A dispute with the Quest's previous booty supplier caused the Canadian HQ to farm out the job to several smaller outfits. Manufacturing delays, a screw-up over Fulda's logo requirements and customs trouble had combined to prevent delivery of the booties in time for mushers to ship them out with the rest of the teams' supplies waiting at each checkpoint.

Most Canadian drivers had received their booties in the weeks leading up to the race. Alaskans were belatedly required to supply the Quest's Whitehorse office with dozens of marked plastic baggies, indicating what types of booties we wanted shipped exactly where. Local volunteers pitched in to sort the goods, but the job threatened to overwhelm them. Mowry, for one, was accused of never turning in his order. The irate musher prowled the Whitehorse office until he found his own hand-marked baggies crammed in a trash can.

Dog booties are essential in a long-distance sled-dog race. With booties worth between 65 cents and $1.20 apiece, roughly half of this year's Quest drivers, myself included, were relying upon the Fulda freebies. We were all nervous about the Quest's assurances that we'd find what we needed waiting at the checkpoints. When Race Marshal Rich declared that it wasn't his problem, his control over the meeting began crumbling.

Questions and charges flew. What about the signed contracts? Why couldn't our handlers deliver the booties? Why did Canadians get special treatment? What kind of scam were Yukoners pulling?

Schandelmeier bucked the tide.

"Take four hundred booties with you from here and take four hundred more from Dawson," he said. "It's your responsibility."

Mowry, who took out a bank loan to finance his seventh bid for a piece of the Quest's $125,000 purse, wouldn't let up.

"When I get to a checkpoint and I don't have booties, you guys better believe you're going to hear about it—from a legal standpoint."

"Tim," Rich snapped, "that's enough. You'll get your booties."

My old kennel partner, a Fairbanks outdoors reporter known for good reason as "The Mowth," continued to harp on the booties until Rich exploded.

"Mowry," he said, "one more word and you're fined right now."

Gwen found the tone of the exchange shocking: *These guys are taking this race a lot more seriously than I am.*

Rich and the other race officials went on at length about general tactics for dealing with the media, especially the blundering European television crews. Everything possible was being done to limit access, they said. Rules had been prepared for reporters and cameramen. Any problems were to be reported.

Larry Carroll, a Willow musher returning for his second Quest, tossed out a last bit of advice for camera-shy colleagues. "Those who don't like the media should stay with the middle of the pack because *I didn't see anybody*," said Carroll, who had placed a respectable twelfth. "There wasn't a soul watching when *I* went over Eagle Summit."

Laughter filled the room.

Jim Hendrick, a manic veteran from Denali Park, leaped up to warn newcomers about camping anywhere near Mackey's dogs, or Schandelmeier's, any of the big name teams. "When you park next to celebrities, nobody gives a damn about you," Hendrick whined. "People will step all over your dogs."

Rich put us on notice that Whitehorse officials planned to boot unauthorized visitors from the fenced staging area an hour before Sunday's 1:00 P.M. start. "You get three arm tags," he noted, holding one up. "Make sure your handlers each have one."

His declaration drew more protest. Turner, a Yukon musher whose local popularity was apparent from the huge mug painted in the front window of a supermarket near my host family's house, spluttered that three armbands wouldn't begin to cover his numerous sponsors and starting-chute handlers.

He wasn't alone. Most of us from Alaska had a dozen or more friends and family whom we considered entitled, if not vital, to assist in our final preparations.

Hendrick's complaint proved uniquely compelling.

"My psychologist must come!"

Rich's stern expression softened. The race marshal promised wailing Jimmy he'd make special allowance for that undeniable need.

❖ ❖ ❖

The banquet was a sell-out. Fulda was responsible. At least that was the excuse I got at the Quest's Whitehorse office. Hundreds of Fulda dealers and members of the European media were expected as part of the company's promotion of its new Yukon Quest tire. To entertain those guests, I was told, the "bloody Germans" had bought out all available banquet tickets months in advance.

Kate's parents, two sisters, and a brother-in-law were flying in from Southeast Alaska for the pre-race festivities, first and foremost of those being the mushers' draw for starting positions. My wife anticipated filling a whole table with our guests.

And I was staring at a measly pair of tickets.

My team handler, Mark Freshwaters, was with me when I learned of the banquet-seating snafu. I had to take care of other errands in town. I asked Freshwaters to pass the news to Kate.

"Oh no," he said, enjoying the situation as a committed bachelor would. "I think I'll let *you* do that."

The banquet was held at the Mount McIntyre Recreation Centre. Domestic harmony was preserved when our friends in Whitehorse, Gene and Andrea, smuggled Kate's relatives into the hall bar through the adjacent curling rink.

Kate had envisioned taking pictures while I let Rory, our twenty-one-month-old son, draw the team's starting number from the hat. But she was off chasing our antsy toddler when the speeches from race sponsors abruptly ended and I was summoned to launch the main event.

The hat was thrust at me. I drew chute position No. 10, an unpressured spot in the front of the thirty-eight-team field. I was addressing the crowd, vowing to beat somebody, anybody across the finish line, when Kate finally delivered our squirming son to the podium. I held Rory up, intending to explain his inspirational role, my hope that he might someday appreciate that his dad once dared chase dreams.

Rory briefly marveled at the faces turned his way—then kicked and squirmed for freedom like a snagged twenty-five-pound coho salmon.

Plopping him down, I launched into a story about N.C., the last addition to my Quest team.

I had picked up the big black husky on trial from Lloyd Charlie, an Athabascan musher from Minto. The seasoned eight-year-old sled dog had come on strong during the last weeks of training, prompting several conversations with Lloyd concerning the price tag attached to using N.C. in the Quest.

"You just say something nice about me at the banquet, Brian. That's all. Can you do that?"

He had my promise.

Then Lloyd heard about the Fulda freebies and asked for "couple of those fancy dog coats" when I was done from the race. Again, I was glad to accommodate him.

On the eve of my departure from Fairbanks, Lloyd called back once more time. If N.C. should happen to *save my life*, he said, how about I promise him that "fancy new parka." He was referring to the custom-tailored Apocalypse Design coats Fulda had commissioned for each musher. That coat was worth $600.

"Nice try, Lloyd," I said. "Forget it."

At the banquet, I raised the stakes. "If N.C. helps me *win* the Quest—you guys are witnesses here—Lloyd gets the new parka."

Returning to my table, I found Kate steaming. Rory was in my arms so briefly she hadn't snapped any pictures at all. And my wife was cruelly disappointed that our charming son had missed the chance to draw Rip O'Roaring Kennel's starting number. Why hadn't I stalled? What was I thinking about rushing through the long-anticipated moment?

"To tell the truth, I wasn't thinking about anything," I said. "It all happened pretty fast."

Kate couldn't understand that. *How can anyone be so dense?*

The only certainty was nothing had gone the way my wife wanted. She realized unpleasantly, and not for the first time, that her boys, like her dogs, had minds of their own.

The hour was late when Tim "The Mowth" Mowry claimed the last slip of paper in the hat. The last musher to enter the 1998 Quest had chanced into a coup, drawing the No. 1 starting position.

NO STOPPING ZONE

MARTIN

Rusty Hagan had heard stories about mushers starting a major race with untested gear, but he never did understand it. Testing was so basic. Take the cooker used to melt snow for dog food. Hagan, a forty-six-year-old home-shop machinist and inventor, wasn't satisfied with conventional designs. He built his own, tinkering with air vents and pot suspension until he had a ring of flaming jets, hot as a welder's torch, licking the bottom of his water pan.

Most of Rusty's equipment featured similar personal refinements. The one exception was his Quest sled.

Rick Armstrong, a local sled maker, had approached Rusty with an offer to trade two of his own lightweight tubular models for one of the inventor's used training carousels. The trade appealed to Rusty on several levels. The particular carousel was an eight-dog model, a prototype for the units Rusty recently sold to Susan Butcher and Jeff King. He had been thinking about expanding on it, building a double-ringed sixteen-dog model. Parting with the old one would free up the necessary space.

Having someone else take charge of the sled also meant that Rusty could concentrate on putting more miles on his team, which was good because even he acknowledged that running circles in the dog yard was no substitute for bona fide trail miles.

The first of the year came and Armstrong's sleds weren't ready. Rusty paid the sled maker a visit in mid-January. Armstrong had a sled nearly finished, but that one was reserved for Tony Blanford, another Quest rookie. Rusty's was still in the works. "You'll have it when you need it," Armstrong said.

The evening before he was leaving for Whitehorse, Rusty's dog truck sat in the driveway fully packed except for the dogs, and the slot reserved for his Quest sled. Rusty turned in for the night, brimming with self-recrimination. *How did I let this happen?*

When he got up at 6:00 A.M., Hagan found a new sled in his front yard. That surprised him because he had slept poorly, yet hadn't heard a thing. Well, he had the sled. That's what mattered.

"Maybe we can test it in Whitehorse," he said, strapping the sled to the roof of his dog truck.

Defending champ Rick Mackey and a lot of mushers, including myself, squeezed in one last short run on the sprint track outside Whitehorse. Rusty wanted to get out there, but he kept finding more and more left to do.

On the morning of the start, while his dogs howled and pawed the snow freshly spread on the streets near Whitehorse's old train station, the musher was wishing his sled showed a few scrapes and other signs of wear. Rusty Hagan, a mature man of modest build, whose tired eyes, weathered face, and dirty hands conveyed a willingness to tackle the next job, whatever it might be, stood in the street staring at Armstrong's shiny bundle of tubes and cables. *How is this thing going to hold up over a thousand miles, hard miles, Quest miles?* That question led to another mental howl: *How on earth did I ever let this happen?*

Khan was my best leader. Hands down. But the Savage One was also eight years old, meaning he was past his prime, and a tad slow for the starting-line command. He might hurt himself laboring to stay ahead of his younger, swifter teammates, stirred into a frenzy by the sensory bombardment of thirty-seven other howling dog teams, strange city smells, and the crowds massed along the barricades.

I figured to save Khan for the second or third day on the trail, when a steady workhorse might just power ahead of the homesick youngsters leading the competition.

My fastest *reasonably* dependable leader was Cyclone, the little leader I'd leased from McKee for three hundred dollars. Cyke's presence at the head of the team leaving Whitehorse was a given. The question was whom could I pair with him?

Danger, a loaner from team veterinarian Mark May, was my speed demon. But his past antics were legendary. In one race back home, Danger hauled a full dog team right through the front door of Valley Center store.

"I wouldn't trust that dog anyplace but wheel," May warned.

Mere miles from the finish line in the 1997 Quest, Mark May had been in first place, driving what most folks agreed was the fastest dog team in the race. Danger chose that moment to initiate a series of crazy turns and mutinous strikes. Doc finished a discouraging fourth.

"Danger has *everything* it takes physically to be a champion-caliber lead dog. *Everything.* But his head isn't there," the vet said glumly. "It's a mental thing."

This year Doc was training for the Iditarod, the race his father Joe won in 1981. He couldn't bear the thought of watching Danger explode another race. Hence came the offer to use the dog at my own peril.

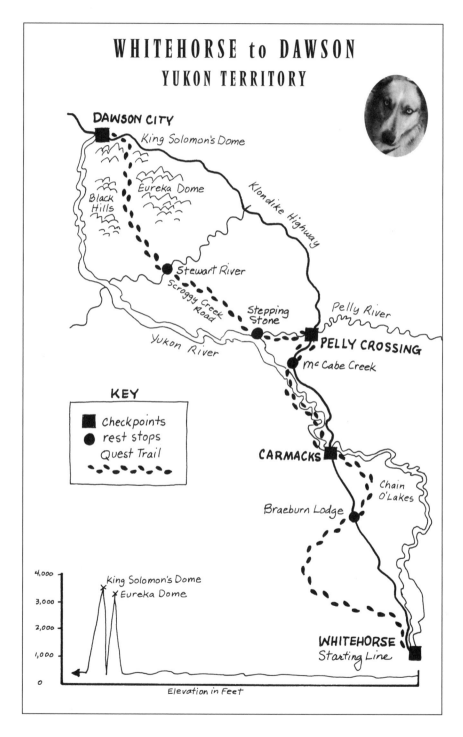

WHITEHORSE to DAWSON
YUKON TERRITORY

DAWSON CITY

King Solomon's Dome

Eureka Dome

Black Hills

Klondike Highway

Stewart River

Scroggy Creek Road

Stepping Stone

Pelly River

PELLY CROSSING

Yukon River

Mc Cabe Creek

KEY

■ Checkpoints
● rest stops
Quest Trail

CARMACKS

Chain O'Lakes

Braeburn Lodge

4,000

King Solomon's Dome
Eureka Dome

3,000

2,000

1,000

0

Elevation in Feet

WHITEHORSE
Starting Line

I caught occasional glimpses of Danger's mania during training. Paired with Cyclone on the second leg of the Two Rivers 200, he set a blistering pace for thirty-five miles and then, before I could hardly react, sat down, took a roll in the snow, and shot off into the woods.

In the mid-1980s, my handler Freshwaters made a name for himself as a racer, finishing Iditarod in the money his only two tries. He knew sled dogs from the perspective of a man who bet his life on their performance, observing their individual quirks over more than a decade of checking and setting traps, and clearing his own trails outside the Yukon River village of Ruby.

Health problems and the falling price of fur flushed the lanky Bush Rat out of the woods some years ago. He now alternated between jobs through the Laborers' Hall and hunting guide assignments, a lifestyle incompatible with keeping a team. But no change of address could diminish Mark Freshwaters' intuitive feel for sled dogs.

From the first day he lent a hand with the team, Freshwaters liked what he saw in Danger. Hearing about the dog's instability, he felt sure I was exaggerating. He changed his tune after an easy chase in the White Mountains.

"He wasn't tired or anything, but he dived off the trail and absolutely quit on me," Freshwaters said, sounding incredulous. "Never seen a dog do that before."

He agreed that Danger wasn't to be trusted leading out of Whitehorse. Which left whom? *Rick?* He was slower than I wanted for the start. *Searchlight?* She was too shy. *Hobbes?* It was a battle just passing a snowmachine with my spooky girl up front. Hobbes leading through city streets lined with screaming crowds? Not in this life.

I had trained Martin for a swing slot, running just behind the leaders. Freshwaters sensed greater potential and began running him in solo lead. "Martin might just be your speed," he said.

Endorsement notwithstanding, Freshwaters looked worried when I mentioned using Martin in lead leaving Whitehorse. "You think so, huh? Well, I guess it's your decision."

On the appointed day we arrived downtown early. Rusty Hagan was the only other musher on the street when I parked my dog truck in the curbside space reserved for team No. 10. I walked over and wished Rusty luck. He wore his usual smile, but weariness showed in his eyes. He confessed that he hadn't slept more than ninety minutes in days. "It gets easier from here," I told him, not letting on that I had deposited eight hours in the sleep bank two nights running. I knew where Rusty was coming from.

Seven long years separated me from the insane morning I mushed the first team out of the chute in the 1991 Iditarod, feeling more wired, more tired, and at least as worried as I've ever been. I felt older entering Nome, scabbed from the wind but triumphant.

Then came marriage. Watching Kate contend with the marathon demands of pregnancy put my casual trek in perspective. Holding her hand that last long night, as she tried so hard for hour upon hour. Seeing the nurses scramble when the fetal monitor squealed and blood appeared in the telltale tube. Stroking my wife's wan face, while machines clicked and, on the other side of the blue curtain, doctors opened her up and reached inside. Accepting the purplish-gray stranger in my arms. Beholding his transformation into our perfect pink son. "Oh, Rory," Kate woozily crooned, ripping free of the surgical restraints.

That was momentous, heralding responsibilities beyond reckoning and satisfactions beyond imagination. *This is just another dog race.*

We unloaded the sled first, followed by harnesses, feed pans, the cooler, and the cooker. We still had nearly three hours to go, so I left the dogs in the truck, resting.

Officials came by several times checking my required gear, briefing me on the starting chute arrangements and other aspects of the ongoing countdown. My picture was taken wearing two different bibs, each bearing the name of a different race sponsor. "What's that, a Canadian firm?" I asked, as officials handed me a bib sporting the name "EELMAN."

"Oh no," the woman said. "I believe that's *your* Bob Eley? Doesn't he work at your newspaper?"

"Of course!" I said, embarrassed. Eley, the *News-Miner*'s sports editor and president of the Alaska Quest organization, had sponsored team No. 10. The luck of the draw had the Eel Man literally riding with us; I couldn't beat that for a positive omen.

McKee showed up with his video camera to document the moment. "You're not going to use Topher in lead?" he joked, referring to his goofy seventy-eight-pound monster pup.

"Topher's definitely not in lead for the start," I said. "He may make it up there by the end *if* I don't shoot him first."

Bill laughed.

It was about ten degrees. Wind gusted through the downtown streets. Under his rabbit-fur hat, Rory's cheeks glowed like shiny red apples. Kate knew she and the little man ought to seek refuge at the Dairy Queen across the road, but she hesitated.

"I wish I could stay," she said.

"It's all right," I said. "Everything is under control. Really, I'm OK."

A red-jacketed Mountie launched the fifteenth Quest. He paraded past the crowds powered by a team of bearish, thick-furred Inuit dogs, a majestic breed evocative of Jack London's Yukon, but little better than waddlers against to the mongrel-blooded Alaskan huskies ruling today's racing circuit.

The Mowth's golden moment came next as the first team to leave the chute. In a departure from his six previous Quest runs, this year my old kennel partner concentrated on speed over power. His dogs averaged a mere forty-one pounds apiece, making Mowry's team the lightest and slightest entered from the Fairbanks area. Led by old Alf and young Figaro, Mowry's team rocketed after the Mountie's burly prancers.

The Iditarod opens with a meandering dash through the streets of Alaska's largest city. The start of the Quest alternates direction year to year, but whether racers are leaving Fairbanks or Whitehorse, it's a quick escape onto rivers and into the wilderness.

The Mountie's ceremonial march stretched a few short blocks. Approaching the curve leading down toward the river, he ordered his dogs from the trail, threading between highway safety cones and onto a side street.

Mowry, relaxing as the crowd thinned nearing the river, was caught off guard when Alf and Figaro dodged left through a gap in the cones, chasing after the Inuit dogs. By the time he regained control, Mowry's dogs were clawing and barking at the prospect of catching the panting fur balls in the process of being loaded into the truck up ahead.

The Mowth, still in possession of first place on the Yukon Quest Trail, hastily dragged Alf and Figaro back through the cones and pointed them at the pair of snow berms erected to guide Quest teams through the curve. Resuming their manic charge, Alf and Figaro entered the berm at a bad angle. Mowry's sled clipped the leading edge of the wall and flipped. He clung on, belly surfing down the short ramp feeding onto the river, where a lone spectator dashed forward and helped the Quest's embarrassed frontrunner right his sled.

"I'd stay right here," Mowry shouted, pulling away, "you should see some fun."

My thirty-second countdown was underway. A half-dozen, beefy volunteers gripped my sled under the Quest's starting line banner. Most were leaning backward, using boot heels and balance to counter the pressure of fourteen dogs leaping and straining to go.

Entrusting my sled to the chute crew, I ran up the line, petting dogs, then hurriedly sought Kate. She was standing a few steps to the side, looking a bit lost as she bounced on her heels, rocking Rory in the backpack. I kissed him, hugged her, then jumped aboard the runners.

Noise faded. I sensed rather than heard or saw the surrounding crowd. My vision narrowed to Cyclone, Martin, and Freshwaters, all of whom were waiting for a cue fifty-six feet in front of the sled. I gestured at the handler. He nodded and slowly backed away.

Moving in what seemed like slow motion, I squeezed the handlebar with my left hand, crouched and cupped my free fingers under the bar welded between the snow hook's double prongs. The Quest's old time-keeper became a towering presence as he slowly raised the checkered flag.

His arm dropped, bringing a slicing return to real time. Cheers thundered. I yanked the hook free. "All right. All right!" I shouted need-lessly. My dogs were already digging forward, showering the sled in loose snow.

The Yukon Quest Trail lay dead ahead, a narrow white path between parallel fences topped by a mass of faces, hats and parkas, waving arms, and flashing cameras. I briefly looked for someone I knew. Didn't see a soul.

My attention shifted to Martin, a shy dog thrust into unaccustomed command on this the wildest day of his young life. He kept looking over his shoulder at me. "Good dog, Martin. Good boy," I called out, striving to convey confidence I didn't feel. *Man oh man, this is probably a big, big mistake.*

A step or two out of the chute, Martin appeared to stumble. I braced for a pile-up, but he was merely flinching at the first blast from the crowd and kept going. "Good boy, Martin. Good boy!"

Within a block, young Martin's talent and drive prevailed. He appeared to be nosing ahead of his partner, particularly whenever the picket fence narrowed, causing Cyclone, the supposed veteran, to fall a step behind. It wasn't something many spectators would notice because I compensated, tapping on the drag to keep the team stretched out.

The dogs made it through the zigzag drop to the river unscathed. But I hit the berm and launched airborne, glancing off the far wall of the chute before finally landing upright on the river. More disturbing than the near crash was the realization accompanying it: *This sled is so goddamn heavy, I can't steer worth a damn.*

With the city behind us, Cyclone reverted to his usual strutting form. A team took shape in the distance. My leaders joyfully pursued.

As the team settled into a calm trot, I took stock. A handful of dogs had thrown off an odd booty or two leaving town, but none of them had problem feet. I glanced at my watch. "Fifteen minutes, max," I said, "then I'll stop."

No more than five minutes later, Picard kicked off his first booty. I winced, because his big feet were always on the mend. Less than a mile later ol' Snaggletooth threw another. This one came flying at me and I snatched it out of the air. The booty felt unusually dense and heavy; it was filled with snow. *I don't like that!*

"Whoa," I cried, jamming my weight on the sled's twin-bladed brake. Cyclone happily obliged, dragging Martin aside to contentedly chew on the fresh powder coating the river. I didn't mind. The shallow crust overlaying the ice offered little for my snow hook to grab. I needed the leaders' cooperation if I was going to replace booties.

Holding a wad of the Fulda freebies in my teeth, I straddled Picard and set to redress his huge, naked paws. I had him taken care of when I saw a team closing fast. There was plenty of room to pass, so I didn't particularly worry. But Cyclone's thirst was quenched. He and several other dogs began barking as the other team passed us. The hook's fragile purchase crumbled and my team gave chase. I stepped aboard my sled as it passed, then caught the bouncing snow hook before any of us was speared.

Continuing along the river, I probed the snow cover with the brake, testing for spot better suited to anchoring the team for the ten minutes or so I needed to finish replacing booties. The blade's screech announced ice and nothing but ice. *This is going to be tricky.*

I was about halfway done dressing paws when Denali Park musher Bruce Lee flashed by. This time I anticipated Cyclone's move and grabbed the gang line. I succeeded in restraining the leaders, but Danger, Topher, and other members of the team's rear guard popped the hook anyway.

I rushed to reset the hook. Another team passed. The hook again popped loose, allowing a cluster of dogs to gather in middle ranks of my team. They were milling about, sniffing each other.

"Easy, easy now," I said sternly, spying Khan nose to nose with Feets.

Old Harley was my canine ideal. After he and Rainy led me into Nome in 1991, Mowry had taken the big dog from Minto on three Quests, finishing with him twice. I took him back after his racing days were over, and Kate learned to mush with Harley, the steady trucker, in front. I often warned her she was getting a false impression; lead dogs are more often erratic, eggshell-spirited companions, reducing a musher to curses or tears on a regular basis.

We often talked about breeding Harley. But raising sled-dog puppies is a demanding task, and Kate and I kept putting it off. Age caught up before Harley got his shot at fatherhood. He was a trembling wreck, far too stiff to consummate anything with the nimble gal we hoped to breed. As a fellow male, I found his mating-game rout depressing.

So I recruited my Quest team, applying a simple criteria to select the candidates: I wanted dogs possessing Harley's work ethic. The sort that pull as surely as they breath, with each step offering all they have, offering too much if a musher recklessly allows it.

Give me fourteen honest dogs, the term mushers give such fine companions, and I figured the Quest would take care of itself.

With that theory in mind, I brought home Goliath. As his owner promised, the big male pulled like an ox. But three days of non-stop barking brought an ultimatum from Kate. "I don't care how well he pulls. I hate that dog and I want him out of here."

By late September I had a core group of somewhat quieter dogs assembled. One blustery Sunday found me unhooking dogs from the Honda four-wheeler after a beautifully uneventful training run. The Mowth could turn most of his dogs loose and trust them to run to their houses. Among my Quest candidates, only Beast and Searchlight, two sweet-natured females that Kate and I had owned prior to the season, were to be trusted with anything. The snarling collection of new recruits demanded strict supervision. Thus I was working from the rear of the gang line forward, returning dogs to their posts one at a time.

Beast was hunched down, head buried in her front paws, as she tried to ignore her larger and louder partner in lead, Khan. He was whining and jerking sideways at their shared neckline, acting as if we were just hooking up rather than finishing a run, living up to his billing as a hard-charging veteran Iditarod leader well worth his five-hundred-dollar lease. I'd called on Lynda Plettner, one of the mushers I chased to Nome, saying I didn't care about speed. What I lacked was a mentally tough leader that I could count on to haul tired comrades out of checkpoints.

Plettner led me through her sprawling dog lot to a sixty-eight-pound male boldly astride his doghouse. He was bigheaded like a Siberian, mostly black-furred, with sky-blue eyes gleaming through the dark mask framing his long white snout. He puffed his chest at

Plettner's approach and spread his pearly teeth wickedly. "Khan isn't fast enough for my A-team anymore, but he's the dog you want."

The restless, pointy-eared barbarian knew commands, providing control that made for smooth training runs with the younger dogs, that September day being no exception. I had put away the wheel dogs. Feets, a skittish five-year-old, was next.

Feets was a gift from Dave Sawatzky, a top-echelon Quest and Iditarod driver. The dog was such a hard worker that I always watched for signs he was overheating on our training runs during those warm days of early fall.

His back was unusually long and his legs seemed short. Walking him, even for a short distance, was difficult because Feets dodged all contact with his kennel mates. I was bent over, feeling my wrist on the verge of spraining from his crab-like evasions, when Feets and I passed Khan.

The leader lunged.

Feets yelped and tumbled backwards, spitting blood. Khan, the assassination complete, strode about at the front of the team, hackles raised as if inviting another challenge.

Feets lay quivering in the dirt. Blood streamed from his mouth, where I saw his tongue was newly forked like some devil-dog cartoon. Worse than the wound was the pattern it confirmed.

Three weeks earlier Khan had wrapped up a training run with a sideways dash to bite old Harley, who'd been relaxing atop a doghouse overlooking the kennel's outbound trail. Thirty-three stitches later, I told myself it was a freak thing: Harley must have made some gesture Khan mistook as a threat.

The second incident involved Rick, a four-year-old, seventy-pound male. I had Rick by the collar and was returning him to his post when Khan sunk his teeth in the younger dog's ass. Lashing out, Rick bit me across the palm. The pair turned on each other and I feared a bloodbath, but Rick yelped and fled into the woods.

He was whimpering when I caught up, and I cradled him like a scared child. That's when I realized how much my hand hurt. It was on fire.

"Are you all right?" shouted Kate, overhearing the commotion while tending plants on our back deck.

"No, no," I wailed, shaking my throbbing hand. "I just got bit. I JUST GOT BIT!"

In all three incidents, Khan escaped punishment amid the turmoil. That weighed on my mind as I took Feets into Doc May's. Mending his tongue took five stitches, costing sixty-five dollars, and May couldn't guarantee that Feets wouldn't rip them out before we got home.

The situation was grim. My main leader had become what mushers refer to as an "alligator," liable to attack anything or anybody.

And Khan was just part of the problem. The recent influx of Quest recruits had transformed our dog yard from a relaxed retiree kennel into a hard-core training camp, populated with young studs eager to claim rank. Snarls and low growls had replaced the joyous group howls that marked Harley's benign reign.

Over the next few days I canvassed other mushers about Khan's behavior.

"You got a fighter?" said Sawatzky. "Oh, man, you can't have that. Can't have that, Brian. Did you discipline him?"

I explained that, in each case, the particular circumstances weren't really conducive to cracking down. Sawatzky reacted with silence. "Well, Brian, you can't have a fighter," he repeated.

At Mowry's suggestion I called Plettner. "Khan's *never* been a fighter," she said, genuinely surprised.

Plettner proceeded to interrogate me about the kennel's overall attitude. It didn't take her long to diagnose a problem. "There's only room for *one top dog*, Brian, and that's gotta be you."

The bossy, seven-time Iditarod finisher had plenty of suggestions. I needed to stare down troublemakers. To proclaim my own dominance by hauling cantankerous males right through each other's space. I liked her tactic for disciplining dogs best.

"If you've got a big male giving you trouble—sit on 'em," declared Plettner, a small, wiry woman with a raucous voice. "Use your weight to squash them against the ground and hold them there. No better way to remind a dog who's the boss."

Jack Studer, an old friend, had all but quit coming over to our house because he couldn't stand to watch my unruly departures. He happened to call the day Khan assaulted Feets. "Your whole dog yard is the problem," Jack snapped. "You have to stop all that growling, Bri. You can't just let them sit there cussing at each other."

As it happened, it was my forty-second birthday that weekend. Jack showed up for the dinner party thrown by Kate with a potent gift. "A lot of good dogs have felt this whip," he said, watching me heft the worn leather instrument. "Now here's how you use it."

Standing by her truck in Whitehorse, Gwen Holdman felt tears welling. Her sled was surrounded by dog food, snowshoes and assorted stuff-bags of gear, every bit of which she considered vital for the first two hundred miles of the race. And it wouldn't fit.

Schandelmeier came over see if he could help. "Gwen, you're not doing this right," he said, rooting through her sled bag. "How many dog coats do you have? All fourteen? Leave half of them. How often do you put a coat on every dog?"

Gwen didn't just have coats for her dogs. She had sewn large blankets for them to rest upon, as well as ten foam mats to insulate them from the cold. Schandelmeier shook his head, pointing out that she was skimping in a more crucial department.

"You don't have enough dog food here!"

Gwen squeezed in more food. But she ignored the former champ's advice about cutting back on camping amenities. Her dogs were going to sleep comfortably—that wasn't negotiable. She managed to pack it all, stuffing her sled bag until it puffed like a long blue balloon, with her own sleeping bag and other bundles strapped on top.

She had drawn the twentieth starting position. Teams were leaving at two-minute intervals, so Gwen had a few extra minutes to prepare herself. She needed to find a bathroom, but became diverted. Her bladder was ready to explode at the starting line.

I'll hang on until the hot springs, she told herself, passing clusters of spectators on the Takhini River. *I'll just run into the little lodge there. Someone will hold my team.*

As it turned out, the trail was routed away from the hot springs this year, disappointing a lot of people, and none more than Gwen. "Oh my God," she cried, seeing the lodge wasn't getting any closer before the trail reentered the woods. "What will I do now?"

Gwen had planned to drive five or six hours before camping. Instead she parked her team at the first place she saw other drivers resting, and plunged into the woods.

She was anxious to keep moving, but Mowry and Dalton were taking a full break, and they were Quest veterans. So Gwen camped for two hours, using the opportunity to pencil her first Quest Trail notes in the hardcover field book serving as her journal.

"Trail is beautiful, day is beautiful, although Hootch is running funny . . .

The other mushers left before Gwen, whose barking dogs had driven Mowry nuts. She thought they'd slept surprisingly well. But they sure were wild to go. She inserted Ruffian into lead with Moxie, shifting Jojo, her main leader, back inside the team. Her control was better with Jojo, a six-year-old dog willing to do anything for his doting musher, but he tended to burn himself out. Gwen wanted to spare him the pressure of leading until it was absolutely necessary.

Ruffian and Moxie charged out of the campsite like bandits fleeing a posse. Gwen's sled flipped, but she hung on, bouncing hundreds of yards on her chest until a musher camping farther up the trail intercepted the runaway team.

Gwen, like most mushers, usually trained with fewer than fourteen dogs. This was her first introduction to the raw power harnessed to her sled. She found it scary.

❖ ❖ ❖

"Easy boys," I repeated. Stepping between Feets and Khan, I took the big leader by the collar and roughly swung him clear. Crisis averted, I again lined out the team behind Cyclone and Martin. We didn't get far before I was catching nervous glances from Martin, whose eyes shouted discouragement. The booty mishaps had resulted in one tangle too many for the young leader. Cyclone, in contrast, was strutting about merrily, seizing every chance to circle back and sniff the butts of the ladies within reach. The fact all four of my girls were neutered made no difference to the half-pint Romeo, whose shit-eating grin, and I mean that literally, was getting under my skin.

Another tangle. Another trio of teams skipped past. "Enough of this," I cried, straightening Cyclone and Martin out for the last time.

The solution lurked three pairs back, pawing the ground and baying with frustration at our shabby progress.

"OK, Khan," I said, accepting that control had become more desirable than speed.

Shifting Martin back inside the team's middle ranks, I took Khan by the collar and marched him to the front, where I paired him with Cyclone. The little rooster's grin vanished and his tail sank between his legs. Boss dog was back.

On cue, Khan jerked Cyclone toward the trail. The team fell into a smart trot.

Approaching Takhini Hot Springs, I spotted McKee in the crowd flanking the trail. He'd found the perfect vantage to videotape *his* dogs on the Yukon Quest trail. As my team trotted into view, Bill couldn't contain himself. "Hey, look at that dog leading right there! That Cyclone dog!" he shouted, dipping the camera lens in his excitement to recording only voices against snow. "And there's Topher there!" he cried.

The trail left the river and continued along a snow-covered road where Kate was waiting for us, flashing a gorgeous smile.

"Hi dogs," she sang, snapping our picture.

"Take a look at the front of the sled," I called to my wife. "We picked up our first ding. Tell Freshwaters he's going to have some work in Dawson."

My plastic brush bow, the dogsled equivalent of a bumper, was badly dented on one side, where a wooden inner support had splintered. I wasn't sure exactly how or where the damage occurred. In any case, it wasn't serious. Repairs could wait until I reached Dawson City, where handlers were allowed to lend a hand during the mandatory layover.

I passed Kate without stopping. She rejoined Freshwaters and her father having only a vague idea of the sled's damage.

My handler took it upon himself to call Ray Mackler, the sled's maker back in Fairbanks.

Ray, who was hard-of-hearing, considered his Starline Ultralight model sleds all but unbreakable. Not only did he refuse to speculate about the nature of my unimaginable problem, he refused to ship any spare parts. "Besides," he declared, "it wouldn't do you any good, because I'm the only one who can fix that sled."

Freshwaters hung up the phone angry with Mackler, and himself. *We got off on the wrong foot, that's all.*

But he couldn't get over the old buzzard's attitude.

"What's a guy supposed to do if he does break one of his sleds?" Freshwaters wanted to know. "Quit and go home?"

EXPERIENCE TELLS

3

DANGER

A dog was dragging in the middle of my team. I jumped on the brake with both feet, spraying snow from the blades. It took another ten yards before the team finally stopped. Hurling the hook down, I ran forward.

The dragger was Danger and he looked bad, real bad. He was on his side, completely limp, with his tongue spilled out through bared teeth. Blind white showed in the eye turned my way. "Jesus," I whispered. "He's dead. I've got a dead dog. Oh, man. I've got a dead dog."

Only minutes earlier the team had finished a three-hour dinner break. We were flying when the trail unexpectedly dropped, turned, then threaded between two posts framing a tiny footbridge. Negotiating the entrance, my eyes were on the sled. *I bet Danger bashed his head on one of those posts.*

Then I saw the tug line wrapped around his neck. *He didn't smack his head, he strangled!* He must have overrun the dog ahead of him. It had probably happened on that sudden drop, which meant I was to blame for failing to string the dogs out. With proper braking I could have absorbed the slack and prevented the team from bunching up.

The corpse twitched. "My God! You're alive."

Dropping to my knees, I fumbled with the line wrapped around his neck. *I should have my knife out. I could just cut it.* No time to find that knife now.

He stopped twitching before I finished loosening the line. "Oh Danger, I'm sorry. I'm so sorry."

The victim's back suddenly arched. He twitched a few more times, then stopped, seeming to deflate and flatten into the snow. I cradled him, praying for some sign of life, detecting none. Danger's head, utterly limp, slipped through my fingers and plopped onto the snow. "Probably broke your neck," I whispered. "Oh, I'm so sorry."

The other dogs were pumped from their recent rest stop. A few were already barking to go. Picard and N.C., the wheel dogs, were lunging forward, trying to pop the hook.

"No you don't," I said, rising from the corpse. "Easy, easy everybody."

I unclipped Picard's tug line and used it to tie off the team on a tree. Then I grabbed a spare tug from the sled and used it to fasten the gang line section behind Khan to a bush. With the team anchored front and back, I had time to think, to digest the awful, awful truth: *I've got a dead dog and it's all my fault!*

A motion caught my eye: The corpse, was—he was *trying to get up!* No, he was up! On his feet! Looking bewildered, yet calm.

"Danger. Oh, Danger boy," I said, hugging him, laughing. "You scared the living hell out of me."

I loaded Danger in the sled. Between the mass of dog food and gear it was a tight fit. He immediately squirmed out and dangled on a neck line. *This isn't going to work because he's not tired.* I put Danger back in the team, resolving to watch him closely.

Danger didn't pull with his usual abandon, but he kept pace without any trouble and before long, it was like nothing happened. *What a dog!*

My attention gradually shifted toward N.C., the dog from Lloyd in Minto. He'd favored his right wrist during the team's dinner stop. That wasn't unusual; N.C. occasionally showed hints of a limp after long training runs without lasting effect. To be on safe side, I massaged his wrist with Kris Krestensen's mystery juice.

Drawing upon chemical expertise perfected while bootlegging LSD in the 1960s, Krestensen claimed to have developed a liniment superior even to Algyval, the ungodly expensive peanut oil used by top sled-dog racers. The new juice hadn't really been tested, but I'd often used the old hippie's Trusty Husky paw balm.

"Maybe it's a kink that will work itself out," I said, noticing N.C.'s limp had returned.

Within a few miles, N.C. was struggling. "Guys," I announced, drawing a quizzical glance from Feets, "this is going to suck."

Braeburn Lodge, the closest place I could drop N.C., was another sixty or seventy miles. *Danger used up the nightly miracle allotment.* Tying off the team, I made room inside the sled bag for a passenger.

The teen mushing queen was barely twenty miles out of town, just past the Yukon River's junction with the Takhini, when her fatigue took hold. Sensing she was verging on drifting off, possibly losing her team in a spill, Brenda Mackey stopped to feed and change booties. The activity left her feeling more alert, but she knew that wouldn't last. She needed tunes. Brenda was scrounging through her sled bag for a tape worth plugging into her Walkman when her dogs, who weren't the least bit tired, pulled the hook.

Mike King, a swaggering, bushy-bearded, thirty-seven-year-old Quest veteran—better known for having the trail tattooed across his back than he was for his accomplishments as a sled-dog racer—was camped up ahead. He saw Brenda's dogs coming and positioned himself to grab her leaders. They ducked King's initial lunge, but somehow he managed to get a hand on their tug lines. He was holding the team when Brenda caught up on foot.

The near disaster provided enough adrenaline to keep the Quest's youngest musher kicking behind her sled until she caught up with her dad and Schandelmeier at their campsite, which had been Brenda Mackey's plan all along.

That night Brenda was chasing her father through the woods—her headlamp switched off so as not to blind him—when Star, a dog leased from McKee, and one that she regarded as her best chaser, ducked down on a side trail, sending Brenda's sled riding up a small tree. She had to use her ax and chop it loose.

Rick dubbed his daughter "the little shadow" when Brenda again caught them resting by a lake, roughly thirty-five miles from the lodge.

He and Schandelmeier took care of dog chores, then sacked out. Though exhausted, Brenda remained too keyed-up to rest. Instead, she kept watch on the movements of rival mushers, particularly those of William Kleedehn, an Austrian expatriate now living in the Yukon. Though he'd lost one leg in an accident years before, Kleedehn, the thirty-eight-year-old owner of Limp-A-Long Kennel, had finished as high as eleventh in two previous Quests. Numerous victories in shorter sled-dog races made him a long-shot threat to win.

"Dad," Brenda said, awakening Rick Mackey, who lay snoring on his sled, "I really think William's getting ready to go."

The defending champ shrugged and pulled a towel over his face.

About that time, I mushed onto the same lakeshore toting N.C., whose restlessness was giving me fits.

Brenda burst out of the darkness. Schandelmeier, too.

"How's Searchlight doing?" Brenda asked, referring to Star's litter-mate. "Are you using her in lead?"

"No," I said. "Maybe later. She hadn't been into leading lately."

"Star's not eating at all," Brenda confided glumly, "and she dragged me into a tree."

I was tempted to camp, but the timing wasn't right. "I'm going to push for another hour," I said. "See you guys later."

Maybe forty minutes and five miles farther, I found Mowry camping under the steep bank of another lake.

"O'D," he cried merrily, "I can't believe you caught me!"

It wasn't true, really. Mowry's dogs had been resting there two hours already, sleeping off a full meal. All things considered, that put his team well ahead of mine. But I appreciated the generous fiction.

Terry McMullin, sixty-three, the gray-haired musher I knew but couldn't quite place at the mushers' meeting, was even then camping at Braeburn Lodge. The retired school principal from Eagle, Alaska, hadn't planned on playing the rabbit, as the saying goes, gifting his younger rivals with somebody to chase. McMullin had simply chanced into a good draw, leaving Whitehorse in fourth place, and afterward Riley motored through the moonlight looking more like a pup than a ten-year-old leader.

A lot of teams passed McMullin during the team's first short break, some forty miles out. Even after leaving Schandelmeier at the lake, the rookie reckoned he had plenty of company. The oldest musher in the Quest was as astonished as anyone when he led the entire field into Braeburn.

There's a thrill attached to the rabbit's role, but experienced dog drivers put little stock in the standings early in a thousand-mile contest. Mowry, for one, got a kick out of leading the race out of Whitehorse, but he was relieved when defending champ Mackey overtook him twenty-four miles from town. Holding the lead that early mainly put a guy first in line for trouble.

The whole night long, people were trading places. At the moment I stopped on the lake, the bulk of the field, including two of the three former champions entered this year, remained behind us. Reveling in that knowledge, Mowry and I lazed upon our sleds, enjoying a magnificent moon cloaked in wisps of clouds, and bantering about our escapes from town, Danger's near death and other adventures of the day, all the while basking in the murmurs of dogs resting in the deep, powdery snow.

Perhaps an hour after I arrived, Kleedehn, then Stan Njootli, Mike King, and Brenda dropped over the bank and rolled out across the lake. Schandelmeier and Mackey were close behind and, though it was hard to tell from the distant headlamps, it looked as if the proven champions passed up those pretenders before the far shore.

Mowry was pulling his own team toward the trail when Lee joined the moonlit parade. The musher with the neat black beard cut a dashing figure flashing through our headlamps in a red jumpsuit, outfitted with an open hood framed by a thick fur ruff.

"Looking good, Bruce," I yelled, uncertain if he even saw us.

Amy Wright got off to a fast start. Expo, her husband's old leader, had the puppies rolling. The trail *was* rougher than any she'd seen before, but Peter had warned her about that. *You didn't come to the Quest expecting the Fur Rondy*, Amy told herself, flashing on the sprint races through Anchorage's groomed trails as she maneuvered her long sled past the stumps lining a fresh-cut forest section.

Actually Amy hadn't come to race at all. Not in her mind, though Peter might have argued the point. As Amy saw it, her mission was preparing Terrapin Kennel's younger dogs for his 1999 bid. Seeing the Quest trail was her payoff. That was her thing: running fresh trails and races. Each new experience increased her insight into breeding and selling sled dogs, and that was the chief passion for this member of the Wright racing clan.

It was dark when Amy arrived at Braeburn Lodge. Between the dog chores and her own craving for sleep, she lost track of what was happening with everybody else. When she awoke from her nap, her husband filled her in. Amy, the avowed non-racer, had trailed McMullin into Braeburn by less than two hours, claiming fourth position close behind three other surprising rookies.

Amy wasn't swayed from her plans by the team's impressive first-day performance. The schedule she and Peter had worked out before the race called for five- to six-hour runs, followed by successive rests lasting ten hours, two hours, then ten hours again. It was a conservative formula designed to keep their young dogs happy.

McMullin and the other frontrunners left long before Amy. She couldn't help but think some of them were being foolish. Particularly that French guy. She'd heard that Andre Nadeau claimed his team could march seventeen hours a day, which confirmed the worst of her first impressions.

"The guy's never going to make it to Dawson," she predicted. "He'll be lucky to make it to Carmacks."

Later, boosted by their long rest, Amy's dogs overtook Nadeau on the Chain of Lakes. Her rest-heavy schedule put Amy camping alongside former Quest champions Turner and Schandelmeier. She was fetching water from a hole chopped in the lake when Nadeau's team caught up.

The speed of his dogs was nothing to boast about. Amy saw that right away. Entering the camp, however, she saw Andre Nadeau's dogs execute a sharp left, mind you, a brilliantly sharp left. They weaved past other parked teams, before finally stopping *exactly* where the musher ordered.

"That was perfect," Amy muttered, thoroughly impressed. "And it wasn't just the front end. His *whole team* is very well trained."

The Mowth's sled was resting on its side outside Braeburn. Shed of his coat and gloves, the musher was on his knees patching together his sled brake using the parts he'd collected when the dang paddle fell apart on the trail. He could see he was going to need another bolt or two. Well, that was one thing to be said for sharing the damn parking area with twenty or thirty teams, *somebody* had to have an extra bolt.

Mowry's sled was a sturdy Mackler, one of the old craftsman's Quest prototypes. It showed the wear of a half dozen thousand-mile campaigns. Fact is, the whole sled needed an overhaul. But who had time for that? Not a deadline-pushing reporter still knocking out Outdoors page features when he should have been on the road to Whitehorse. He'd go over the sled with a wrench in Dawson. Sure.

He had the brake together and was leaning on his sled when I finally showed up. *About time, O'Donoghue,* thought Mowry, who'd been at Braeburn three hours already.

While I paused to talk with race officials, Mowry studied my outfit. He noted that big Plettner dog was in lead. Could have predicted that.

He saw my sled bulged with excess gear, not to mention that big dog Lloyd first sought to loan him. He saw Freshwaters pointing out a decent parking spot. *O'Donoghue's lucky to have him along.*

Last of all, Mowry noticed my pained expression as the sled slipped past, and N.C.'s squirming attempts to escape the sled bag.

Bruce Lee happened to be walking past. His eyes were also drawn to the big passenger. "I gave him that dog," Mowry announced, grinning fiendishly. "Heh. Heh. Heh."

Two hours later, it was my turn to watch as Mowry hooked up to leave. I knew Tim was berating himself for staying around so long. His young dogs sure looked primed, barking and leaping in harness. The team tore through the parking lot and across the highway, trailing sparks off the rebuilt brake.

"Hey," someone shouted. "Looks like Mowry's missing something."

The brush bow was resting in the straw vacated by The Mowth's dogs. *How the hell can you go anywhere without that,* I wondered, having witnessed my own brush bow deflect trees countless times in the last twenty-four hours.

Gwen Holdman's team was turning down a hill when one of her snow hooks tumbled and slipped free. The double-pronged claw bounced a few times then bit firmly on a stump, stopping the team dead and flipping Gwen over the handlebar onto her wheel dogs.

Though winded, Gwen forced herself to her feet; every second increased the chances of another team piling into them.

Her sled was pinned. She couldn't drag it uphill to free the snagged hook, not with fourteen dogs pulling the opposite direction. So Gwen used her second hook to anchor the team on the slope. Then she grabbed her ax and began chopping.

As the stump crumbled, the second hook held just long enough for Gwen to grab it. The dogs dragged her down the hill, hook in one hand, ax in the other. On the lake below, the team made a hard right, leaving the trail and dashing under a fallen tree, which finally arrested the sled in its branches.

Gwen hadn't lost the team. Her sled was merely stuck, rather than shattered, as it easily might have been by the impact with the tree. Yet, standing on the lake not far from Braeburn Lodge, she didn't feel lucky. She felt endangered by the immensity of the journey to come. "Oh my God," she said, trembling. "I can't do this."

Two teams dropped onto the lake. Both mushers saw Gwen's predicament—they couldn't miss it—and continued.

Gwen didn't necessarily expect, or want, a hand freeing her team, but it struck her that none was offered. *This is really a race*, she again realized. *There isn't going to be anybody out there helping me if I really screw up.*

On Schandelmeier's recommendation, Gwen had packed a folding bow saw. She used it to cut an opening through the tree's branches, saving for last those that were pinning her sled. The operation took quite a while, and her dogs were going crazy by the time Gwen's saw bit into the last restraint.

The weakened branch finally splintered under the dogs' pressure, and Gwen's team surged out into the lake's unblemished snow. Following her commands, Ruffian and Moxie brought the team around and rejoined the trail.

Braeburn was a short haul. Gwen could have used more time to regroup. Instead, she pulled in behind the lodge full of self-doubts, convinced that she lacked whatever it took to go the distance.

"Has anyone scratched yet?" Gwen asked officials.

The answer was no, which came as a huge disappointment. The first hundred miles of the Quest had reduced the ambitions of the pretty blonde driving the fast dogs to a face-saving gesture. Gwen Holdman wanted nothing more than to avoid being the first Quest driver to quit. "I'll keep going until, like, I'm in the middle," she told herself, "then I'll scratch."

Using my sled for a mattress, I napped in the sunshine bathing Braeburn's parking lot. It wasn't a deep sleep. Part of my mind registered the crunch of feet moving through the snow and clicks of cameras aimed by the spectators gathered outside the restricted area. I was conscious that Rusty Hagan, the musher camped closest to us, was fixing his own dogs a meal.

He was still at it when the onset of leg cramps forced me up. Boy, it was bright out. I had to squint to make out the digits on my watch. I was 3:56 P.M., only minutes ahead of the watch alarm's programmed onslaught of beeps. That meant I'd slept the better part of ninety minutes, the first such rest for me in the last thirty-six hours.

Rusty looked up, grinning as usual. "Have you seen my booty applicator?"

"What?"

"It's neat," he said, fingering some sort of cone-shaped tool dangling from his neck. "Watch, I'll show it to you."

"You're telling me you got a machine that puts on booties?"

"Slips them right on. Spares your fingers," said Rusty, beaming at the chance to show off another invention.

Kneeling over one of his sleeping dogs, Rusty took a booty, placed a paw inside his device, then, yanking on the tool's neck strap, popped it back off.

I stared, unable to follow, much less comprehend, his deft movements. And suddenly I didn't care. "It's *way* too early in the morning for this, Rusty." I lurched off to find a suitable tree, or maybe a bush, out of the tourists' line of sight.

"Booty applicator, huh?" I muttered, fumbling with zippers and drawstrings. "Odds are this is a dream."

I was repacking the sled when Freshwaters updated me concerning N.C.

"Everything was square with that vet who looked at him this morning," he said, referring to Steve Swank, the West Virginia veterinarian who'd placed N.C.'s wrist in a cast, stabilizing the injury until Doc May could see him in Fairbanks. "But that Steve guy is gone and we got another lady vet who wants to take the cast off again.

"I told them they should talk to you," the handler said, adding: "I don't think these vets have any right to keep poking that dog. Their authority ended when he was dropped."

Freshwaters had a point, but it never pays to pick a war with the veterinary corps. I went looking for them to straighten things out.

The vet not only wanted to examine N.C. If it looked like his wrist was broken, she advocated transporting him to Whitehorse for X-rays. The open-ended nature of her proposal was alarming. X-rays were going to show a break—I could tell that much by just looking—followed by what? Surgery to reconstruct the joint? Life as a house pet? It would take a lobotomy before Lloyd's village commando filled that role.

Doc May, a sled-dog specialist, would give me a realistic assessment. I knew that was likely to be grim, because N.C., at the age of eight, was likely on the downside of his racing career.

My thoughts turned to a comment I heard years ago from Jeep, another musher in Lloyd Charlie's village. He was offering me a puppy.

"How do I know the dog is any good?"

Jeep smiled. "He's alive and he's in Minto, isn't he?"

I knew where Lloyd would come down, but for all I knew this Quest veterinary volunteer doctored lap dogs at home. Could she handle a reality check?

I decided to be candid. "I want N.C. to be comfortable, but there's another issue here," I said. "N.C. is a village dog. If this injury keeps him from racing, his owner would probably put him down before considering cosmetic surgery."

The vet's face hardened. "I'm not sure this can wait until the dog is back in Fairbanks. I think I'm going to ask you to talk this over with Marianna as soon as she's free." The door closed before I formed a reply.

Great. Now the *chief vet* was going to be on my back. *Way to smooth the waters.*

I sought out Joe May, my veterinarian's father, a race judge, and most significantly at this moment, a trapline-schooled musher. "You know what Lloyd's going to say about this—that dog's wrist is never going to be right," I said. "He's a shooter."

The judge brokered a compromise with Marianna: N.C. was to be medicated to ensure his comfort and produced daily for the examination by the vets. So long as no crisis developed, however, he'd be riding in the dog truck under Freshwaters' personal care.

My handler was pleased.

"He's already coming around, doesn't seem to hardly notice that splint," he said. "To tell you the truth, I'm glad to have the company."

The last fingers of the sun were reaching across the Klondike Highway as a Yukon musher's handler helped shepherd my team across the road. The dogs looked refreshed after their seven-hour break. Before long, most were loping toward the rolling hills. We soon caught and passed Tony Blanford, a fellow rookie who was some kind of doctor in Fairbanks. Less than a mile later, however, I noticed Martin's tug line sagging. Rather than pulling, he was being pulled on the short line clipped to his collar, neck-lining as it's called, a most unusual, entirely alarming, behavior for a hard-working husky like Martin.

I stopped the team and checked him out. No cuts showed on Martin's pads. His wrists weren't particularly sensitive. Neither rubbing his back, nor flexing his shoulders produced telltale yelps. I was perplexed.

"What's that matter, Martin? If there's something wrong, you'd tell me, wouldn't you?"

His big, blue eyes appeared mournful. But that was Martin's way. I scratched him behind the ears, then returned to the sled.

Khan, in solo lead this evening, was whining as I reached for the hook. Invigorated by the brief pause, he leaped to work along with most of the crew, whipping my sled forward like a tin can strung from a bumper. Martin's tug continued to droop. He just wasn't cutting it.

"Damn," I whispered, watching the young dog, the one leader in whom Freshwaters detected a promise of "speed," struggling to keep up.

There was a chance I was witnessing the effects of a tight muscle, a fleeting gastric pain, perhaps nothing more than doubts burdening a young dog unfamiliar with the pressures of racing. Martin might rebound.

I balanced that possibility against the fact that we had some eighty miles to go before reaching Carmacks. Martin's behavior suggested I might soon find myself packing a passenger for the duration of that trip. The memory of N.C.'s squirming load was too fresh to tolerate that thought.

Returning to the lodge, I met Blanford head-on. He looked startled. "I'm taking one back," I said.

❖ ❖ ❖

In the years I covered the Quest as a reporter, the trail to Carmacks was generally described in apocalyptic terms, a veritable valley of destruction for the best-made sleds and the hopes of the luckless mushers driving them.

In 1989, Krestensen played the hero on this stretch, guiding Charlotte Fitzhugh, a lady whose Quest dream sunk under weight of her iron cookware and other bizarre accessories, into position for rescue. Soon afterward, however, Krestensen sunk his sled, upside down, in a nasty creek hole. Ol' Kris tried to leverage the kit free using knots and rigging learned as a merchant seaman. It didn't work. So he plunged into the frigid water, unloaded his sled from the bottom, and manhandled it out. Hours passed before Kris found a cabin to warm up. He wasn't ready to quit, but the damage was done: His heels were frozen. He hobbled as far as Dawson before the pain from his thawing extremities forced him out.

So leaving Braeburn I prepared for the worst, stuffing my sled bag with clamps, bolts, duct tape and Freshwaters' roll of all-purpose utility cord.

Nightfall found us threading craggy bluffs and dark, brooding forests. Mushers hadn't ever mentioned the raw beauty of this passage up the Yukon's Chain of Lakes, pearl white stepping stones each, framed by trees bowed in a snow-caked death embrace with the frozen waters.

Resting and running alone as I traveled four to five hours at a shot, I leapfrogged up the chain, passing and being re-passed by Tony Blanford, Rusty Hagan, and Bill Steyer, three mushers whose speed and rest schedules best matched mine.

Fatigue caught up in the hours before dawn. I dug out the Walkman that my brother Coleman had thoughtfully shipped from Washington, D.C. He's a professional drummer and his audio care package left nothing to chance; I had three sets of head phones, all the batteries I could want, and a collection of tapes recorded for moments such as this.

Coleman's first selection was a live performance by Little Feat, a band we both knew well. The lyrics catapulted me to another place and time.

"Your daddy said I'm no good. Your mama says keep away. I've got to tell you truthful girl—you could never make me stay. I've got something up and down this coast. Bet you my last dollar girl I can love you love the most."

"That was me, guys," I told the dogs. "You didn't know me then."

Dancing between the sled runners, I recalled lightning visits to New Orleans: blasting though garbage cans in a Caddy driven by the daughter of a judge; fleeing across Lake Pontchartrain toward the swamps with another girl I knew as The Beast; squeezing more than seemed humanly possible into the hours before my cargo ship sailed for other ports and girls.

"Don't the sunrise look so pretty. Never such a sight. Like rolling into New York City with the skyline in the morning light. Roll right through the night. I said roooooool! Roll right through the night. I said roooool!

That was me, too: Racing dawn to Manhattan via the New Jersey Turnpike, feeling rich from scoring that last fare to Newark Airport. Move to Alaska? Get outta here. I took life a dime at a time, cameras ever in reach for the spot-news photo that would make me famous.

The trail behind had more curves and surprises than anyone could count. And it all led to this moment, this gliding ride on the runners under a Yukon moon, chewing through miles and memories, dancing to a familiar tune.

"Give it to me gently, feets don't fail me now. Feets don't fail me now."

Gwen wasn't far off schedule. She had planned on a long break at Braeburn Lodge, eight to ten hours minimum. From what she had heard, most mushers stayed there at least eight. Her team figured to have plenty of company.

She couldn't believe how fast most teams cleared out. Dieter Dolif and a handful of other mushers were the only ones left by the time Gwen ducked inside the lodge for dinner. The meal wasn't especially good or anything, but Gwen lingered over it, feeling calm for the first time in days, reluctant to move.

"Is Dieter getting ready?" she idly asked an official.

"Dieter? He left fifteen minutes ago."

"Is *anyone else* here?"

"Just you."

Gwen shot outside. Trampled snow and scattered chunks of straw marked vacated campsites. The emptiness was unsettling. The night sky loomed vast and dark.

Pitching gear into her sled bag, Gwen Holdmann rushed to get on the trail.

True to their breeding, Gwen's dogs virtually flew in the hours that followed. Some of the overland sections were tricky; she had to wrestle her sled past countless trees, through the hidden dips and sharp rises. But the trail's technical difficulty was a boon, restoring Gwen's confidence in her abilities as a musher. The lakes, meanwhile, provided a perfect groove to unleash her dogs' speed.

Gwen eventually overtook Dieter's plodding Siberians and the pair camped on a hill, enjoying the warmth provided by the slight elevation gain.

Dieter was having trouble with his brake. Working on his sled together, Gwen realized how glad she was to have company. Her fleeting brush with last place had awakened all sorts of misgivings: *So much can go wrong driving dogs alone in this wilderness.*

Alaska's top sled-dog racers keep huge hundred-dog kennels, where the best of the best are trained together in the musher's A team, while handlers groom the most promising minor leaguers as replacements. This is most true among Iditarod's upper crust. Mushers of Jeff King's and Martin Buser's ilk go as far as entering handlers in the big race to provide their "puppy teams" with precious experience.

The Quest, with its smaller overall purse, attracts fewer professional racing kennels. The Mackeys, with more than a hundred dogs to pick from, were the exceptions among the contenders of 1998. Mushers drawing upon kennels sized from thirty to sixty dogs were more common among the Quest ranks. And there were also mushers in Mowry's and my own situation: filling out the fourteen-dog string with a few that even we doubted would make it, because there simply were no others to choose from.

The Mowth knew going in that Kylash was shaky, Jane was likely too young, and Bonnie, well, Bonnie, whom he'd raised from a pup, hadn't ever learned to pace herself. She'd be resting in the dog truck before Dawson. Bet on it.

When Jane faltered that first night, Mowry was disappointed, but hardly surprised. When Kylash looked discouraged en route to Carmacks, it was more annoying than distressing. The sled-handling required to dodge collisions minus a brush bow kept Mowry from dwelling on Ky's pending exit.

Asia's stumble was another story. She was a key leader. A proven Quest finisher. As he cleared room inside the sled to load her, five miles short of Carmacks, The Mowth was tight-lipped.

Bonnie's not going to make it past McCabes', Mowry realized. *That means two hundred and fifty miles into the race, I'm down to what? Down to ten dogs!*

Keith Kirkvold camped on one of the lakes. Dan Turner picked the same spot. Both men were forty-five and shared the simple goal of finishing the long-distance race, something Turner had failed to do in his first Quest attempt several years before. Keith, a tall, gray-mustached Fairbanks hospital carpenter, found the company of the government assessor from Haines, Alaska, most enjoyable. As far as Keith was concerned, camaraderie was proving to be the best part of the Quest.

Turner was in lead descending one of the hilly links in the Chain of Lakes when his dogs cut the wrong side of a tree, snapping several neck lines before the team halted in a miserable tangle. Keith's big fourteen-dog string came rolling down upon them. By the time he managed to stop, half of his big males were mixing with Turner's crew.

Keith hastily separated the dogs before any blood was spilled. Turner carefully edged his dogs around the tree and mushed away, leaving Keith facing a dilemma: The angle for departure was all wrong. *If I take off with these dogs going crazy like this, I'm going right there,* Keith thought, eyeing the damned tree.

Keith had raised most of these dogs from pups. He had more faith in them than he did in rules drawn up by folks who probably never imagined a plight such as this. He unhitched half his dogs and turned them loose.

His control enhanced by the smaller team, Keith manhandled his sled past the tree and resumed his descent. Emerging from the last trees, he felt a stab of fear. His loose dogs were way out on the lake chasing Turner.

Wondering if he'd made a big, big mistake, Keith called them back. Hearing their master's voice across the lake, the fugitives dutifully turned around.

As he hooked the dogs back up, Keith felt vindicated. *That saved my buns right there on that tree, and it was the safest thing for the dogs.*

BUM TIRES

4

SEARCHLIGHT

Dawn lit the frosty trees on a bluff overlooking the Yukon River. My spirits were running down with the batteries in the Walkman. Stevie Ray Vaughan's artistry was being savaged, but I kept the tape rolling in a perverse tribute. Any distraction was welcome as I faced a typical rookie dilemma.

Carmacks had to be close, but how close? Ten minutes? An hour? The competitor within argued for pushing through to the checkpoint. *The dogs will rest better on straw. And it won't hurt me to grab a real meal and a warm place to bunk.*

But what's best for the dogs? The team was greatly overdue for a break. The warm meal sloshing inside my cooler was going to spoil if I didn't feed soon. *So how far is too far?*

The Walkman expired. I rolled for ten more minutes, then parked.

While the dogs were eating, I got out the maps, along with my handheld global position system tracker, which, theoretically, ought to give me a satellite fix on the team's location.

More often than not, the Garmin 12 XL gave me nothing but a speed check. It showed, for example, that Cyclone generally loped at about thirteen miles an hour, while Khan seldom cracked ten on his best days. More complicated tasks were hampered by the gadget's tendency to lose the satellite fix if I carried it under my parka, triggering annoying beeps. And if I didn't keep it warm, the damn Garmin conked out.

The space-age gods looked upon us favorably this morning. The Garmin found its orbital kin through the trees and gave me our coordinates. The result was depressing: Carmacks lay directly across the river. "Another half hour and we would have had it."

Bellies full, my dogs had quietly curled in the snow. Rouse them too soon and it could sour the younger dogs. I settled back on my sled prepared to sit tight for two, maybe three hours.

Bill came rolling up, followed by Rusty, John Nash, and Walter Palkovitch.

"I screwed up. You guys are real close," I shouted to Bill. "Just checked the map. It's only about five miles to Carmacks."

Ninety minutes into the break, Picard, Luther, and several other dogs began stirring. That was enough for me. I sprang from the sled and, in less than ten minutes, signaled Khan and Hobbes to move out. Searchlight, flashing worried looks, continued up the trail with her shoulders slumped, head and tail low. *Poor little girl doesn't know what to make of this.*

"Good dog, Search. *Good girrrrl!*" She seemed to straighten at the reassuring words.

The trail stayed on the bluff much longer than the map suggested. The river, perhaps a hundred yards below, appeared choppy. Now that I thought about it, I recalled some mention at the driver's meeting that the trail into Carmacks had to be re-routed past dangerous ice.

The slot between my rear runners normally filled by the drag was empty. A slope bristling with stumps had ripped it off in the hours before dawn. *Oh well*, I thought. *No big loss. You planned to drop it in Carmacks anyway. That stump saved us the trouble of disconnecting it.*

But I hadn't fully adjusted to the drag's absence. Descending a sharp little hill, I stabbed for the missing track and sank my boot deep in soft snow. As the team bounded downward, my other foot slipped from the runner and I dropped onto my knees. Clinging to the handlebar, my torso arched backwards under the team's forward pressure. "Aaaagghh," I grunted, hearing my vertebra crack in shocking sequence.

I don't know if it was something the dogs sensed in my voice, or my body's effect as an anchor, but the team stopped dead.

I gripped the sled, gasping and scared, wondering if the misstep was going to put me in a hospital bed alongside Peter Zimmerman, the Swiss musher whose training injury overshadowed this year's race.

Exiting his dog yard behind a fresh twelve-dog team, Zimmerman had flipped his sled, smashed into a tree, and broken his back. He remained paralyzed in a Vancouver hospital, where the musher's mounting bills—and his ineligibility for Canadian health coverage as a foreign national—had inspired fundraisers on both sides of the border.

I wiggled my toes and flexed my ankles. The old wiring appeared intact. Rolling my neck for good measure, I took a deep breath and hauled myself to my feet. A dozen heads gazed at me. Curious? Or did I detect concern? Either way, the attention gave me a warm feeling.

"Who told you guys to take a break?" I shouted merrily.

Down on the Yukon, the trail continued up river, away from Carmacks, but I wasn't complaining about the detour. Out in the center channel lay a steaming gash of open water, twenty to thirty feet wide.

❖ ❖ ❖

Terry McMullin mushed into Carmacks shortly before 7:00 P.M. on February 9, leading his closest rival by forty minutes. The frontrunner role was heady stuff for an aging pioneer schooled on traplines out near Copper Center and the Fortymile country, a musher who, before many of his Quest rivals were born, used dogs to haul freight for scientists in the ice fields above Juneau.

But the mushing grandfather knew his dogs, Riley and Marcus, in particular, were ready for everything he asked them to do. McMullin, a two-time Iditarod entrant in the mid-1970s and early 1980s, prepared carefully for his return to long-distance racing. He had eighteen hundred miles on this team, mountain miles logged crisscrossing windy American Summit, including more than a few hundred-mile days.

But the old schoolteacher knew his run in the limelight was nearly done. Riley and the bunch deserved a good, long rest and they were going to get it. McMullin recognized, after all, he didn't have a prayer of winning this thing. He merely aimed to capitalize on his tremendous start and try and hang with teams in the front of the pack. That was the game plan, if it even deserved mention as such.

The gray-haired musher could use a snooze himself. He awoke refreshed, aside from feeling a twinge in his throat, and set to work readying the team for departure.

At 5:37 A.M. on February 10, McMullin picked up his snow hook and directed Riley toward the trail. In the ten hours since his arrival at Carmacks, twenty-one teams had trailed McMullin into the checkpoint. None had left. The rookie leading the Quest, now entering its third day, hadn't reckoned on this. *Who is his right mind would?* But he figured he'd run with it. *Why not?*

Some ninety minutes after the frontrunner's celebrated exodus, Andre Nadeau shook the little bells attached to his gang line. On cue, his big Siberians uncurled from their cozy beds of straw, rose and obediently assumed familiar places on the gang line. Each waited patiently as the musher moved down the line, refastening the harness and collar snaps that channel the strength of fourteen individuals into a single powerful unit.

Moving with brusque efficiency, Nadeau returned to his sled, uttered a French word for walk, then hung on as his dogs lurched to work.

Within the hour, five teams were on the move from Carmacks.

Joining the Quest rookies was Yukoner Brian MacDougall, a Canadian veteran of note, having claimed several championships in the Percy De Wolfe, a mid-distance race on the Yukon River north of Dawson.

In 1989, MacDougall's first Quest ended barely two hundred and fifty miles from the starting line. He redeemed himself in 1994, when he placed ninth. While respectable, that one-time top ten showing alone didn't, by any means, qualify thirty-six-year-old MacDougall as a bona fide contender. Crowns collected in the Percy, a race lasting barely a day, offered no proof he could run with the front pack entering the final stretch a true mushing marathon. And conventional wisdom, reinforced many times in the history of both Iditarod and the Quest, held that a musher must first taste victory in the sport's main events to gain the knowledge necessary to actually claim it.

Bruce Lee of Denali Park held that distinction. In his last three attempts at the Quest, Lee had mushed and camped alongside race leaders, sizing up their teams, as they did his, from a calculating front-runner's perspective. Lee finished those Quests in fifth, fourth, and finally, most bitterly, placing second in the 1991 race. In the wake of that last loss, Lee turned to the Iditarod with mixed results. His return to the Quest this year stirred excitement among longtime fans and wariness among rival contenders.

Lee and his handlers, chief of whom was his wife Jeralyn, had mapped out a precise traveling schedule, breaking down the trail to Fairbanks into set runs of roughly fifty miles apiece. The plan reflected both the Quest veteran's grasp of the trail and his best assessment of the team's capabilities.

Lee's confidence in the Yukon Quest organization sagged as the miles mounted. Problems created by poor snow he could understand, but the twisting path through rough-cut forest seemed dangerously crude compared to Iditarod's well-defined lanes.

This stuff was acceptable in the early years of the race, observed Lee, whose own participation dated back to the Quest's third running in 1986. *But not after fifteen years. This isn't a young event anymore.*

When Lee mentioned such concerns to volunteers and fellow racers, they scoffed. Rough trail was part of the Quest's lure, its history, they said.

Lee didn't buy the poetic comparisons to mushers hauling freight or mail between mining camps and roadhouses. *They didn't drive over a thousand miles in twelve days.*

Nomad, one of Lee's most dependable lead dogs, came up lame after a rough river crossing. Miles, his main leader, stumbled on a crack and fell, along with his partner, into a gaping hole in the river's shelf ice. Miles emerged from the hole limping, Lee saw, grimly noting the signs of a trauma injury unlikely to heal out on the trail.

Jeralyn spotted Miles's odd gait as the team approached the clearing at McCabe Creek camp. Hearing the circumstances, she agreed that her husband had best drop Miles, a momentous call because the five-year-old male was Bruce Lee's "go-to" dog, an Iditarod-seasoned leader who never let his master down.

"That's probably it for a win," Bruce said. "I'll go ahead and see how gracefully we can finish, but a major card's been played in the deck."

"Well, you know, do what you can," Jeralyn said. "Maybe somebody else will stand up."

❖ ❖ ❖

GWEN'S JOURNAL   Feb. 10, Carmacks checkpoint

Having fun today. No trouble on Braeburn-Carmacks trail although it was rough. Camped with Dieter Dolif for 6 hours before Frank Lake—warmer there than below. Couldn't get a fire going. Trail not as bad as expected. Carmacks is a great checkpoint—steak dinner, but didn't sleep well. Will probably drop Moxie as his wrist is very sore. Frost is, too, but not so bad

❖ ❖ ❖

Sniffing at a piece of whitefish, Searchlight held her left wrist about three inches off the ground. "Look at that," I said, pointing.

"Oh yeah," Freshwaters said, grimacing.

"I'll wrap it in a minute here and put on some of Krestensen's magic juice."

My handler nodded approvingly.

I longed to rehash details of the team's performance over the last two hundred and twenty miles, but I confined myself to inquiring about N.C. and Martin.

"They're both doing great," he said. "Vets couldn't find anything wrong with Martin."

"Had him in swing and he was neck-lining, " I explained glumly. "I could have tried shifting him to wheel. Probably screwed up there. But Martin just didn't look right. Know what I mean?"

"I'm sure you did the right thing."

Our conversation was stilted; we weren't sure how far the judges planned to take Rich's declared ban on verbal assistance.

"Think you could find me a vet?"

Freshwaters fetched Steve Swank, the West Virginia vet who first treated N.C. This was his first Quest, but Swank had doctored sled dogs on several Iditarods.

"So which race is harder, the Quest or Iditarod?" the vet asked.

"Too soon to say, doc. Both look nasty from here. Ask me in a week."

We laughed.

"I got one with a sore wrist," I said, leading him to Searchlight. "But I'd like you to look them *all* over."

"We can dooo that," Swank said, smiling wide. He bent to work, delicately flexing Searchlight's good wrist, then comparing it to the sore one, manipulating her shoulders, her rear haunches, and examining each paw. He repeated the hands-on inspection with each dog in the team, dictating his observations to an accompanying vet tech, who scribbled them down in the team's yellow logbook.

"You ever heard of Algyval?" Swank asked when he was finished.

"That peanut oil stuff? I saw a lot of guys using that on Iditarod the last few years, but its too pricey for us. I've got some mystery juice supposed to be just as good."

"Right," Swank said, looking doubtful. "This Algyval," he said, "it's proven to be a tremendous anti-inflammatory, seems to penetrate the joints. We don't know *why* it works, but it does. And they gave me some. Great big bottle of it. Tell you what. I want you to experiment for me. I want you to use it on every paw, every wrist and shoulder in your team, starting with that one," he said, pointing to Searchlight's sore foot.

"You serious?"

"Oh yeah," Swank said, winking. "I'll go get that big bottle. Let's test it out."

As the vet squad moved on, I grinned at Freshwaters: Algyval costs thirty dollars *an ounce!* My handler had edged away during the inspection and casually stood off to one side, hands clasped behind his back. I knew his nonchalance was feigned.

"That Swank guy's OK," I said.

"One of the good ones," he agreed.

My regard for Swank didn't change even after the vet repossessed that pricey bottle.

Kate was waiting inside the checkpoint. Rory beamed when he saw me. "My Daddy!" he cried, running for my arms. I swept him up, feeling each of his twenty-five pounds magnified tenfold. He tugged playfully at my fur hat. But the allure vanished as several other kids ran past.

"Down," ordered my son.

I placed Rory on the floor and watched him wobble off in search of adventure.

"He seems to be adjusting to life on the trail," I told Kate.

"Oh, yes," she said, watching Rory hugging a little girl by the end of a bench table. "Our social butterfly."

I polished off a free steak, cookies and salad, magnificently prepared by local volunteers, then stretched out on a cot in a side room. Bliss.

❖ ❖ ❖

Nearing Carmacks, Bill Steyer had noticed that Olaf, one of his three-year-olds, appeared stiff. A long snooze at the checkpoint cured the problem, if there ever was one. Now Olaf looked his usual spry self prancing at the end of Bill's leash, which came as a major relief to his master, a thinly bearded thirty-nine-year-old, doctor-wife-supported house-dad, whose easy-going smile and hippie attire camouflaged a hotly competitive ego. Olaf might not be a leader, but the team's overall attitude benefited greatly from the excitable youngster's presence.

So Bill naturally took Olaf with him, mushing from Carmacks late Tuesday afternoon. Hardly a mile out, Bill had second thoughts. The youngster's steps were tentative and oddly rigid, throwing a pall over the entire team. *Nobody looks good*, Bill thought grimly.

He stopped and loaded Olaf into the sled. McCabe's was only forty-five miles. Hauling a passenger wasn't going to kill them.

The team's erstwhile cheerleader apparently thought otherwise. "Roo-roooo-rooooooo," Olaf whined.

Bill's other dogs did near somersaults trying to identify the cause for their teammate's distress. The team, already moving poorly, slowed to a maddening crawl.

"This is *not* going to work," Bill finally admitted, worn down by a quarter mile of Olaf's intolerable yowling.

He returned to Carmacks and dropped Olaf. Being a rookie to long-distance racing, Bill wasn't sure what to do next. Bunko, his main leader, the dog Bill liked to call The Insurance Policy, seemed lethargic. These dogs all had eight hours of recent rest, so it wasn't a matter of fatigue. What was it?

Bill procrastinated for an hour before deciding that he and the team were losing ground by staying in Carmacks. Once more, he pulled the hook.

This time his team's performance was absolutely terrible. The dogs pooped. They pissed. They paused every few steps to glance warily at their master. Stop and go. Stop and go. Bill tried swapping leaders. It didn't help. Never in all of training had Bill observed his team so flat and discouraged. It unnerved him. Roughly the same place as before, he called a halt to the miserable show.

Bill Steyer sat on his sled, entirely at a loss. He had good dogs. Expensive dogs. There was nothing wrong with their conditioning. A highly competitive marathon runner, Bill had entered the Quest reasonably confident of doing well, of finishing, say, in the top half of the field. But nothing had gone quite right. He'd already had to drop

Lo Rider, one of his key leaders. Bunko looked shaky. So did Lemon, another main leader. Beaver had done all right, but she was subsisting on snacks. More than a day had passed since Beaver last ate a real meal. *How long can she go without becoming dehydrated?* The fact is—he didn't know.

"Do I want to go back?" Bill asked himself at last. "Do I want to scratch?"

Walter Palkovitch, another musher from Fairbanks, came upon Bill's parked team.

"What's going on? You having problems?"

"Yeah," Bill said in a tone discouraging further questions.

As Walter continued toward McCabe Creek, Bill solemnly turned his team around for the second time.

Refreshed from my nap, I was packing when Bill's team loped back into the checkpoint. I knew the other musher from brief encounters at Grubstake Feeds, my dog food supplier, and his recent adventures in the Two Rivers 200, where he used a cell phone borrowed from a motorist to get directions to the finish line.

He'd left the checkpoint a couple times already and wasn't carrying a dog this time, so I had a hunch what was happening: *His leaders are rebelling and Bill doesn't know enough to put down the mutiny.* I went over to talk to him about it.

"If your team won't go after leaving a checkpoint, camp right there if you have to, but don't go back," I told him. "Never, ever, turn around."

Bill took my comments hard. They confirmed his own suspicions, fueled by that glad dash back to the checkpoint, that his dogs' troubles were mental rather than physical, and a direct reflection of his own indecision.

Oh man, he wondered, *did I really blow it?*

Walking back to my own team, I shook my head. *At this rate, he'll be lucky to escape Carmacks.* My own race was nothing to brag about. Ol' Terry had only beat us there by fifteen freaking hours. *And we're only two days into the race!*

Loose straw and brown and yellow blotches in the snow marked the campsites of teams already gone. "Still a long ways to go," I told myself. "We'll catch some of those folks before it's done."

I was retrieving food pans and finishing other last-minute chores under Freshwaters' watchful eye, when a handler from the Yukon asked what I thought of the new booties.

"What new booties?"

He filled us in. Responding to complaints about the lousy Fulda freebies, race officials had brought in several hundred replacements. "You hear anything about this?" I asked Freshwaters.

"Not a word."

The checkpoint manager had just come on duty and hadn't heard anything about replacements. He made some calls while I checked out the booty story with Patricia, who was covering the race for my newspaper.

"Oh yes," she said. "There was a press conference."

"You'd think they might tell mushers about it."

The checkpoint manager subsequently confirmed that new booties had been distributed earlier that day. "I'm afraid they're all gone," he said.

"That's bullshit," I declared. "It's supposed to be equal treatment. I've been here all day and no one said one word to me, or my handler here."

Freshwaters nodded.

"You know this isn't right," I added.

The volunteer offered no argument.

"I want to file an official protest."

"I believe we have a form for that," the guy said, rummaging through the paperwork cluttering the race official's table.

I had just finished composing a complaint to the Quest boards in both the Yukon and Alaska when Dave Rich returned the checkpoint manager's call. He asked to talk to me.

Only a handful of mushers had received the booties, the race marshal said, explaining that the program was limited to drivers who complained about problems with the Fulda gear.

"That's even worse," I said. "That's selective treatment. Everyone using these Fulda booties knows they're crap. I didn't say anything because I figured we're all in the same boat. And you told us you didn't want to hear anything more about booties. "

Rich countered that it wasn't feasible to supply everyone with replacements. And I was wrong if I thought frontrunners were the ones' benefiting. "Most of those guys know better than to rely on something for free," he said. "The teams dependent on those Fulda booties are mostly those, like yourself, traveling near the back."

We went in circles. I finally broke off the conversation telling Rich I needed to get moving.

Replacing the phone, I turned to the checkpoint manager. "The protest stands."

❖ ❖ ❖

GWEN'S JOURNAL   Feb. 11, McCabe Creek Dog Drop.

Rough trail but it went OK. Starting to dread dropping down on the Yukon. Jumble ice was bad on one section and I crashed several times there. Also was not well marked going up one bush trail and I ended up having to backtrack and make a 360° turn to get back. Walter Palkovitch helped. Big hole on slope right out of McCabe, very dangerous, lots of dogs hurt there. Made it. McCabe nice, but couldn't sleep well in shop because of generator.

❖ ❖ ❖

Brenda's spirits were crumbling, along with her team. Three dogs poorer by Carmacks, she was loading yet another when Keith Kirkvold overtook her on the trail to McCabe Creek. He stopped and loaned her a vented stretch bag designed to comfortably restrain unruly passengers.

The grateful teen fell in behind Keith, who was still mushing a full complement of fourteen burly dogs. She was further humbled when he stopped to unclip tug lines before entering an icy section.

"I just have too much power," Keith confided.

Bedding down her team in the clearing fronting the homestead serving as the Quest's McCabe Creek dog drop, Brenda found more cause for grief. Wall Street, a promising eighteen-month-old male, was hobbling on a pair of tender wrists. Though she knew such injuries are treatable, the young musher was stricken with guilt. *He's one of our best young dogs*, Brenda woefully observed. *What if I injure him permanently?*

Brenda was so down on herself that she took little comfort in the homestead's accommodations. The luxury of hot water seemed no great boon to a musher whose fate was tied to a leader as dumb as Star, and a bunch of sour hounds on a hunger strike.

When the chores were done and she joined local volunteers inside the shop building housing the Quest detachment, Brenda found her own appetite lacking. She aimlessly stirred the moose soup, feeling her cheeks burn from the room's unaccustomed heat. Lacking the energy to even move, she stretched out on the thin bench seat, an entirely lousy place to sleep, requiring a balancing act to avoid toppling.

Keith, meanwhile, bunked in a loft within the adjacent heated garage. A woman was sleeping alongside him when he awakened about 3:00 A.M. He assumed it was Brenda.

"Well," he said, shaking her. "Are you ready to go?"

He repeated the question several times with increasing urgency.

"Nope," the woman finally said.

Keith shrugged and made for the ladder. Brenda must have changed her mind about leaving together. Inside the shop, he was startled when he came upon her sleeping on the floor. Keith could only imagine what the other gal in the loft thought he was asking for. It made him smile.

Dodging the big hole in the ice, Khan bounded up the slippery entrance into McCabe Creek. My sled slipped sideways exiting the Yukon and smashed into the bordering brush. I managed to keep it upright and, shoving from behind, plowed over saplings back onto the trail.

The dogs smelled a camp. We were gaining momentum when Kahn barreled past a well-marked turn, breaking a fresh trail on up the creek. Low branches sent me hunkering down. I got a foot on the brake, but the snow covering the creek was powder light and the claws feebly scraped against ice. The channel was narrowing fast. "Whooa, whooa!" I cried.

Finally stopped, I could hear water rushing beneath me. "Great, watch us break through now, " I muttered, crawling toward my errant leader. "We shouldn't even be here."

Taking Khan by the collar, I pulled him around and began reversing the team, maintaining a merry front as I squatted on the thin ice, shoving pairs of dogs past the sled.

Race Judge Joe May was waiting when I pulled into the McCabe camp at 3:20 A.M. on February 11.

"We've got booties for you," he said. "Go ahead and finish your chores, then come talk to me."

I fed the critters, treated Searchlight's wrist, then joined May inside a big truck, purring with heat. He filled me in on the dilemma confronting officials.

By Braeburn, Stan Njootli's dogs had such pervasive foot problems—which he blamed on the poorly fitting Fulda freebies—that the Yellowknife musher warned he'd have to scratch unless he was allowed to scrape together some replacements.

With the exception of Dawson City, where practically anything goes during the thirty-six-hour layover, the approval of the race marshal or a judge was needed to add anything to the supplies shipped prior to the race. A decision was made to try and outfit Njootli and other mushers facing a similar bind with better booties.

May sympathized with my complaints over being excluded. He stressed that the goal was to keep teams in the race. And he granted that plan wasn't well thought out; the demand for replacements had quickly outstripped available supplies.

It was easy to understand why. Fulda had given each of us fifteen hundred booties, which varied widely in quality and design. Multiply fifteen hundred times the seventeen teams known to be relying entirely on Fulda's dog boots, tack on the uncertain requirements of the other twenty teams on the trail, and the Quest's misguided rescue had created a potential demand for tens of thousands of new booties.

"This whole thing has blown up in our face. We're doing the best we can," judge May said.

The snafu was unnecessary. A few mushers might have scratched, but the rest of us would have made do by identifying the booty designs that worked, or running dogs without them, stopping as necessary to hand-clean paws. I'd been doing just that with Topher and Picard, owners of the biggest paws in my team, because large-sized Fulda booties were the worst of the lot.

"You know, Joe," I said, "I was figuring everything would work out if I could put my hands on a roll of electrical tape."

Following our chat, the judge introduced me to Marcus, the Quest's newly designated Booty Man.

"I don't even know what we have here," Marcus said, revealing a stash of cartons packed with new booties imported from Whitehorse and Fairbanks. "Bring me the booties you don't like and I can trade them one for one."

Some two hours after my team's arrival at McCabe, I finally made it inside the shop building. Brenda, rummy-eyed and listless, was seated at the bench table with her mom.

"Having fun yet?" I asked innocently.

Brenda lifted her head and stared. "No, Brian, I can honestly say I'm having no fun at all."

"Oh, it'll get better," I assured her. "The first days are *always* the roughest."

I could tell she thought I was insane.

A big dog dropped from Njootli's team lay stretched out on the floor by the stove. Like Brenda, he appeared shell-shocked, staring at nothing as his chest rose and fell.

SUN DANCERS

5

HOBBES

From McCabe's the trail paralleled the Klondike Highway for seven miles. Mid-morning found my team trotting alongside the pavement. The sun was out. It was a balmy day, well above zero. I stripped down to my old Iditarod vest and danced on the runners, keeping time with a Neville Brothers concert tape.

I found myself mugging for dog trucks and other passing vehicles, standing on one foot, clowning and imitating Superman in flight. One motorist jumped out with a video camera. I obliged with a show, delighting in my own balance and the team's fluid progress up the Yukon Quest Trail.

From the road, the trail veered off into a forest scarred by wildfires. The swampy, skeletal realm offered no shelter from the sun, which was rapidly softening the trail.

I was beginning to regret my seven-hour stay at McCabe's. Leaving even an hour earlier would have reducing the time spent running in the day's heat, which I sensed was already bumping the freezing point.

"It's only thirty-five miles," I told myself. "I'll broth them in a bit here."

I used the GPS to locate our position on the map. We weren't far from the mid-way point, which fell on the far side of the first of two broad lakes. That seemed the logical place to serve out the soup sloshing inside my cooler.

Trail markers stretched out across the middle of what was indeed a large lake.

Khan and Hobbes, sharing the lead, slowed as they repeatedly broke through the weakening, punchy crust. "Go ahead! Go ahead!" I shouted, fearing we'd stall if I didn't keep driving. Nearly all the dogs were gobbling bites of snow every few steps. All were panting hard before the lake's far shore took shape.

"Not much farther, guys, and I'll give you a drink."

I kicked to lighten the team's load, and sweat was rolling off my chin before we reached the chosen spot.

"Whooa," I called softly. The dogs stopped on the word. Most of them rolled in the nearby cool powder while I dug out the pans. All but one was soon lapping the soup greedily. Only Scrimshaw refused. She was an old gal and the team's smallest dog. I didn't like her listless appearance. I tried wetting Scrim's lips with the soup—a trick I picked up from Freshwaters—but she wasn't interested in drinking.

Scrim generally preferred meaty, or at least solid, meals. I threw her a chunk of whitefish. It never hit the ground. "That got your attention, girl," I said, both pleased and relieved watching her chew it, because whitefish is an excellent source of moisture. *I need to remember that.*

Outside the ice rink temporarily serving as Quest headquarters in the Native community of Pelly Crossing, Freshwaters frowned. Twenty-five teams had checked in, fifteen of those were already down the trail, but the handler was more concerned about the clear, sunny sky. "I kinda hope I don't see Brian before this evening," he muttered to himself, noting it was barely noon and already thirty-five degrees out.

Respect was growing for Andre Nadeau. Even before leading the field into Pelly Crossing the previous afternoon, a whopping three hours ahead of fellow rookie and closest challenger Louis Nelson, Sr., word began getting around about the Frenchman's accomplishments on the far side of the continent.

For starters, Nadeau, forty-two, was five-time winner of the Labrador 400. Little was known about the race other than the distance: four hundred miles, which in the very least demonstrated the guy was more than a weekend dog driver. The biography Nadeau submitted to the Quest described his occupation as a roofer, contractor, and campground operator. It also stated he was four-time champion of the Maine CANAM Crown 250. Even less was known about that particular event, but multiple victories in any dog race weren't to be scoffed at.

Furthermore, Andre Nadeau wasn't, as most presumed from his French growl, a clueless European in the mold of Joni Elomaa, that Finlander who crashed in 1997. The musher driving the well-trained Siberians hailed from Ste-Melanie, Quebec. Hell, that made Nadeau a goddamn American.

Terry McMullin had commanded the media's attention through the initial days of the race while the language barrier also served to keep reporters off Nadeau's back. By Pelly Crossing, however, McMullin's team was slipping in the standings and he looked worn. Voice diminished to a rasp, the old principal turned to a sympathetic veterinarian for personal doctoring.

Reporters hardly noticed. The Quest's mysterious new frontrunner was the man of the hour now.

When Nadeau sat down to eat inside the Pelly ice rink, print and radio reporters swarmed the table. They were joined by Danielle, a bilingual handler as curious as everybody else. She served as translator during an impromptu press conference.

Do you think you're going to win? Can you keep this pace?

Nadeau responded that he viewed the Quest as two separate events: The first being a 450-mile race between Whitehorse to Dawson City; the second, the 550-mile race from Dawson to the finish line in Fairbanks. With the thirty-six-hour break in between, the musher said, his dogs ought to handle both stages with ease.

Jack Studer, the friend whose whip proved so invaluable bringing my kennel under control, thought reporters were missing the mark. "Let's hear about your dogs. Tell us how you train."

Nadeau patiently explained that the dogs were his own breed. The team had more than three thousand miles conditioning, he said, describing his reliance on long, long runs hauling heavy loads, and always pulling a tire for good measure. His dogs were trained seven days a week, sometimes twice a day, he said.

The response impressed Studer, whose no-frills approach to mushing came from driving dogs across Nome's unforgiving tundra. He abandoned his notion of the newcomer being a damn fool pushing his dogs toward collapse. If what he said were true, Nadeau's training regimen amounted to double the conditioning of most Alaska long-distance kennels.

Studer, a jaded dog man who once toured Europe handling for the legendary Roxie Wright, liked to believe that he'd heard and seen it all. Listening to the newcomer, his mind quaked: *This Nadeau guy he's going for it.*

It wasn't just the technique. Jack Studer found himself marveling at the rookie's cool demeanor. *This guy is 100 percent cement. He's real. His boots are full.*

Gwen couldn't imagine how her team ended up on the wrong side of the highway. Who knows how far she might have strayed had those Yukon motorists not flagged her down and pitched in to guiding her team back across the road?

The trail to Pelly was supposed to be a breeze. It seemed that way as Gwen followed the Quest's broad backwoods lane into the burned-out forest.

It was hot, but the sun was low. Cresting a small hill, she nonchalantly stuck her foot out rounding a curve. The boot caught an exposed root and, just like that, tore Gwen from her sled.

Her dogs made the turn, but the heavy sled continued straight over the edge, dragging the whole team with it. "Thump, thump, thump," she heard the sled roll.

Running forward, Gwen saw her sled nesting between birch trees at the bottom of a steep gully. Her dogs looked startled, but otherwise appeared all right.

It was a nasty climb down. Tying off her dogs at the bottom, Gwen chopped down three trees to extricate the sled, bringing her logging tally to six trees in the first two hundred miles of the race. *Probably some kind of an record.* Then she hand-carried her gear up the slope. The mishap set her back an hour. So much for catching those mushers ahead. "This was supposed to be the easy section," the depressed musher muttered.

Ten minutes later, the team entered a section of the forest carpeted with icy glacial seepage. Water, a lot of water, was flowing over top of the ice. Suddenly, a geyser spouted from the ground ahead. A bizarre, waist-high fountain of water gushed before Gwen's eyes, and the trail led straight into it.

Skirting the geyser, Gwen's dogs understandably strayed from the trail, wrapping the gang line around dead trees. "God," she cried, more in frustration than fear, "I'm *never* going to get out of here!"

The heat was ridiculous, but I figured it was best to push for the checkpoint. That last soup break ought to quench the dogs' thirst. If not, well, there was there was plenty of snow to chew.

Trail sections open to the sun were deteriorating fast. We got maybe a hundred yards out on the second lake before the packed crust fell apart, plunging the dogs into sloppy powder. Hobbesey, who'd been doing great paired with Khan in lead, didn't like it one bit. She quit pulling and wallowed on her back, sun bathing.

Running forward, I plucked Hobbes out of the snow, unclipped her from the gang line, and moved her back inside the team. Khan gulped a mouthful of snow and strained forward, snapping his line tight. "Good boy," I said, scratching between his ears.

Returning to the sled, I shouted: "All right." The dogs that weren't ready picked themselves up. Onward we plowed.

From the second lake, the trail entered a healthy spruce forest. Dan Turner was camping in the shade.

"It's too hot for them," he said.

"I'm not stopping before Pelly," I said. "Can't be more than ten miles."

Leaving him behind, I felt inklings of doubt. "Turner must be crashing," I whispered, but I wasn't sure I believed it.

About 3:00 P.M., roughly four and a half hours after leaving McCabe, the Pelly River came into view, snaking across the floor of the valley below. Khan charged down the hill, conjuring images of ten thousand Mongol riders storming Kiev. He looked magnificent, anyway, leading my dozen dogs spilling onto the road at the foot of the hill, where a blazing line of Quest markers pointed to town.

We passed several houses before I saw Kate standing under a distant banner suspended high over the street. "Let's go home," I called, spurring the dogs into a lope.

"Dad-dy!" Rory sang out from my wife's backpack, watching me skid to a stop. Who'd imagine two syllables could hold such sweetness?

"We need to look at your gear," said a guy with a clipboard, reminding me where I was.

The checker, a friendly member of the local Yukon Indian band, rattled off helpful tips about the checkpoint, pointing out the water house and such, when I noticed one of the vets squatting over Scrim.

Her performance had fallen off the last few miles. The vet acted more concerned than I cared to see. At least three vets had surrounded us. They were trading disturbing glances. *And what are they whispering about?*

While I bedded the team in fresh straw, vets were examining the dogs' gums. I was tossing out whitefish chunks when Marianna, the chief vet, approached with the news I'd been dreading.

"Three of your dogs are a *bit* dehydrated," she said.

Hours earlier that same day, Ned Cathers had arrived in Pelly seriously concerned about his team. The fifty-four-year-old wilderness guide hadn't dropped any dogs—fourteen were still hitched to his sled. But all of them were short on training miles. Blame that on Lake Laberge's late freeze up. Cathers sought to compensate with short runs through the first miles of his tenth Quest. He aimed to keep his younger dogs happy while they gained the conditioning and confidence to compete down the stretch. He couldn't pull that off without help from Falcon, his main leader and one of the few seasoned dogs in the team. But Falcon was acting like a pup, constantly stopping to socialize, generally driving his master nuts.

Cathers waited to see how the dogs responded to dinner and a good rest. Alas, sleep wrought no change in attitudes. On the morning of February 11, Cathers signed the paperwork becoming the first to scratch from the 1998 race.

"For my ego, I would like to go on," the musher told a *Yukon News* reporter, "but to me that shouldn't stand in the way of making a good judgment for the dogs."

The previous afternoon, Mike Hyslop found ten other mushers lingering in Carmacks when he arrived mushing the last dog team on the trail. Sixteen hours later the company was long gone, leaving Hyslop, a forty-three-year-old frame shop owner, on his own. He soon joined Cathers on the scratch list, tossing the figurative Red Lantern forward like a hot potato to be juggled by the thirty-six mushers left in the Quest's grand elimination game.

Three years before, Kurt Smith's team faltered climbing Eagle Summit, the infamous mountain outside Central, Alaska. The forty-year-old federal park ranger was back for another try, but the road to vindication was proving rough. First, a virus weakened Smith's team.

Breaking up a dogfight outside Carmacks, the musher received a deep palm bite. Though veterinarians stitched him up, handling that sled was a bear.

The ghostly Red Lantern, touched by Gwen, then batted between Dieter and Hyslop, settled in Smith's sled before he reached McCabe Creek. But it wasn't the ranger's to keep. He soon loaded his dogs aboard a truck as Day Four's toll mounted.

Keith Kirkvold rolled into Pelly in the cool morning hours. He didn't plan an extended stay, but that changed when he checked his dogs at noon. The heat was brutal, way beyond anything his big dogs were exposed to training in Alaska's cold Interior, and it promised to get worse. Keith immediately decided to let them sleep through the afternoon.

He was surprised to observe a three-time Quester like Mike King preparing to leave.

"Michael," he said, "don't you think it's a little warm. Maybe *too* warm to go?"

King, already eight hours into his own stay, wouldn't hear of further delay. The race was getting away.

I was feeding my dogs—taking particular care to ensure Scrim, Picard, and Topher slurped the electrolytes prescribed by the vets—when a commotion drew my attention to the road. A dog team was inbound from the wrong direction. King had turned around.

His dogs looked strong passing mine and that was disappointing; King was the musher I most wanted to beat. It had to do with his kennel name, Trail King, and the huge Quest tattoo etched across his back. Everything about him was too damn loud.

"It's no good!" King shouted in this thick Maine accent, demanding attention as usual. "We sat out there under the bridge for *five hours.* These dogs are done."

No doubt the heat, thirty-eight degrees above zero, had a lot to do with it. I had three listless dogs to remind me of that. But King's demeanor suggested a deeper spiritual collapse.

I turned to my handler. "Can you imagine quitting on day nice as this? Putting a year of your life into something and just quitting."

Freshwaters was an old trail hippie. He once mushed from Ruby past Nome clear to the Eskimo village of Barrow, living off scavenged walrus and Bush hospitality. He shook his head.

"You see it happen, but I never did understand it," he said. "OK, maybe your dogs aren't ready to race, but you've got a marked trail and all your supplies waiting for you, why not make a trip out of it?"

Depression has a contagious effect on stressed dogs and brain-dead mushers. I'd seen the first signs of an outbreak back at McCabe Creek, where young Brenda appeared so down on life. Bill Steyer, likewise, though he impressed me by making it *that* far after all the reversals leaving Carmacks.

Huddled by their teams at McCabe, Brenda, Bill, Tony Blanford, and John Nash all reminded me of the ripped-off tourists that occasionally landed in my old cab, uncertain where to turn next, yet wary of trusting any New Yorker. Now paranoia isn't a bad thing to bring with you to the city, or the wilderness, but start acting like a victim in either environment and it's self-fulfilling.

Jim Hendrick, looking haggard, stopped me entering the Pelly checkpoint.

"Any of your dogs look sick?"

"Nah, Jimmy, the sun zapped a couple, but none of them are sick."

"Half my team's got diarrhea. The rest are limping," Hendrick moaned.

I was in flight mode when I spied Gwen Holdman fetching hot water for her team. "Look around," I blurted, "people are falling apart. It always happens the third or fourth day into a big race. People lose faith, their dogs sense it and start looking terrible. The whole thing's a vicious circle. Before you know it, teams are scratching."

Gwen nodded. She recalled hearing something similar from Joe May.

I continued: "You've got the dogs and I think, Gwen, that you have what it takes to make it the distance. Just hang in there through the next few days.

"Good luck," I added, "hope to see you up the trail."

Only that last part was a lie.

Lining out my dogs for departure that evening, I shared my own greatest fear with Freshwaters. "We're doing OK, but the back of the race is catching up," I said. "Same thing happened to me on the Iditarod. Every time I passed somebody it was like the kiss of death.

"If I want to beat anybody at all, I need to keep Gwen and as many of these other teams in the race as I can."

"Oh, I wouldn't worry. Brian," he said. "Take care of the dogs and I think you'll do fine."

The darkness felt tangible. It pressed upon the tunnel punched by my headlamp. *You've got fresh batteries*, I reminded myself, *and it isn't as dark as it seems.*

There's a cure for night blindness, but it requires an act of faith: I smacked the power switch on the battery pack, killing the lamp.

The tunnel immediately gave way to a dimmer, but broader, starlit landscape. My dog team was a furry blue-white blur, floating along the shelf overhanging the wider river below. My vision improved, along with my sense of balance, as we continued without the headlamp's glare. But this, too, was an illusion of sorts. Absent the headlamp I couldn't make out details of the trail ahead. Markers essential to staying on course might go undetected without their reflective gleam. I smacked the button again. Now that my eyes had adjusted to darkness, the beam appeared more powerful, reaching several times as far up the trail.

Khan kissed Hobbes, and both looked frisky sharing lead. All twelve of my dogs looked alert and happy, exchanging more kisses and sniffing the reminders of twenty-five previous teams.

We'd leaped in the standings, reflecting both the day's casualties and my six-hour stay in Pelly. As I had expected, most of the other rookies lingered a good while longer before attempting the Quest's intimidating two hundred and twenty-mile jump to Dawson City, the longest run between supply points of any major sled dog race.

I had one additional bit of strategy in play: Though my sled felt as if it weighed a ton, the load was lightened by freeze-dried meat. It was a new product and outrageously expensive: ten dollars or more per pound, compared to fifty-five cents for similar amounts of conventional meats, but the tiny cubes were light as dust.

I had bought three hundred dollars' worth, roughly thirty-three pounds of the space-age beef, and shipped it out to key places on the trail. For the Dawson run, I took fifteen pounds, enough for five full team meals—one more than the mileage indicated was necessary—yet sixty pounds lighter than the same amount of conventional meat.

The sled glanced off a piece of hardened crust. I saw it coming but reacted clumsily and launched sideways, momentarily teetering, then dropping off the shelf's jagged lip. The sled crashed hard on huge chunks of ice, but the total fall was only about four feet, which came as such a relief I almost burst out laughing. That mirth was snuffed as the dogs continued along the shelf above, flipping the sled, dragging it and me another ten feet until the brush bow finally wedged under an icy boulder.

My shoulder and hip stung, but the sled was intact, if stuck.

"This could be a bitch," I whispered, wondering how I was supposed to restrain a well-rested twelve-dog team if I had to disconnect the goddamned sled.

Seizing the brush bow with both hands, I placed my foot against the shelf's edge for leverage and, with a desperate yank, wrenched it free. Khan and the other dogs felt the movement in the gang line and surged. I danced to avoid being pinned as they hauled the nose of the sled up onto the shelf. The bulk of its weight remained below the lip, anchoring the team from going a step farther.

"Looking good, very good," I chirped, studying the alignment.

Taking position behind the sled, I gripped the handle bar with both hands for an all-out push. If this failed, I could always unload the frigging thing, though I dreaded that.

"Ready!" The dogs leaned forward, familiar with what comes next.

"All right!" The dogs pulled. I pushed. The sled popped over the edge, dragging me along on my belly.

Again, the brush with disaster left me feeling absurdly giddy. "We've gone what? A mile, guys?"

Feets glanced back at me.

"That only leaves about two hundred and nineteen miles to Dawson! Piece of cake. Right?"

Realizing I wasn't addressing him, Feets turned back toward the trail. He had tracks to follow. Other dogs to meet.

Brenda Mackey was walking in circles. She kept mentioning how tired she was, but wouldn't sleep. Watching her, Gwen, a worldly twenty-five, felt sorry for the poor teen.

If she appeared scatterbrained, Brenda had cause. The nine dogs she had left were giving her fits. Coming over from McCabe they moved OK, but seemed weak. When she attempted to really gorge them in Pelly, most refused to eat.

If that weren't enough, Roland, the family's toddler, had some kind of flu, making life miserable on her mother. While Brenda empathized with that—she worried about the little guy herself—her mother was driving her crazy!

Brenda longed to scratch and go home. College, which she put off attending to concentrate on sled-dog racing, suddenly beckoned. Anything to escape from this nightmare.

Even Brenda's grandfather was on her case.

"Scratch?" Dick Mackey had cried, looking angrier than she'd ever seen him. "You haven't earned the right to scratch. Go home now and you'll be a quitter. That's all. A quitter."

It wasn't like that. The teen figured she was being realistic. If her team folded mid-way to Dawson, a possibility she *had* to consider, chartering a rescue flight would be horrendously expensive. She *had* to factor that in; her bills from this Quest were *out of control*.

Late in the evening, the third time she offered them a meal, Brenda's dogs showed an appetite. Everyone, that is, but Star, the lead dog she'd leased from McKee. Star merely nibbled on snacks.

The young musher's outlook was fatalistic. Her mother picked up on that and the pair really got into it. At last, feeling she'd lose her mind if she didn't escape her mom, Brenda pitched her gear into the sled and was gone before anyone knew it. Her fury made the even the Quest Trail inviting.

Gwen slept six wonderful hours and awoke feeling chipper. She had dropped only one dog so far. The thirteen she had left were doing great. Other mushers in Pelly were having a tougher time, that much was obvious.

Maybe I can do all right, Gwen told herself for the first time since leaving Whitehorse.

Only minutes away from leaving, Gwen noticed a sheared bolt at the base of her sled's rear stanchion. Her dogs, refreshed by their four-teen-hour stay in Pelly, were whining and bouncing in their harnesses. Two other good bolts shared the load on the bracket attaching the stanchion to the runner. Repairs could wait, judged Gwen Holdman, reaching for her snow hook.

Under a brilliant moon, I glided past old farm buildings perched overlooking the Pelly River. Compared to the Yukon's jarring brutality, this was mushing on a cloud. I ran most of the night with my headlamp switched off, reveling in the blur of shadowy fur rippling along the river's deep groove.

The temperature had dropped to about ten degrees. I was dancing to another of my brother's new tapes, listening to some bluesy woman belt it out. The only blemish on the ride was our speed.

How many times had I said it? "Khan's not real fast, but I don't think he'll lose much either." It became my standard line, one I repeated so often to Kate and everybody else that I took it as an article of faith: The Mighty One would deliver a steady eight miles an hour on the trail.

"Wrong!" I said, beholding the digital truth. On this absolutely flat, well-compacted trail, the GPS showed my team was traveling precisely 7.1 mph. *Boy, that'll throw fear into the competition.* Khan was paired with Hobbes, but she wasn't about to push him. I could tap Cyclone for a boost, but he and Khan had been trading growls recently. And

I was content to leave Danger in swing, feeling fortunate to see him alive.

Picard and Topher occasionally allowed their tug lines to sag, as did Scrim. All three still showing the effects of that hot run into Pelly. I was lucky they retained their appetites. A few more days of dosing with the powdered supplements provided by the vets, and the trio ought to bring them around. In that respect, Khan's leisurely cruising speed couldn't hurt.

The markers steered us into a forest. Stepping Stone, a traditional Quest hospitality stop, had to be close. The trail broadened, cutting a broad swath through ancient trees. This was confirmation, because Stepping Stone was located on the Old Stage Trail, one of the big stampede routes into Dawson. "Cool," I whispered, wondering if any ghosts were watching.

We entered a cluster of cabins. Lamps glowed in the windows of one of them. Seconds later, I came upon the hand-written sign directing Quest mushers to the riverbank below.

Several other teams were camped on the frozen beach overlooking the Pelly's broad mouth. I directed Khan to the end of the line and tied him off on a piece of driftwood.

A curl of northern lights flickered along the sky's lower edges. I was flexing my back, watching the electric flower blossoming overhead, when a volunteer from Whitehorse joined me on the beach.

"How long until the next team?"

"Oh, I'd say, a good hour or two. Didn't see *anybody* behind me out there."

That very moment a dog team spilled from woods.

"Shows how much I know," I said sheepishly. Walter Palkovitch had been shadowing me for hours and I never had a clue.

It was 2:30 A.M., green and yellow tendrils swirled above, basking the frozen beach in surreal, shimmering light.

"We've got stew waiting for you in the cabin," the volunteer said.

❖ ❖ ❖

Eighty miles ahead, Canvas and Clovis, a pair of surprising two-year-olds, led Bruce Lee's team on the rolling, twisting, largely overgrown road to Scroggy Creek's closed mine.

Lee liked what he saw bounding ahead of him. These dogs were happy, well-rested, and possessed speed rivaling any team on the trail. Lee had run enough races himself, and watched others do it enough times as a judge, to appreciate the significance of this performance some three hundred and fifty miles into the Quest.

"This team is prime right now," he observed quietly, cautiously, as if to acknowledge such a thing was dangerous. "Prime."

The game was also going well. He could hardly believe it, but Rick Mackey, the defending champ, Schandelmeier, MacDougall—all of them stopped at Stepping Stone. And that made no sense. With the recent addition of Pelly as a checkpoint, the old homestead arrived too soon to justify camping, particularly in a year as warm as this. The way Lee saw it, Stepping Stone's hospitality was positively dangerous.

Lee's schedule carried him three hours farther up the trail, where he refilled his cooler using the watery overflow always seeping from the hillside in that area. He ran straight through the morning and camped as the day's heat set in. It pleased him to see his dogs stretching lazily on their backs, bellies soaking in the sun.

Mackey and the others didn't show up until sundown. By then, Lee was breaking camp. The timing suggested his chief rivals were badly off schedule. Confirmation arrived as Mackey and the others declined to chase him up the trail.

Whether by design or ignorance, another musher had skipped past Stepping Stone; Nadeau's runner tracks stretched before Bruce Lee now.

Lee was too shrewd to blindly dismiss anyone. He made note of Nadeau's departure from Pelly, then paused just long enough at Stepping Stone to check on the rookie's time through. The Quest veteran was pleased to note his own team covered the same section ninety minutes quicker. *His dogs are slow!*

There's only one way a musher driving slower dogs holds the lead, and that's by running the team longer than resting, a formula whose side effects inevitably catch up over a thousand miles. If Nadeau was doing that, well . . . *He's in way over his head.*

Following Nadeau's tracks mile after mile, however, inklings of doubt nibbled at the veteran's complacency. *What if he took a long break between Pelly and Stepping Stone?* Speed comparisons would, of course, be meaningless, Lee realized. So Nadeau's dogs *might* be swifter than he assumed, and *that* would explain why he hadn't overtaken him. It was something to keep in mind.

Surveying the competition in Pelly, The Mowth saw few surprises. Teams he'd be lucky to beat were mostly ahead of him. Those with less experience were, with few exceptions, falling behind. His team, well, it wasn't setting any records, but Rudy, the reddish-haired, barrel-chested male who'd led most of the way a year ago, looked rock solid.

Mowry accepted that his hopes for a top-five finish were out of reach. The goal now was collecting a paycheck by finishing in the top fifteen. He'd been here before. Oh yeah. He'd been in this same position enough times to know some guys ahead of him were bound to fold. Cathers, who'd beaten him into Pelly, was history. McMullin was already showing the signs. Nelson, the old villager from Kotzebue, was another guy ripe for picking off.

Nelson was the target as Mowry pulled out of Stepping Stone near sundown on February 11. They'd pulled in together, but ol' Louie cut rest by about two hours and bolted. He still hadn't figured out this was a thousand-mile race.

The revelation concerning Mowry's own race came on Scroggy Creek Road.

Rudy stopped and sat down

Mowry couldn't believe it: That was way too deliberate for an injury time-out. He shifted Rudy back in the ranks. The dog responded with his usual all-out effort, which wasn't at all reassuring to his master. The lead dogs Mowry that had left—Laverne, Figaro, and Alf—were cream puffs, great during training, but all known to crumble in past Quests.

Rudy was no quitter, Tim "The Mowth" Mowry would swear to that, but his number-one dog had just delivered a great impression.

SHIFTING FORTUNES

CINDER

Cinder noticed first. He sprung to his feet, staring at the river. Other heads turned. Searchlight's snout remained buried under a paw, but her ears twisted, probing like a radar station, until they locked onto something beyond my own ability to hear. I quit collecting food pans and scanned the Yukon, which twinkled with golden crystals in the morning sun.

A dog team was cutting down the river's far side.

Dropping the pans, I followed the team's progress. "Has to be bad news," I whispered, squinting as I tried to make out just who was returning to Stepping Stone, and whether the musher was packing any dogs.

The team was practically on the beach before I recognized old Terry McMullin. The Quest's one-time leader was hunched over the handlebar, his upper body teetering with each dip in the trail. His face was grayer and whiter than the mop of hair showing above the collar of his big, loose parka.

Terry didn't brake and his team raced up the beach toward mine. I intercepted his leaders to prevent a tangle. "Want some help parking?"

McMullin nodded. If he said something, I couldn't hear it. I pulled his leaders over to a stick of driftwood embedded in the hard snow. Terry got his hook down, then leaned on his sled, wheezing.

"Got up into the hills," he rasped. "But I couldn't help the dogs. Too sick. Had to turn back."

One of the volunteers led the ailing musher inside.

Soon as I finished packing, I joined them. Terry was slumped in a chair, looking defeated.

"Too sick," he croaked, shaking his head.

"Hey, you had a hell of a race," I reminded him. "You led the Quest for what, two hundred miles? Not many people can say that."

He smiled weakly.

As early as McCabe's, the retired principal knew he was contending with more than a passing cold. McMullin drove himself, hoping to just work through it. He was so out of it in Pelly that he broke up a scrap without noticing that one of the combatants had suffered a wrist bite. It swelled something awful, and McMullin wound up leaving the dog, a good swing dog, behind. He still held seventh place at that point, but the great slide had begun. Another ten teams leaped past before he first left Stepping Stone.

McMullin was already zero for three on the Iditarod. One of those scratches resulted from a similar bout with illness on the trail. The Quest, his grand post-retirement adventure, was meant to erase those past disappointments.

Woozily weighing his options at Stepping Stone on February 12, McMullin divided the meals left in his sled by miles yet to go. The effort made his feverish mind swim, without changing his plight. The next food cache was Dawson, one hundred and eighty miles away. Even if McMullin shook this bug over the next few hours, Riley and the crew were sure to run out of food. His race was finished.

Down on the beach, I cursed my own sluggish movements. Nash and Walter, two teams I passed overnight, were already making tracks out on the river. "Get your shit together, man," I told myself. "The race is getting away."

Packing nearby, Brenda, another musher who had trailed me into Stepping Stone, railed about oversleeping.

"Did you hear anyone try to wake me?"

"No," I said, chuckling. "But I heard them talking about it. The guy claimed he shook you really hard."

Brenda frowned and resumed fastening booties. She was brooding about a comment made by one of the Quest volunteers. "You must have needed your sleep, dear," the woman had said.

Hearing that, she'd almost choked on a thick slice of homemade bread. "Oh no, I didn't," snapped Brenda, whose competitive nature was returning now that she and the dogs were on their own.

Coming over from Pelly, Brenda *had* repeatedly dozed, but she couldn't afford to relax, not if she wanted to catch up with Rusty and Keith. She'd been thrilled to find the pair still camping in Stepping Stone. It was a huge bummer watching them leave before her team was even fed. The volunteer's subsequent failure to wake her compounded the disappointment.

"I'll follow you out," Brenda called, seeing me position Khan and Hobbes facing the trail.

It was 10:30 A.M. Even before I crossed the river, I realized the heat was against us today. Khan and Hobbes settled into their usual plugging gait. Brenda overtook us on the first hill.

"Brian," she called, "mind if I go ahead of you?"

"Nah," I said. "We both know who's faster. Heat's going to shut us down before long anyway."

Her team passed mine and immediately left us. Khan, savage conqueror of the Klondike, couldn't get close enough to bite a Mackey team unless it was parked.

A few miles later, another dog team passed us head-on. It was Nash. Two dogs eyed me from his sled bag.

"I'm scratching," he said grimly.

"You sure you don't . . . "

"No."

"I'm sorry to hear it. I was looking forward to a rematch out on the Chena River," I said, reminding John of our duel down the final miles of the Hahn 200.

A smile flickered on his face. Then Nash shook his head and resumed the long march home.

The sun steadily intensified. Before long, Picard's tug line sagged so low it left marks in the softening snow. Topher and Scrim, the other dogs zapped out on the lakes, performed only marginally better.

I began resting the team a full five minutes out of every thirty. Most took advantage of the breaks to chomp snow. All of my dogs were panting. Khan, hardest of all. Each breath released a cloud that hovered like an indictment. *If I had stayed six hours instead of eight—cut loose two hours earlier, two hours cooler!*

"Face it," I said, "you screwed up again."

Brenda drove to roughly the midway point between Stepping Stone and the Quest's Scroggy Creek camp. She was pulling out cooking supplies when she heard dogs barking nearby.

Walking forward, she saw marks indicating quite a few teams had camped in this same area. In one campsite she saw a packet of batteries, supplement powder and—this was incredible—Blue Heron tablets, an herbal formula for combating diarrhea in sled dogs.

"Oh my gosh," Brenda cried, recognized the combination. "This is where Dad camped."

That put a smile on her face.

Brenda's mood brightened even more when she traced the source of the noise to Walter's team, camping not far ahead. Another musher picked that moment to stroll back from the opposite direction, curious to see who'd joined his group's balmy afternoon siesta. "Oh, Rusty," Brenda cried. "I'm *so* glad to see you.

Bill Steyer was reeling. With the glow on the horizon signaling the dawn of the Quest's fifth day, Bunko, his best dog, an expensive veteran dog, was barely keeping his feet. Bill had already moved the big guy out of lead. He'd made that change made midway from Pelly with positive results.

But now, perhaps an hour shy of Stepping Stone, Bunko was having trouble keeping up. At first, Bill simply stared; The Insurance Policy was neck-lining.

As he stopped and loaded him, Bill searched his memory about the status of Stepping Stone. *Is it an official dog drop?* He didn't think so, but wasn't sure. *And if it isn't, what does that mean?*

He knew provisions existed for leaving ailing dogs at the tent camp set up near Stewart River, but that was another seventy or eighty miles up the trail. Bill couldn't fathom carrying sixty-five-pound Bunko all that way. *Maybe I should turn around?* Pelly *was* closer, but Bill had already experienced the damage of backtracking.

Bill mushed into Stepping Stone in time to watch Brenda chase me out.

The beleaguered musher hardly parked before a volunteer broke the news he'd been dreading: Stepping Stone wasn't a dog drop.

Feeling low, Bill tended his dogs then trudged up to the main cabin. Inside, he met a Quest volunteer of longer standing, who recalled mushers leaving behind injured dogs in past races.

"I've got to call in an update to Dawson," the woman said. "Maybe you'll want to talk to the officials?"

Hope flared within Bill Steyer.

They managed to get Rich on the radio phone. "You can drop the dog," the race marshal said, "but you have to make your own arrangements, fly the dog out at your own costs, *and* you're going to get a penalty."

Rich was unspecific what that penalty might be. They could settle that in Dawson.

Bill was discussing transport for his dog when Nash showed up. He had an entire team to evacuate. What was one more dog? Nash agreed to take Bunko with him to Pelly Farm, the closest place his handler could meet him with the dog truck.

Gwen had trailed Bill into Stepping Stone by about two hours. They agreed to travel together as soon as it cooled off.

Bill had little confidence in his remaining leaders, but he put on a bold front that afternoon, leaving Stepping Stone before Gwen. The dogs fulfilled his worst expectations, putting on their "stupid act," as Bill called it, farting and pissing, looking lousy and dispirited in general as they meandered out onto the river.

Gwen's dogs were yipping and leaping in harness. She caught Bill within the first mile and then had trouble holding them back. He finally waved her ahead.

Gwen passed him on the fly and continued, maybe, a hundred yards before stopping dead. "My God," she said, staring down at a stanchion attached to a bracket completely severed from the runner below. "My sled's broken."

The world around me was melting. I was fortunate that my bibs were water-resistant, otherwise I would have been soaked from kneeling to tend paws. It was 6:00 P.M. and hadn't cooled off that much, but the sun was dipping and I was fed up with waiting.

Khan bellowed merrily and threw himself at the trail. Hobbesey briefly neck-lined before joining the big guy's effort. *Better watch her.*

The dogs were freshly brothed. Usually that served to quench their thirst for a few hours, but not in this weather. I had dogs nipping snow from the get-go. Hobbes, whose beautiful thick gray coat was a major liability tonight, gulped another mouthful with nearly every step.

"Damn this weather," I muttered, grudgingly checking my watch. If this heat didn't let up, I might have to stretch the breaks to ten minutes out of every thirty.

Hobbes seized upon the first stop to leap into the deep snow bordering the trail. She planted her belly in it and wiggled happily. "Good girl," I coaxed, motioning for her to rejoin me on the trail, where Khan, panting with a toothy grin, rested on folded front paws.

Turning heads alerted me to another team's approach. I ran to the sled, crouched, gripping my fingers around the hook. "All right," I called, yanking it free. The sled jerked forward.

Whistling Khan and Hobbes into a lope, I attempted to shake the pursuit, but the other team gradually gained ground. I was resigned to being passed when Hobbes suddenly launched sideways, sending her teammates careening into each other. I barely dodged ramming Rick and Feets. Glancing over at Hobbes, I saw my burly girl playfully wallowing in snow.

"Maybe you should pass," I called to Tony Blanford, whose leaders were sniffing the back of my legs.

"Oh, that's all right," he said. "We'll be taking a break soon."

"You came straight through from Stepping Stone then?"

"That's right," Blanford said.

The news cheered me up. Considering their recent rest, my team remained significantly ahead. I pulled Hobbesey out of the snow, hopped back on the sled, and off we went.

Less than a mile later, Hobbes dove for another belly-rubbing session; she was losing her mind in this heat. "Got to change leaders," I called to Blanford. "Sure you don't want to go ahead?"

He waved me off and flipped open his sled. He was tossing out snacks as my team pulled away, this time with Khan leading solo. Riding backward, I watched Blanford's team shrink in the distance. His dogs appeared faster than mine, but that wasn't proven yet. He might be drafting on us; a close chase makes any dog team look good. "Let's see what he's got," I said, swiveling back toward Khan and the crew. "Go ahead! Go ahead!"

We made good time until Khan halted on the edge of a wide clearing. The hillside glistened with ice, bathed by rivulets of trickling water. "So much for those new booties," I said, sighing.

I joined Khan in front, surveying the hazard. A flat pool of overflow, perhaps fifty-feet wide, covered the trail. The pea-green color of the slushy seepage signaled it was fairly fresh. I edged out onto it warily.

Like a spongy wrestling mat, the surface gave slightly, but supported my weight. Even if we did break through the surface, it *couldn't* be all that deep. *Right*, I thought. *Tell yourself that.*

Some leaders balk at crossing wet surfaces. We hadn't seen anything like this in training, so I had no idea how Khan might react. On cue, he marched right out into it. The Savage One didn't care for the slippery footing, however, and veered downslope. Treading upon small bushes he skirted the pool's lower edge. *It works for me.*

Emerging from the far side of the pool, I stopped and began stripping off booties before they could freeze to the dogs' feet. The evening's balmy temperature made that unlikely, but conditions might change.

A dozen dogs equals forty-eight booties. I was changing booties when Blanford appeared on the opposite side of the pool. I stood up and waved as he left his sled to inspect the obstacle.

"What you want to do is circle it to the left," I called, pointing to the broken bushes.

I couldn't tell if he understood me or not.

The rookie was standing there, frozen with apparent indecision, when I pulled the hook.

Khan charged. I smiled. The gap opened anew.

Lee wasn't chasing anyone, not yet, but the rookie had his attention.

Trailing Nadeau all those miles into Stewart River, Lee found his curiosity growing for both the man and his dogs. The frontrunner's team was sleeping when he reached the remote tent camp. Lee couldn't tell anything about the dogs from that. He needed to watch those dogs leave, that would tell him all he needed to know about the rookie's judgment.

Nadeau, with whom Lee had yet to even make eye contact, was either sleeping or eating in one of the tents. The veteran finished his chores and went to join the volunteers for a promised steak. He returned to find the frontrunner's campsite empty; Andre Nadeau had cunningly slipped away.

Well, that's interesting.

Mushers Cor Guimond and Paddy Santucci showed up during Lee's five-hour stop at Stewart River. The real opposition, in Lee's opinion, remained unaccounted for: Mackey, Schandelmeier, and Turner, the three proven champions.

Nadeau wasn't merely a Quest rookie, he was mushing his first-ever Alaska sled-dog race. *It's like a surfer coming to Hawaii for the first time,* Lee reasoned, *I don't care how good you are, you haven't seen the best.*

Lee was reconnecting tug-line snaps, when Schandelmeier and Mackey finally pulled into Stewart River. The defending champ stopped directly alongside.

"You just get here, too?"

Lee searched Mackey's face for signs the other musher was kidding. What he read amazed him: *Rick actually doesn't know I'm six hours ahead of him!*

Lee honestly described his last runs, and the advantage he now possessed; lies being so common in sled dog races, he figured Mackey wouldn't believe him anyway.

The champ followed Lee out, but only went as far as the tree stand across the river. Lee presumed the move was aimed at throwing off pursuit from Schandelmeier and the other mushers camped back at Stewart River. *Rick's just messing with them,* Lee deduced, admiring Mackey's willingness to forgo the hospitality waiting in the nearby tents.

The schedule Lee worked out prior to the race called for resting and feeding his dogs at Granville, an open cabin in an old mining settlement roughly halfway to Dawson. He pulled over just shy of the junction.

Although he couldn't see the cabin from where he stood, Lee felt reasonably sure he'd find the frontrunner there, soaking up the hospitality. And everything he'd seen so far suggested that Andre Nadeau would hook up and go the minute anyone caught up.

The veteran decided to explore what might happen if he failed to cooperate. He camped alongside the trail, positioning his sled where he could lean back and observe the rookie's next move.

Forty minutes later, a helicopter made a low pass before touching down at the cabin. Lee heard barking and imagined the conversation sure to follow: "Oh, there's another team right around the corner."

A snowmachiner from Granville buzzed over to talk with Lee. The helicopter was packed with German tourists, Fulda people, he told the musher. Lee was more interested in hearing about Nadeau.

"So when *did* Andre get here?"

The information indicated Lee's team had covered the distance two hours faster, which fit with his previous calculations about their relative speeds. As the snowmachiner roared off, Lee heard the frontrunner's dogs barking and howling again. The racket made Lee smile.

Nadeau was on the run.

The rookie's team trotted past. Lee automatically checked his watch. *Stick with the plan.* He had another two and a half hours to kill. He was sorely tempted to scrap the schedule. That pouch of nuggets beckoned.

Lee got up and nervously paced, suppressing instincts inflamed by the rookie's predictable flight. "You're not going to do this. Nope, you're not going to do this," Lee muttered while his dogs slept. "You're *going* to stay here."

In Stewart River earlier that same afternoon, The Mowth prepared for the hundred-mile run to Dawson with dread. Though Rudy performed like a champ inside the ranks, he sat down every time Mowry put him in lead. Laverne and Figaro weren't much better. That left only Alf, an older sled dog prone to injuries, a leader whose forward movements were proportional to the volume of the musher's commands, a furtive pace-setter inclined to fall apart in situations far less demanding than the Quest. This was the same lead dog, in fact, that quit on Tim "The Mowth" Mowry the last time they tackled Eagle Summit together.

And Alf was his best shot.

Contemplating the dog's many faults, Mowry grimly added the extra gang line section needed to place a single leader at the helm of a ten-dog team. It was the logical step, the musher knew, but he made the adjustment with a heavy heart: *I'll be lucky to get to Dawson.*

❖ ❖ ❖

Like winged Icarus of Greek myth, the so-called Flying Finn soared to intoxicating heights before plummeting. "The speed of the dogs is not surprising to me. It is my breed," bragged Joni Elomaa, charging into Braeburn ahead of the 1997 field, as if the lodge marked the finish line, rather than the first choice camp. Those racy dogs never saw the Quest finish line, though there was more to that story.

A rookie actually won the 1994 Quest. But Lavon Barve, a perennial Iditarod contender, was a seasoned long-distance racer. He began conservatively and let others set the pace until the situation was ripe for a decisive surge across the finish line.

The few comments that Andre Nadeau made about his strategy—combining long marches and short rests—struck most observers as foolish. His poor dogs couldn't keep up the pace, they said, smugly circulating the field reports radioed from Stewart River and various cabins, which showed Bruce Lee steadily gaining ground.

Other rookies soaring through the early checkpoints—McMullin, Nelson, Wright—had all tumbled in the standings. If Nadeau's comeuppance didn't happen in the Black Hills, where the team faced 3,550-foot elevation Eureka Dome, said the handlers and reporters dissecting the race in cafes and cozy truck cabs, wait until those hapless dogs hit King Solomon, the intimidating 3,800-foot gateway to Dawson.

It came as a shock, 8:10 P.M. on February 12, when Andre Nadeau mushed the first team into Dawson, claiming the pouch of gold nuggets awaiting the first musher to the Quest's midway point. Far from being exhausted, all but one of the race leader's dogs remained on their feet as officials checked his sled for required gear. As the minutes stretched, those Siberian-blooded demons grew impatient and actually howled.

"We don't usually see that in Dawson," a race judge wryly observed.

The master of those dogs exuded confidence.

"No problem," Nadeau said, describing his team's journey in clipped English. "The dogs just work, work, work. There was no push."

More than two hours passed before Lee trailed the rookie into town. While he missed out on the gold, the veteran had chopped Nadeau's lead in half over the last hundred miles, carefully positioning his team for the yet-to-come run through the treacherous ice reported north of Dawson.

"It's kind of like playing chess, playing chess against someone very good," Lee told KUAC-FM's John McWhorter. "When they move a piece, they're not moving just that piece, they're manipulating the whole board to where they want to be four or five moves from now. That's what you have to be doing all the time."

Even before Stewart River, Lee began adjusting his runs to enter Dawson as near as possible to midnight with the goal of completing the team's mandatory thirty-six-hour layover at high noon or thereabouts. "I wanted the heat of the day to slow the dogs down," he explained to the radio reporter. "And I wanted the light so I can see."

Lee's 9:30 P.M. arrival, while not optimum, fit with his strategy to leave town in the calming sun.

He had spotted Nadeau two hours and thirty minutes at Granville. Given previous running-time comparisons, Lee figured his team would knock that down substantially during the sixty-mile run into town. Yet, the time sheet revealed his swift runners trimmed a mere ten minutes off the rookie's supposed plodders. *This guy is a serious competitor.*

Once again Lee confronted the possibility the stealthy musher from Quebec might possess more speed than he was showing. *That* held particular relevance for Lee, who still nursed the wounds of his last Quest.

"Face it," Bruce Lee reminded himself, "you *never* saw Charlie coming."

Gwen was flummoxed. She risked breaking a runner if she continued. But she didn't have the right bolts or tools to reattach the stanchion bracket. This situation was the pits. Her race was looking up—and now this!

Bill came over to look. He agreed her sled needed immediate repair, not that he had any idea how that might be accomplished.

The pair heard the whine of an engine. Gwen ran down the trail and flagged a passing snowmachine. It was a family from the nearby farm, a father and two kids. The man took a look at Gwen's sled then buzzed off to get his cordless drill. In less than an hour, the grateful sled dog racer was good to go.

Gwen was about to leave when Bill, who'd been quietly brooding on his sled, got up to announce that he was scratching. "I've lost my main leader, and my other dogs aren't doing anything for me," he said, looking woeful and shrunken.

The problem isn't the team, it's the driver, thought Gwen, sensing Bill's judgment was clouded by depression. "Let's just go fifteen minutes and think about it again," she suggested, betting the other musher would come around if she lured him far enough from Stepping Stone.

The first few miles Gwen held her dogs back, presenting an enticing target for the team behind. The chase worked its magic. Thereafter, Bill had no trouble keeping up.

Later, rolling along Scroggy Creek Road, Gwen spied a fur hat on the trail and neatly snatched it as she passed. "Somebody is missing this hat right now," she whispered, examining the hat for a clue to its owner.

Schandelmeier had briefed Gwen in the trail, sharing tips about campsites. She carried notes from that conversation on waterproof cards. His next recommendation called for camping on the same ridge Brenda and Rusty chose earlier, an area Schandelmeier touted for its great firewood.

Bill's team perked up and nightfall saw him leading en route to the ridge, when the pair came upon a bewildered and nervous Tony Blanford. "You've got to help me build a fire," the musher said, explaining that he was *really* cold from losing his hat.

Gwen smiled and fished out the mystery hat. She and Bill urged Blanford to join them a few miles up the trail, where they promised a big bonfire.

That was agreeable to Blanford, a tall, chunky thirty-eight-year-old musher with a light mustache. He'd tried to get a fire going, he said. Had botched it. Should have done more camping with the dogs prior to the race, that was obvious, he confessed. Hadn't been time for it, Blanford added, now babbling, or so it seemed to Gwen, about the demands of his full-time job as a Fairbanks psychiatrist.

Gwen and Bill were bustling about, preparing meals for their dogs, when the rattled doctor caught up. Gwen dispatched Blanford to collect firewood. He returned with armload of damp branches, apparently gathered off the ground. *That's why he couldn't build a fire*, Gwen realized. *He doesn't know what wood to get.*

She sighed and gathered fuel herself, snapping dead lower branches from nearby trees, a ready source of dry tinder. Gwen soon had a crackling fire going.

Bill was again resting on his sled, which he had parked ahead of the other teams. Gwen was wondering if she should invite him over when he appeared toting his sleeping bag, and promptly stretched out near the fire.

Wanting everyone to be cozy, Gwen rummaged through her sled and pulled out foam pads she had brought for her dogs to sleep upon. The dogs hadn't cared for them, but the pads demonstrated their value as sleeping mats for Gwen, Bill, and Blanford. Snow was falling in huge wet flakes, so Gwen also passed out dog blankets, custom-made from windproof fabric, to keep them all dry.

While she busied about making the camp more comfortable, Gwen asked the men to gather more wood. Blanford was more than willing, but returned with more wood of dubious quality several times. She asked Bill to lend a hand.

"Yeah, whatever," Bill said repeatedly, but didn't stir.

That irked Gwen, but she didn't say anything. It seemed easier to fetch fuel herself.

In the morning, Bill showed irritation as Gwen puttered about, repacking her sled and attending her dogs.

"Just go then," she snapped, feeling peevish.

Bill and Blanford briefly conferred. Afterward, Bill came over to Gwen, who was still putting on booties as fast as she possibly could.

"Tony's not looking too good. He's thinking about scratching," Bill said. "We need to help him out the way you helped me last night. Everyone gets bummed out and he is right now. We need to work with him."

"That sounds great," said Gwen, warmed by the display of camaraderie.

Bill, observing that his own team remained a question mark, tested them by going first. "I'll just wait for you guys a little way up the trail."

Gwen smiled; everything was cool.

Blanford followed Gwen out of the camp. As usual, her dogs were keyed up and ready to race. Merely hanging on was demanding.

Within minutes of breaking camp, Gwen realized Blanford *was* in trouble. *I've never seen a dog team move so slowly.*

She parked until he caught up. Then she ran another hundred yards and stopped to wait. Another hundred yards. Another stop. It was bad, really bad. Blanford's team seemed worse off than Bill's had ever been. Which raised another issue: *Where is Bill?* He had made such a point of them teaming up to help Tony . . .

At last, Blanford's team achieved steady, albeit sluggish, progress.

"I'm going to find Bill," Gwen shouted.

Calling up her dogs, Gwen Holdman streaked forward, chewing up the miles with the team all three knew was the fastest in their group. It took her more than twenty minutes racing at a bounding, rolling lope, to overtake her erstwhile campfire companion.

"Hey, how are you doing?" Bill yelled back to Gwen, grinning pleasantly.

"Where the *hell* have you been?"

The pair stopped to discuss matters. Gwen, incensed at Bill's apparent blindness to his mounting offenses, unloaded.

"I'm sorry," Bill spluttered at last, "my team was going really good and I just wanted to keep 'em rolling."

"Well, thanks for remembering us."

Gwen was done waiting. She and Bill wrote Blanford a note and stuck it on a trail marker. But the mushing psychiatrist finally had his dogs figured out. He caught up before Gwen and Bill were finished.

Gwen led on the high ridge overlooking Valhalla Creek, where the forest hadn't ever recovered from a wildfire. Mushing through the thinned trees she was awed by the sweeping view. She noted the net effect in her February 13 journal entry:

"Valhalla Valley is grand country, very big. Makes me feel so small . . . "

DAWSON OR BUST

7

RICK

Listen to yourself!" I shouted at Larry Carroll, whose team was parked across the clearing. The bearish musher from Willow, Alaska, was bending a volunteer's ear concerning Rick Mackey's alleged deceit in treating the Quest as a race.

"You're whining," I said. "It's five o'clock in the morning, and you're sitting out here whining, Larry."

He spluttered. "I am *not* whining, it's, it's just . . . "

"Give it a rest, Larry. Booty your dogs or something."

The exchange earned curious looks from Cinder and Danger. None of my dogs were sleeping. Though most were exhausted, my dinner preparations had even the weariest in the group keeping an eye peeled for further developments.

Five other dog teams resting in the clearing below the Quest tents at Stewart River signaled to the crew that it was time to kick back and savor the rewards of another job well done. That awareness accounted for the lazy sprawls I saw along the gang line, postures radiating a casualness different from the tight curls characteristic of trailside camps.

It helped that it was warm out—no colder than zero. In this starry wee-morning hour, Kate's pregnancy, the working world, truck problems and other issues pressing at home—it was all so far away.

Two irritants nibbled at my joy: Somebody's goddamn dog kept barking, and Big Larry wouldn't shut up.

Larry Carroll, a thirty-seven-year-old contractor, was the only musher I'd seen moving about in the forty-odd minutes since our arrival. He immediately rubbed me the wrong way, suggesting there was no reason to rush; my dogs could no doubt use a long break and no place was better for that purpose than Stewart River, he said, adding that, of course, the real race had passed us all by.

It was a crock. Big Larry was looking over his shoulder. I would have liked nothing better than to snack my dogs and roll. But he was more right than he knew.

My niche in the Great Cosmic Scheme was defined by two maintenance responsibilities: sled and team. Both showed the wear of three hundred and fifty miles on the Yukon Quest Trail. So, swallowing the bile, I smiled when Larry piped up with his unsolicited advice. "Don't worry," I said, "we're staying a while."

Some fifty miles back, three bolts had sheared from the rear stanchion of my sled, leaving the basket floating above one runner. The problem was identical to Gwen's, who was also driving an "unbreakable" Mackler sled, but I hadn't heard anything about that.

Rather than weaken that runner with new holes in a makeshift attempt at patching it—a job I wasn't certain I could finish with the limited tools at hand—I settled for lowering the brake claws until they were lightly brushing the snow's surface, creating a spacer separating the runners. The quick adjustment, combined with delicate steering and a bit of fancy footwork on the good runner, had carried me most of the night. *What's another hundred miles?*

"A hundred miles of terror, that's what," I said, dreading the resumption of that nerve-wracking balancing act. *But what choice is there?* Freshwaters would be meeting me in Dawson City, where he could give the sled a complete overhaul.

As I squatted on the cooler, nibbling banana bread and waiting for the hot water inside to soak the mash of freeze-dried meat and dry kibble, my team's condition was a greater concern. Khan's howling drive had kept his weaker-minded teammates going straight through the night. Riding the cool hours for all it was worth, I pushed eleven hours, traveling virtually non-stop after that last woeful glimpse of Blanford.

A marathon run is the ultimate test of a sled dog's mettle. The long charge proved everything I ever believed about Khan, but others showed cracks under the pressure. Hobbes and Cyclone, for example, performed well inside the team, but neither one of them wanted any piece of leading. That was ominous. *One misstep by the Savage One . . .*

An hour short of Stewart River, Rick, the young leader I'd been saving, began favoring his front left paw. I examined him, but couldn't identify any cuts or obvious sprains. He'd limped into camp.

Marie, an upbeat vet from Vancouver, traced the ailment to a bum shoulder. Rick's injury might respond to massage treatments and lineament, she said hopefully, but we both knew that shoulder problems tend to worsen with the miles.

The busted sled compounded the hazards and hassle of carrying even a tiny dog, let alone a seventy-pounder like Rick. With Dawson more than a hundred miles off, the decision was a no-brainer. "I'd appreciate it if you could look him over again in the morning," I told the vet, "but unless we see a miracle, I'm dropping him."

I also had her check Picard, who hadn't pulled a step the last thirty miles. He wasn't limping, but hadn't been himself since that hot run into Pelly. His appetite remained great; dehydration wasn't an issue. I blamed his listlessness, that failure to pull, on a spiritual malaise not uncommon three hundred to four hundred miles into a dog's first major race. Snaggletooth was shell-shocked.

My depressed laddie yelped as the vet flexed a leg.

Marie took that as an answer: "How hard would you pull if your shoulder was hurting?"

I didn't necessarily buy it—Picard hadn't acted like he had an injury—but it was reason enough to ship him home. I couldn't tolerate slackers, not with our approaching reckoning with King Solomon's Dome.

Marie was joined by Veronica, another Quest veterinarian. When they finished examining my team, they moved over to inspect Larry's. He was, theoretically, in the process of leaving. Blessed with an audience, however, Big Larry launched into his Mackey-bashing tirade.

Another time I think I might have enjoyed Larry's performance; obviously his own race wasn't going as planned. But I wasn't in the mood at Stewart River, where I was down to nine dogs for the duration, all of which needed rest. So I called him on the whining.

Stung, Larry turned to another sore subject: his kennel's mysterious rash of training-season injuries. He pressed the vets for their expert opinions. Could the injuries stem from some dietary deficiency?

In the middle of the night, nursing a team staggered by unforeseen calamities, mushers often brood about such things. But the consequences of nutritional deficiencies, fascinating as they might be, weren't eating away at the other racer's soul tonight. Larry returned to his preferred topic: Rick Mackey's corruption of our beloved Quest with his evil Iditarod ways.

According to Larry, the Quest of yore, an idyllic camping trip, was being trampled in the front pack's newfound zest for speed. The defending champ was to blame for it. "I've lost all respect for him," he declared, loud enough that Searchlight's ears twitched.

"Larry," I interrupted testily, "you're whining again."

The dog that wouldn't shut up belonged to Walter Palkovitch. He barked the entire time I was tending the team. He was still barking when I finished my own meal—a steak and macaroni feast prepared by the Canadian rescue team staffing the remote camp—and ducked inside the mushers' tent, which featured not only heat, but a lush bed of spruce bows.

Walter's dog erupted again as Rusty, Keith, and Brenda packed in the hours before dawn on February 13.

Each bark made me twitch, reminding me of the errors in my mushing math. It had seemed reasonable to push through the cool night hours. It felt like a triumph parking alongside those other teams. But they were leaving some four hours, perhaps as much as six hours, before the coming day's heat made travel unpleasant.

I ought to stay at least eight hours, but that put us back on the trail at 1:00 P.M. *Baked by that sun!* The only way to dodge that heat was to cut our stay way short or sit tight until 4:00 P.M. *Should have shut down at midnight, asshole. You could have rolled straight through and camped all afternoon.*

Walter was down there packing with everybody else. His dog continued to bark, rubbing salt in the wound, hurling insults.

Brenda was down to eight dogs, yet life on the Quest Trail had never seemed better. From the first delicious sip of Tang in the volunteer's tent, to the joy of slipping on clothes dried while she was napping, the six-and-a-half-hour stay had worked wonders on her outlook.

Best of all, Brenda was poised to synchronize her traveling schedule with that of Keith and Rusty. The pair had beaten her to Stewart River by about two hours. If she chased them out now and hung on until their next camp, well, that was the break she needed.

For several days, Rusty and Keith had been mushing more or less on pace with Thomas Tetz, a thirty-three-year-old German butcher now working as a Yukon tour guide. Short and sturdy, Tetz's close-cropped haircut gave him the physical appearance of a Marine, which wasn't too far off the mark, considering the musher also dabbled in Ironman competitions.

Tetz was here to race and took off from Stewart River more than two hours ahead of Rusty's group.

He looks like an orphan, Brenda thought, as they all passed the down-cast German several hours later. He hadn't even reached the Black Hills, a mere fifteen miles out, before the group ran him down. Tetz's dogs perked up at the prospect of company. Their master wisely rejoined the folks he'd hoped to ditch.

From a modern mining camp, full of snow-encrusted machinery, the Quest Trail climbed a series of switchbacks into the rolling ridges known as the Black Hills. Brenda's eight kept pace on the flats, but Keith's full string powered farther ahead with every incline.

Thick fog hugged the trail. Feeling sorry for the young musher behind him, Keith came up with a radical remedy, an approach possibly unprecedented in annals of modern sled-dog racing and expressly prohibited under Rule 22 of the Yukon Quest International Sled Dog Race.

He stopped and loaned her a dog to get her out of these hills.

Brenda had shortened her gang line to suit her shrinking team. There wasn't room to quickly insert another dog, not without major adjustments. So she whipped out a spare tug line and ran three dogs together in the team's middle ranks.

Brenda felt deeply beholden trailing Keith into the misty hills near Eureka Dome. Nothing in her ultra-competitive background had prepared her for such kindness, such unselfish treatment from a supposed rival. The Quest was full of surprises, mused Brenda Mackey, snapping a photo of what she called her "Third Dog."

A bear had me. Awakening with a shout, I found myself staring at Bill Steyer.

"Boy, you were really sleeping there," he said, grinning.

My heart was pounding as I unkinked my aching body from its cramped sled-top perch. Bill and another driver had parked their teams a few yards behind mine on the unplowed road descending Eureka Dome.

"We thought you were Brenda," Gwen chimed in.

And I thought Bill was a goddamned grizzly charging out of the woods. *Jesus, that was vivid.* I scanned the silver gray trees, certain I was missing something. Then it hit me: *Bill and Gwen can't be here!* My watch showed I'd only slept an hour. Last I knew Bill and Gwen hadn't even made to Stewart River. *That means I left holding, what, a ten-hour-lead?*

"What did you guys do? Come straight through?"

Indeed, after resting seven hours at the tents, they had stormed across the Black Hills in a single shot.

This was my second camp in the same stretch. The first stop, we were waiting out the heat. This last time I fed the team a full meal, because several dogs were looking weak. Topher, in particular, seemed close to his limit. That was scary; McKee's black goof was the tallest and, at seventy-eight pounds, possibly the heaviest dog in the entire race.

"We don't want to stop until we get to Granville," Bill said, interrupting my reverie.

Gwen nodded, but doubt showed in her face.

"I wanted to stop before this, but we've come this far already." Her voice faded.

"We better get going," Bill said.

I stretched and watched the other teams skirt around mine. "We'll be about an hour behind you," I shouted as they pulled away.

Gwen had been really mad at herself for letting Bill talk her into this. Of course he'd been wrong about reaching Granville in six hours. Regardless of how fast a dog team might appear, almost nobody averaged more than six or seven miles an hour over the long haul, not when you factored in snack stops and other interruptions. Gwen accepted that and planned her runs accordingly, but guys never did. It pissed her off; men had such inflated opinions about their dogs' speed.

But everything changed, eight hours into the run, when they came upon the dog team parked alongside the road. *Bill was right to insist,* Gwen realized in an abrupt change of heart.

"Wow," she said, leaving my team behind. "We caught another musher!"

It felt so cool.

An hour later they passed a boarded up cabin. Not far beyond it, Bill pulled over and walked back to talk to her.

"Could *that* have been Granville?"

Bill was inclined to think so. He suggested they camp.

"No, let's keep going another fifteen minutes," Gwen said. That closed cabin didn't match what she'd heard about Granville.

"No, that's Granville," Bill insisted. "I don't want to go another step because we've already gone too far."

Gwen couldn't argue that last point. Her dogs weren't moving at anything near their usual happy-trotting pace. That spirit she loved in them appeared lost, maybe for good. She couldn't believe she'd allowed this to happen—driving her poor dogs *nine hours straight!*

At least Bill had promised her a fire this time. Gwen could use one. Her light jacket and goose down over pants were soaked from sweat and wet snowflakes.

An hour later, I too saw the closed cabin and wondered if it might be Granville. We weren't stopping in any case. Out of curiosity, I checked the cabin's coordinates against the map. Granville lay a couple miles farther up the trail.

I told Gwen and Bill as much when I came upon them minutes later. I even showed them our position on the map, not mentioning that I fixed the location using the GPS, possession of which wasn't addressed in the Quest rules.

The pair was already cooking meals. "I'm not going to move my dogs unless I *know* Granville is close," Gwen declared.

Both mushers beseeched me to stop at the hospitality cabin, if it was indeed close, and send someone back to fetch them.

I was reluctant. Khan was starting to roll. There was nothing to be gained by stopping so soon.

"Please," Gwen said, "tell them we're really wet and cold."

"Tell them we have money," Bill chirped brightly.

"I'll see what I can do," I said.

I asked what they knew about teams still behind us.

Blanford made it into Stewart, they said, but he appeared ready to scratch. Dieter, the German doctor driving the purebred Siberians, was last reported out of Stepping Stone.

Gwen knew Dieter and was worried. "I don't think he wanted to be alone," she said of the musher saddled with the Red Lantern.

A few yards up the trail, I threw down the hook and ran back.

"Hey, either of you guys have tapes to trade?"

I was sick to death of Little Feat, Dylan, not to mention the Spice Girls tape supplied by my nieces. I had another music stash waiting in Dawson, in the meantime I craved fresh tunes.

Both mushers shook their heads.

"You guys aren't listening to anything?"

"I never use a Walkman," Gwen said.

Never? That was unthinkable as far as I was concerned. Music was my spiritual crutch, at times the only shield against the demons of the dark, sleepless hours. *No wonder they sound stressed.*

Granville was distinguished by a handful of scattered, mostly shuttered, dwellings and quaint road signs, interlaced with snowmachine tracks. Approaching the main intersection, I paused before a large hand-written sign inviting Quest mushers to stay a while at a cabin located "right at the intersection."

The trail forked at the intersection. The few structures I could see in either direction were boarded up. Quest markers led toward the left. "Haw," I said.

I continued several hundred yards without coming across the hospitality cabin. Realizing I must have misread the sign, I stopped the team and firmly planted both hooks.

Khan looked back, puzzled. "Take a break guys," I said.

"This sucks," I muttered, walking back toward the intersection. I didn't know if anyone would even be at the cabin. Sometimes local residents merely leave the door unlatched for mushers in need of a place to warm up. "This really sucks."

As I thought, the sign stated the hospitality cabin was "right at the intersection," whatever that meant. I read it and re-read the line, too tired to get it. Afterward, I stood in the intersection looking for chimney smoke, paw prints or runner marks, any hint of a cabin concealed in the trees. The cabin had to be off to the right. That was the clue to the damn riddle, wasn't it? But how far?

I looked at my watch. Being a nice guy had already cost me twenty minutes, and I was working up a sweat from tromping around in bunny boots and full gear. "Fuck this," I said and headed for the team.

The dogs were sprawled in the snow, eyeing my approach warily.

"On your feet," I ordered, standing astride the runners.

The dogs were unusually slow to get up. Khan shook himself, then wandered over to nibble snow. Cyclone, Feets, and Searchlight remained sitting down. Hobbes rolled on her back. Only Danger looked ready.

"All right," I said. Khan paused chewing to glance at me, but made no move to obey. *This is serious*, I realized.

Throwing down the hook, I ran to the front of the line, took the old leader by the collar and hauled him forward, lining out the team.

"All right," I shouted. Khan cooperated and the team shot forward, maybe, twenty feet before my leader again paused to chew snow. A mutiny was brewing. I had to regain control, pronto.

I grabbed Khan by the collar and, dropping to my knees, bit him on the right ear. He yelped, sounding more indignant then hurt. "No more screwing around," I said, nose to nose, forcing him to look at me. "YOU HEAR ME, KHAN?"

The third time I gave the order, it stuck.

High noon, February 13, Mowry was so close to Dawson City he could taste the beer. He deserved one, pardner. So did Alf, for that matter. He could have anything he wanted after coming a hundred miles in single lead.

It wasn't just Alf who was doing well. The whole team had done better than the musher had imagined possible during those dark moments at Stewart River. Hey, these dogs caught MacDougall, Funatsu, and Kleedehn at Granville, three teams their master wasn't sure he'd even see again. The Mowth was pretty pleased at that development. *Too happy*, he realized now, wishing he'd made more of an effort to chase them out. *Oh well.*

Here he was climbing the berm into Dawson at last. A guy had to like that.

Mowry was happier still when the checker showed him that sign-in sheet. He was less than a half-hour behind David Dalton, even closer to Keizo Funatsu and Cor Guimond.

Mowry's trusty handler, Mark, had a nice campsite fixed up. The Quest veteran knew he ought to just hand over the dogs and sack out. But it was too bright out for sleeping. He'd be getting up soon enough to feed the dogs again anyway. Instead, The Mowth hustled off to buy beer from that Canadian government store.

He took the beer with him to the campsite. Call it medicinal. The dogs needed their paws tended. Their boss needed to wind down.

The Mowth was well juiced even before the reporter came schmoozing.

The glad-handing fellow from Los Angeles considered himself a colleague. He knew Mowry from last year's race, which the guy had mined for an evocative feature about life in the North. Afterward, he and the *News-Miner*'s Outdoors editor broke bread together in Fairbanks discussing just what it was about these dogs that had people so enthralled.

But the reporter wasn't dealing with a fellow journalist in Dawson. He'd blundered into the locker room of a playoff team down by fifty points at half time. Worse, he didn't know it but he was on *this musher's list.*

Mowry had detected an offensive presumption in the guy's patter. No reporter covering his second sled-dog race had any *business* pretending he *knew* what was going on. Not as far as The Mowth was concerned.

Righteously drunk, Mowry unloaded four hundred and fifty miles of aggravations on the intruder, delivering the critique with both barrels.

❖ ❖ ❖

GWEN'S JOURNAL   Feb. 14, Dawson Trail

> *. . . Trying to get some sleep and keep warm in the wet snow. We ran 9 hours over Eureka Dome to try and get to Granville, but couldn't find the cabin. Hope we didn't fry the dogs in the attempt . . . 50 miles to Dawson. Hope to be there by late tonight.*

Slept very well. Brian came by last night. Stayed warm with chemical
heat packs. They feel great on my neck, too. Waiting for water to heat up.
Will tackle last section at 3 p.m. after 9-hour rest. Plan to water 3 1/2 hours
out and rest at least 2. Snow accumulation about 1" Beautiful country!

❖   ❖   ❖

"Are you the last one?" the lead snowmachiner asked.

"No, there's a couple still behind me yet," I said, sighing at the reminder that the tail-end of the race was catching up.

The guy wished me luck and roared away with his friends.

Stubs of branches were smoldering under a tripod I'd lashed together using scrub spruce trunks. I had used the contraption melting water for the dogs; we were out of alcohol.

King Solomon's twelve-mile climb waited directly ahead, the final hurdle before a long downhill run into Dawson City. I hadn't wanted to camp again, but it seemed prudent after the sun burned away the morning haze, turning the day into another forty-degree scorcher.

Most of my dogs were smart enough to refresh themselves with quick sips from the seeps flowing over the unplowed road above Sulfur Creek. Not Topher. Moving like a zombie, he seemed ready to keel over if we didn't stop. Hence, the unplanned camp.

So I dug out my emergency packet of freeze-dried beef and brewed the team a soupy meal. Topher watched as I served it out, but he didn't get up. I slid the food pan right under his nose and he ignored it. Dipping my fingers in the soup, I used Freshwaters' trick and wet his lips. Toph's tongue flickered, he boosted himself on his elbows, then proceeded to lap the pan clean.

"So you've got an appetite, eh?" I refilled the big dog's pan. Every bite improved the odds on him climbing the dome on his own, and the broken sled made that essential.

"You can do it, Big Guy," I whispered, watching Topher's reposition himself in the snow. His eyes closed. His broad chest rose and fell.

I melted more snow and warmed Kate's last two vacuum-packed meals, savoring the Little Smokie sausages and bacon bite by bite. Then I popped open the beer I'd been saving for the top of the dome and toasted the burning of the tripod. The sun was on the decline. It was time.

Topher didn't pull a lick, but he stayed on his feet and the dreaded climb proved anti-climactic. It was still light out as Khan led us past the radar tower crowning King Solomon.

It had become cloudy and wind rose before we cleared the exposed summit ridge. The temperature was falling. From my position on the runners, I scanned the dogs' feet. White dots showed on the pads of about half the paws I could see. *Snowballs!*

Trees were several hundred yards ahead. If we could just make it there, I could deal with this out of the wind. But Cyclone had begun limping. Scrim, too. *This can't wait.* Placing my toe on the brake I stopped the team.

"Aw, damn," I said, kneeling beside Cyclone. Flakes of red showed in the snow by the little dog's feet. He wasn't the only one surrounded by red spots. The snowballs, formed in the last few minutes, were already causing bloody splits.

It wouldn't have happened if the dogs were wearing booties. But I was running short. The changes necessitated by all those wet patches had seriously depleted my supply.

I had just enough left on King Solomon to protect Cyclone and the half-dozen other dogs showing blood. That meant I'd have to keep close watch for snowballs on the dogs running without booties and stop, as needed, to clean their feet by hand. *One last hassle down the stretch.*

Between the wind and the temperature plummet, my hands, painfully exposed picking out snowballs, stiffened into claws before we escaped the ridge. Descending the mountain, I used my teeth to tear open chemical warmers for the first time in the race. I dropped them inside my mitts, which also saw their first use in days. After a while my hands prickled with renewed life.

The trail descended from the dome along an unplowed road paralleling creeks feeding into ever-larger creeks, all of which betrayed increasing signs of historic mining. I'd been curious about the "waste" designation given to scattered irregular circles on my Canadian topographic maps. Vast piles of rusting machinery and twisted iron, crumpled buildings and heaps of old tailings rose alongside us now, an enduring souvenir of the Klondike gold rush and ample justification for the map maker's cryptic reference.

Nightfall arrived as the trail bottomed out in a wide valley. A gleaming line of Quest markers pointed the way through an open pit mine of gigantic proportions. Speaking about ruins: My neck and back ached from the contortions of days spent steering a broken sled.

Growing up in the Washington, D.C., suburbs, I spent entire summers fighting for rebounds under the basketball hoop bolted above our garage. At one time I was a rock climber and I've always enjoyed hiking, but I've never been a monster athlete.

Not like Mowry. He's an animal, the kind to stay up all night drinking with his frat brothers in Ohio, pile into a car, and drive non-stop to the starting line of the New York City Marathon, which he proceeded to finish. That's a true story.

The Mowth loves blitzkrieg sporting endeavors. Ever since we both landed at the same Alaska newspaper in 1986, he's taken pleasure recruiting me to share the pain. Take the Chena Dome Trail: The map at the trailhead describes the twenty-eight-mile route as a three- to four-day endeavor. Mowry somehow persuaded me to leave the backpack at home and "go for it," subsisting on candy bars and a few slices of Curry pizza. I've got a half dozen years on Tim. He's always been in better shape, but this lean machine of mine will rise to the occasion.

We completed the loop in something under eighteen hours, and it wasn't until the last mile, stumbling down pavement toward the car, that Mowry started claiming my grunts reminded him of cows back at Mowacres Farm in New York.

His taunts rolled off my back. I went the distance. So what if the machine was flashing warning lights.

Tonight the machine was acting a mite sluggish, I must admit. Oil was thickening and the bearings connecting my arms and legs felt loose. Fumbling with another packet of hand warmers, I dropped a blue suede glove, an expensive member of a favorite pair. I stabbed for the brake and missed, slipping to my knees. By the time I recovered my balance, the glove didn't seem worth bothering about. I had spare work gloves, not my first choice, but sufficient; Dawson was within reach.

I stuffed more warmers in my baggy military-surplus mitts and zipped the Fulda parka tight, donning the hood to fend off wind for the first time since Fairbanks.

It wasn't enough. Nearly a week of sweat had reduced the effectiveness of my gear. My right foot felt like a wad of ice; the bunny boot, a worn Iditarod holdover, was shot. "Thank God for Dawson," I whispered, recalling the provision for replacing gear there.

Part of me recognized that I ought to stop and make some adjustments to counter the cold. But the horizon's glow took priority—it had to be Dawson, had to be. *Keep pushing and we've got it.*

An immense dark shape was rising in the distance, something manmade, towering above the ruins and silhouetted against the navy-blue sky. Drawing closer, I saw it was a gold dredge, similar to ones I've seen in Fairbanks and Nome.

I was staring at the rusting giant, wondering about the men who tramped north to toil in its shadow. Topher wobbled, then slipped. I fumbled for the brake. He was dragging by the neck line when I stopped the team.

The big dog lay prone, open mouthed and panting, his dry tongue draped across his teeth. After a moment, he focused on me and struggled to get up. "That's all right, Toph," I said, stroking him. "You made it over the mountain. I'd say that's good for a ride into town."

Even though I was out of dog food, I had to lash my sleeping bag and several other bundles to the outside of the sled bag before I could squeeze Topher's bulky frame inside.

Clutching his collar with one hand and riding with both feet on the good runner, I wobbled onward. Like a prospector of old, I felt spent, hell yes, but that golden glow drew me. In my case a rich payoff was certain: I had a warm bed waiting in Dawson City alongside a gal named Kate.

"Let's go home," I called out, as the trail finally emptied onto the Yukon River, where a blaze of reflectors lined our path into town. "Let's go home."

Khan's Horde swept across the frozen plain. Topher shook off his lethargy and flailed with his front paws, attempting to climb out of the sled bag.

"Down," I said, pinning him by the collar and smacking his nose with my free hand to emphasize the point. He quieted and I scratched my big passenger between the ears. "Easy boy, easy," I whispered, ignoring the stabbing pricks of iced whiskers splitting under pressure of a widening smile. *Can't blame a Quest dog for showing excitement entering Dawson.*

"Let's go home!" I shouted, passing an old paddlewheel boat locked in the ice.

A few minutes shy of 9:00 P.M., Khan charged up the levy, gleefully trading the dark river for those delicious city lights.

❖ ❖ ❖

GWEN'S JOURNAL   Feb. 14, Dawson City

Arrived in Dawson around 11 p.m. with Bill after an 8-hour run over King Solomon's Dome. The Dome was a piece of cake, but it was a long run down from the top. I don't like being perched on a mountain with a team of dogs. We went up in the daylight, so you could see how high you were up, then we zoomed down in the dark, zigzagging down the mountain. Put Panda in lead at the end and she did great...

❖ ❖ ❖

Peering out the second-story window of the Downtown Hotel, I suppressed panic. Snow was streaming past the street lamps outside. It hadn't appreciably accumulated while I was sleeping, but that was a small comfort to a Quest musher sentenced to sit tight for another five hours in Dawson, while the clock slowly counted off the mandatory thirty-six-hour layover. From my vantage, each falling flake was another bullet for the enemy camp. Out on the broad Yukon River, it wouldn't take much more than a gust of wind to mold loose snow into a weapon.

As I gathered up gloves, neck warmers, and other gear drying on the hotel room heater vent, the snowfall stirring my apprehensions had already begun ambushing those ahead.

Preparing to leave Dawson City, shortly before 2:30 A.M. on February 16, Walter aimed on breaking away, once and for all, from the other eight teams wagging the tail end of the 1998 Yukon Quest field.

He had every reason for confidence. His dogs were fast, faster than any of the teams left in town. He demonstrated that on the trail over from Stewart River, where he spotted Rusty Hagan and those other happy campers a solid hour, then leapfrogged past them. True, they overtook him in the Black Hills. But his dogs had the final word, bypassing the bunch of them at Granville, and streaking ahead into Dawson. The time adjustment left Walter holding a fat ninety-minute lead over Thomas Tetz, the musher due to leave next.

Walter also knew this trail from the Percy De Wolfe, the Dawson-to-Eagle race named for a mail carrier who once mushed the same route. That trip was windy the entire way, so Walter didn't give it a thought when the weather soured in the hours before his Quest team's departure.

Light snow was falling as he rocketed from the campgrounds and down an icy road, missed the first turn, and followed a driveway into a French woman's front yard. Oops. He'd made the same mistake in the Percy.

Walter circled the woman's yard and shot back out the driveway. Paying closer attention this time, he soon found the marker, along with the reason his leaders, Hera and Anise, first missed it: New drifts covered the trail out of town.

Walter hadn't counted on that. Wind whipping across the Yukon during the Percy hadn't really affected the trail. But there hadn't been any fresh snow to push around that year.

Hera and Anise, good girls both, obediently busted a new path. Walter dropped onto the Yukon River and plugged along, step by disappointing step. The few markers were hard to see. Dawn was hours away yet. Walter repeatedly had to stop, get off his sled, and search out the trail on foot.

A little more than two hours out of Dawson, Walter Palkovitch parked his sled and stripped the booties from his dogs' feet. He wanted company for the hard trail ahead.

The posse wasn't long catching up. "Why are you stopping?" asked Tetz. His dogs remained frisky, finding travel easy in the groove sliced by Walter's crew.

"Go ahead, I'll be right behind you."

Rusty, Keith Kirkvold, and Brenda Mackey passed before Walter gave chase. They all stacked up behind Tetz.

The German's dogs no longer looked so chipper. They were plodding through elbow-deep powder, which blanketed the Yukon as far as Tetz could see. He had his answer concerning Walter's early camp.

How much of the trail was affected? That was the pressing question. Ten miles? Twenty? Tetz knew it was fifty miles from Dawson to the Fortymile River, where the Quest Trail peeled off the Yukon. Surely, the wind's damage was localized. Race officials hadn't said anything about needing to break trail for fifty miles. If that were the case, they would know about it. Wouldn't they? Surely, the entire Yukon couldn't drift in a single night. Could it?

The morning sky hovered murky and gray above the trio of Quest teams resting across the Yukon from Dawson. The wind and snow had finally slacked. Streams of flakes gave way to orphans fluttering on errant currents.

I'd mushed into Dawson some thirty-four hours earlier, bone tired, hobbled by a cold foot and nursing a team half-filled with discouraged or injured dogs. All but the eight fastest Quest teams were then still in town, converting Dawson's public campgrounds into a tent city reminiscent of the scene here in 1898, the mad summer after steamers carried news of George Carmack's discovery on a nearby tributary of the Klondike River.

As I walked along the campground road, a sack of freshly washed harnesses slung over my shoulder, the boomtown was fast disappearing: Garbage sacks bursting with used straw had replaced sleeping dogs, and handlers were breaking down tents and tarps.

Bill, Gwen, and I were the only active racers left in town. I took it in stride. The Quest's layover—a wondrous respite, providing me with a grand total of twenty-four hours sleep—had restored the bounce in my legs, and revived my faith in Mighty Khan's destiny to conquer.

I found Freshwaters ladling out another meal, the team's fifth and their last Dawson dining indulgence. My poor handler looked beat from his round-the-clock mission.

Kate's father, Rudy, was off chasing down another set of batteries and select bolts in case the other stanchion runner bracket failed. The sled, neatly overhauled by Freshwaters at the Gas Shack, stood ready for packing. Even the old green sled bag looked spiffy following a spin in the hotel washer.

In truth, the entire thirty-six-hour pit stop couldn't have gone any better with paid actors and a script. From the moment I turned Khan and the team over to Freshwaters—everything simply fell into place. Kate had steered me to our room. I clowned with Rory, chatted for a few minutes with John McWhorter, the reporter from KUAC-FM radio, set a freshly opened beer on the bedside table, and after that, a twelve-hour gap exists in my life.

Over breakfast at the Jack London Grill, I spied Blanford, looking wind-burned, puffy-faced, and generally forlorn after scratching at Stewart River. I also noticed that the musher's father wore bunny boots the same size as my own. "Excuse me," I said, "any chance I could persuade you to loan me one of those boots?"

Blanford's pop drove a hard bargain. "I want your first born, there," he joked, nodding toward Rory.

"Done!" I cried. We traded boots on the spot, adding to the ambiance of Dawson's finest restaurant.

By now, everybody on the Quest Trail knew Rory. His outgoing nature, wobbly steps, and blossoming vocabulary had become a prime amusement during the checkpoint vigils that inevitably accompany a long-distance sled-dog race. The veterinarians at Stewart River greeted me with accounts of his new antics. On the sidewalk fronting the hotel in Dawson, my son casually waved to a pair I assumed were strangers.

"Hello, Rory," the guys both said.

Kate, battling a cold and coping with her fifth month of pregnancy, escaped her own miseries showing off his new tricks.

"Where's Daddy?"

"On the trail!"

"What's he doing?"

"Mushing doggies!"

Rory Patrick O'Donoghue, middle name taken from a grandfather he'll never meet, barely filled his baggy snowsuit. He was still mastering his pack boots, baby bottles only recently swapped for cups, but his leap from the cradle had begun. My Quest learning curve, steep though it sometimes felt, was nothing in comparison to a toddler getting his first glimpse at the big world yonder.

"Ask him where we are," Kate suggested as we returned to the room.

Rory needed no prompting. "Dawson City!"

I caught another nap, awakening just in time to catch the mandatory drivers meeting on the afternoon of February 15. Everyone left in the race was in attendance: Larry, Walter, Rusty, Gwen, Brenda, Amy, Keith, Bill, Tetz, and myself. Rich and the other officials had good news concerning the trail. No sleds had been broken leaving town, they said. New snow apparently cushioned the worst of the Yukon River ice.

We'd see for ourselves soon enough. For all but a hundred of the next three hundred and thirty miles, we'd be chasing Quest markers down the belly of the vast white beast herself.

I wanted to update my maps on cabins and known hazards, but I waited too long and the race marshal's entourage cleared out of town. Fortunately, local volunteers introduced me to a guy involved in the actual trail-breaking effort. He sketched in the rough outlines of three new overland portages cut around truly impassable jumble fields.

When I returned to the camp, shortly after 6:00 A.M. on February 16, all I had left to do was pack.

"I put all the food over there," said Freshwaters, frosted down to the rims of his glasses and gesturing toward a heap of snow-dusted sacks. "You'll want to go through it."

"The dogs are all eating," my handler said reassuringly. "I imagine they're ready to go. After thirty-six hours I guess they ought to be."

I threw in four full meals for the team, all of which featured freeze-dried meat, a pair of vacuum-packed personal dinners, and the same number of pre-packed snacks, battery and glove packs, topped off by ready-to-grab team snacks, including three small sacks of beef nuggets and all the whitefish that fit.

By 8:00 A.M., almost two hours before my team's schedule departure, the sled was good to go. "We've got time," I told Freshwaters. "Let's swing by the hotel and grab breakfast with Kate."

Walking back to the dog truck, we discussed strategy.

"I'm going to do everything I can to catch Rusty and those other guys by Fortymile," I said, referring to a cabin fifty miles down river in the ghost town of that same name. "If I can pull it off, I'll cut rest, whatever, and chase them out. Coming off the layover, the dogs ought to be able to handle it."

Freshwaters agreed. "A lot of people make the mistake of thinking a race is over as soon as they fall behind. Well, it's not. That's been proven many times," he said, grinning.

"People ahead of you are going to make mistakes. You'll be surprised how much can change—long as you keep racing all the way to the finish line."

YUKON OFFENSIVE

8

FEETS

The first drivers' meeting in Dawson, three days earlier, found Bruce Lee preoccupied. He searched the faces around him trying to match one with the mystery man, that "Ghost," as he and other veterans had taken to calling Andre Nadeau.

Lee, competing in his first Quest since the disheartening loss seven years earlier, was struck by all the new faces among the mushers, veterinarians, and race officials gathered in Dawson. So many, in fact, that he couldn't identify the surprising rookie.

Reports collected by his handlers suggested this Nadeau was a formidable adversary. His record as five-time winner of that four-hundred-mile Labrador commanded respect, as did his multiple victories in the CANAM Crown, the big Maine race. Of course, Lee didn't believe the quality of the competition was anywhere near comparable, but Nadeau had proved he had that killer instinct all champions share. That was a characteristic well understood, if not claimed, by Bruce Lee, who at times felt cursed to play eternal runner-up.

It didn't sound like much now, but in Lee's day as a high school runner in Ohio, a sub-four-minute mile was every sprinter's goal. He surpassed that magic threshold, but only in training. When it mattered, when the teenager lined up at state meets, the second hand on the clock always beat him across the finish line by a few lousy ticks.

Lee forgot about those disappointments until the 1991 Quest crown slipped through his fingers, unlocking all the memories. In the aftermath, Lee, whose mushing reputation rested upon top-five finishes, questioned himself anew. *Is second the best I can do?*

He had to assume his rival's big Siberian-blooded dogs were seasoned finishers. If the race came down to a grinding march into Fairbanks, Lee recognized that the youth and inexperience of his own dogs figured to be a disadvantage. But he also possessed significant assets: faster dogs and intimate knowledge of the trail.

Lee reasoned that his best approach was to preserve the team's blazing speed, which meant shunning long runs, particularly where breaking trail was required. But neither could he afford to let anyone get too far in front on the Yukon. From those axioms came a strategy: Stay within striking distance on the river—no more than two hours behind, and catch the frontrunner entering Circle City, where the Quest Trail left the damn Yukon once and for all.

A late-morning departure gave Lee the daylight he sought negotiating the rough sections of ice. And Nadeau, who left Dawson holding a three-hour lead, handed Lee's young leaders a fine set of tracks to follow. When Lee appeared outside Sebastian's cabin at the mouth of the Fortymile River, fifty miles later, he'd cut the frontrunner's margin in half.

"You had a fast run, huh?" observed Nadeau, whose English, though accented, was evidently better than many believed.

Lee, making his first eye contact with the Ghost, sensed that the big-shouldered rookie was playing cat and mouse with *him*. The suspicion grew as Nadeau began fiddling with his sled as if ready to go immediately, but didn't follow through. *If that's what you want to do, great,* Lee mused. *It's taking you a lot longer to get places.*

Nadeau gave his team a bit more than three hours rest before setting out about 8:00 P.M., February 14, on the hundred-mile trail to Eagle, Alaska.

Lee lingered until midnight, giving his team almost twice the rest. Once again, young Canvas and Clovis set a swift pace, slashing the frontrunner's edge from four hours to just two by the time Lee reached the checkpoint at Eagle's former one-room schoolhouse.

The apparent speed differential further persuaded Lee that his rival was living dangerously, repeatedly cutting rest to keep his slower team in front. Nadeau wasn't the first to take that risk. "It'll catch up," the veteran told himself. "It may take a while, but it always does—usually on Eagle Summit."

The behavior of Nadeau's dogs outside the schoolhouse offered additional support. For the first time that anyone watching could recall, the frontrunner had difficulty getting his dogs to eat.

Aw, that's it, thought Lee.

No one else knew it, but Andre Nadeau *was* coping with the repercussions of a grievous error, having run short on dog food during the hundred-mile haul from Fortymile cabin. In the parlance of sled-dog racing, Nadeau had committed what's known as a "rookie mistake," a miscalculation easy to make on an unfamiliar trail. His dogs persevered, conquering American Summit on empty bellies, working so hard, so faithfully, their appetites were extinguished by exhaustion.

Nadeau camped eight hours in the old school yard. Appetites returned over the long break, but the team's spirit wasn't the same. As the musher hooked them up to leave the checkpoint, about 9:30 P.M. on February 15, John McWhorter, the Fairbanks public radio reporter, astutely picked up on the blue mood gripping the frontrunner's team.

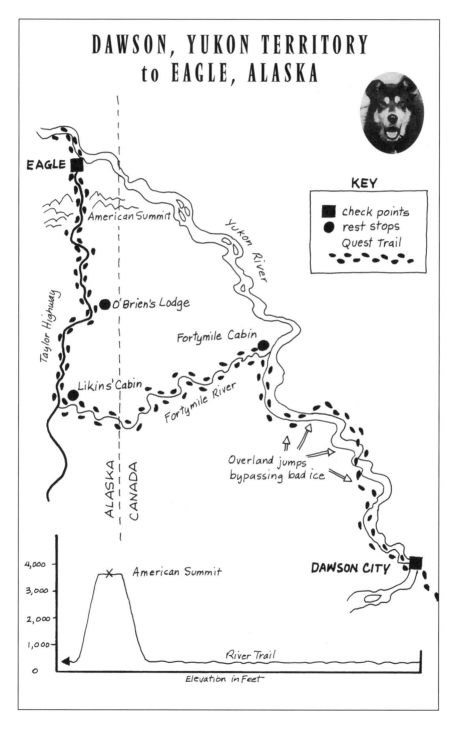

DAWSON, YUKON TERRITORY
to EAGLE, ALASKA

EAGLE

American Summit

Yukon River

KEY

☐ check points
● rest stops
    Quest Trail

Taylor Highway

● O'Brien's Lodge

Fortymile Cabin

● Likins' Cabin

Fortymile River

Overland jumps
bypassing bad ice

ALASKA
CANADA

DAWSON CITY

4,000

American Summit

3,000

2,000

1,000

River Trail

0

Elevation in Feet

"He had two dogs just barking their heads off, but that contrasts with the many dogs he used to have barking their heads off," McWhorter told listeners, reporting live from Eagle. "They're not as happy as we've seen them go out. They didn't all stand up on command. They didn't all get up. Yeah, they're just tired."

Mushing from Dawson, tall Ty Halvorsen's doggerel rang through my mind.

"When it starts to blow, you gotta go. And *if* snow starts to fall," Rusty's handler had boomed in Pelly, delighted with his own wit. "If snow starts to fall—haul."

His mirth was short lived. "That's right," Ty said, towering over me like Rasputin, his thick eyebrows arched, hinting menace. "Snow falls—you haul."

The consequences were seared in Ty Halvorsen's memory. After falling behind early in the 1987 race, he smacked into blizzard after blizzard. While seventeen other racers quit, the stubborn six-foot, seven-inch trapper strapped on his long snowshoes and broke a new path for the dogs. Ty's overall time of twenty days, nine hours, made his the longest Quest of record. Some might smirk at that, dismissing his accomplishment as a leisurely camping trip. Having claimed my own Red Lantern surviving that stormy Iditarod, I appreciated Ty's accomplishment: He faced the Quest Trail's worst and triumphed.

On all but a few sections of the Iditarod Trail, a musher contending with a blown-in trail can generally count on an assist within, I'd say, forty-eight hours, in the form of villagers blasting through on snowmachines. Sometimes it's an organized rescue party, but more often the trail is reopened by snowmachiners engaged in routine local trips.

Ty chuckled at that notion.

"On the Quest you're on your own, boy."

It felt that way leaving Dawson. Rusty's group was six hours ahead, allowing a lot of room for drifting. The fun started right out of the campgrounds, when Khan hauled the team into some lady's front yard.

Dodging kiddie toys and a snowmachine, I mushed around the

house. Khan was headed back out the driveway as the woman came outside to greet us. "You are not the first to do this," she called in an amused French lilt.

On the second try, I found the markers that delivered us to the river. Snow wasn't falling just then, but drifts were advancing on every gust of wind. The trail was patchy, with tracks running for twenty or thirty feet then vanishing into waves of fresh powder. There were enough markers for me to identify the general direction, but Khan lacked the talent some leaders possess for deciphering an invisible trail.

"Rainy, I bet you're enjoying this," I said, wishing I still had my bossy little Iditarod lead dog. Until cancer got her at the age of thirteen, old Rainy was my seeing-eye gal, the leader I depended upon to nudge hulking partners like Harley on course.

Khan had Harley's tendency to charge straightforward. We had such light snow during training, I hadn't caught that. But it was obvious breaking trail out of Dawson. Khan kept plunging off into powder, his sheer drive proving a liability on the drifted sections. *Better do something before our Main Man gets discouraged.*

On a hunch, I shifted Hobbesey up front. Schandelmeier, her former master, trained on a trapline. With a background like that, the big girl ought to know something about drifts.

Indeed, she did. Hobbes mystically found the packed trail through the seamless white, literally weaving through mounds of crazy ice. Between her quiet guidance and the Barbarian's snarling enthusiasm, we blasted through the drift sections.

I remained worried. These six-inch drifts could triple on the wind's whim. Neither the gray sky, nor the occasional towering chunks of ice, reminiscent of Godzilla eggs or Easter Island gargoyles, offered any reason for encouragement.

Roughly two hours into the run, the first flakes trickled across our path. Soon my cheeks were tingling and my eyes watering—from the increasing snow shower.

"Oh, man," I muttered, recalling one day on the river during the Iditarod when snow fell so hard leaving the village of Grayling that I wondered how it was possible to breathe.

"Get up, get up Khan," I cried, calling the dogs into a lope.

The snowfall eased, but it was constant enough to keep my fears alive. So I drove the dogs, skipping usual breaks, pressing them hard, noting the team's progress on the map as the trail jumped from the river, dodging areas of impassable ice, onto crude forest paths. I'd wanted to camp in one of these sheltered overland sections. But the sky wouldn't let me rest; it wasn't dark and stormy, reminiscent of the Yukon's rolling punches in 1991, but the shades of gray suggested anything was possible.

"When the Yukon's sleeping, a wise man tiptoes past," I incanted, picturing Dr. Stephen Strange, one of my Marvel comic favorites, weaving spells binding the Dread Dormumu.

Each flake added to my lead over Gwen and Bill, but that wasn't comforting anymore. They were endangered, perhaps even doomed if they gave these drifts any time to grow. *Take this seriously, guys, because I need somebody behind me.*

❖ ❖ ❖

The threat was apparent to the teams traveling with Rusty Hagan. Though daybreak made it possible to take bearings on distant markers, it brought no end to the drifts swamping the trail.

Thomas Tetz and Keith Kirkvold shouldered most of the trail-breaking. They took turns in front, trading off when the stress showed in their lead dogs. Keith spread the work around within his own team, giving every dog at least one bite at solving the Yukon's frustrating riddle.

Mushing at the tail end of the group, Walter was discouraged at the sight of his swift dogs reduced to a fitful crawl. *Racing without a trail is like bowling without an alley, playing basketball without a hoop, soccer without goal posts,* he decided, finding bitter entertainment in the dismal comparisons.

As the afternoon stretched, Walter pondered quitting. The equation looked damningly simple: At the rate the group was moving, dog food was going to run out before *anyone* reached Eagle.

Others in the group shrugged off his concerns.

"People will rescue us," both Keith and Tetz said.

"What are you talking about?" challenged Walter, appalled by their cavalier attitude. "Are you coming out here to get rescued?"

The anger reflected Walter's experience in risky mountaineering rescues, some of which ended with the retrieval of bodies. From his perspective, the approach suggested by Keith and Tetz was ass backwards. *You don't extend yourself to a place that needs rescue—you avoid rescue.*

Brooding over the complacent comments of the other mushers, Walter leaned even more strongly toward scratching.

His companions had their own complaints. The trail was bad enough on its face, Rusty felt. Walter's whining merely added to the misery. The ingrate tagalong wasn't the one doing the trail-breaking. No, Walter was back there muttering about not having fun. *What did he expect? This is the Quest.*

Rusty didn't want to wish ill on anybody, but he was starting to hope Walter might live up to his words for once and turn around.

Walter was still weighing his options when another musher passed the group head on. It was Cor Guimond. He was headed home.

"Cor," Walter shouted as they passed, "am I going the right way?"

"Well, I'm not going the right way," Guimond said glumly.

"There must not be a right way then," Walter shot back, tittering with amusement.

He continued, oddly cheered by the encounter, until he'd gone too far to make it back to Dawson by nightfall. *Might as well keep going,* Walter decided.

The snowfall dwindled. A dog team was bearing down from the opposite direction. The oncoming musher's dogs were clipping right along, drawing a sharp new line on the river's freshly stretched canvas.

It's Cor!

I knew him only by reputation.

Cor Guimond might not have the fastest team, but the forty-seven-year-old musher knew the country as only a Dawson trapper, guide, and fisherman could. He'd be the one to welcome temperatures tumbling into the fifty-below range. Let the Weather Gods test us! Conditions sending guys like me into survival mode would have been Cor's cue to seize the lead.

Kate had witnessed such feats while reporting on the Quest in 1994, when minus forty was the warmest encountered throughout, and again in 1995. Both years Cor dictated the pace, if only briefly, before finishing seventh, and then fourth, continuing his trend of improvement. She also contended, and not unpleasantly that I could tell, with the Dawson musher's shameless flirtations. "He's a rogue," she once confided. "You know he's not that handsome, but there's definitely *something* about him."

And here he was in retreat.

Cor neatly passed me, then stopped. "You're only thirty minutes behind six, maybe, seven teams," he offered.

"That's great. I had no idea."

An awful silence ensued.

"You know, we've never met," I said at last, "but my wife, Kate Ripley, she speaks very highly of you."

"Kate's your wife, eh? I wondered what she was doing on the trail this year. I thought maybe she was reporting, but no?"

"She's just out here helping to keep me going."

"The Wee One, he is yours then?"

"Oh, yeah," I said, smiling at this further evidence of my son's notoriety. Leave it to Rory to make a bigger impression on the contenders than Daddy ever will.

"My dogs, they are sick," Guimond said sadly.

"They look good to me."

"They're feeling a little better today, but I scratched last night. This is the first time we haven't been plodding at five miles per hour."

"Tell me about it," I said, "that's about what we're doing right now."

"Are your dogs sick?"

I laughed. "Naw. Our top speed is, like, seven miles an hour. I got a real slow leader."

The musher's eyes narrowed and his lips curled with puzzlement. He said nothing, but I took it that he, Cor Guimond, was amazed anyone would attempt the Quest with dogs that slow.

So be it. Cor was the one headed home and his misfortune presented us with a gift. For the first time in hours, Khan and Hobbes had a broken trail. Our speed picked up as they took advantage of Guimond's groove. The GPS showed we were moving up the Yukon at 7.2 miles an hour—verging on Warp speed aboard Starship Khan.

I paused at an intersection. Splitting from the main trail, which continued overland, a smaller trail showing signs of heavy dog team use also climbed the riverbank. This had to be Cor's cabin access.

We'd come seven hours with only a handful of brief snack stops. My team was due for a full meal break. Yet, I hesitated. I couldn't see from the river, but there was a chance that Walter, Rusty, Brenda, maybe that entire group, were camping up there. Coming off the long layover in Dawson, these dogs of mine had energy to burn. "Gee, gee," I cried, directing Khan away from the cabin.

Dodging trees in a narrow tunnel through the forest, a grin widened on my face. *With any luck, I've just caught and passed the whole bunch.*

I kept the team rolling an extra hour before shutting down on the Yukon. The campsite was the sort I'd hoped to avoid—too far from either bank to find shelter. But it was dead calm. The evening sky had cleared. And I worried that I might be pushing the dogs too hard. The last mile or two Searchlight, who was in swing, had pulled toward the side a few times, almost balking. Now that we had stopped she was a happy girl, growling pleasantly as she rolled in the snow.

I snacked the dogs heavily and they promptly settled down, pawing cozy nests in the deep powder alongside the trail. While snow melted in the cooker, I dosed Searchlight's wrist with the magic juice, then moved down the line stripping off booties. All nine were snoozing before jets of steam announced the water had reached a boil. I tipped the whole pot into the cooker, soaking the dog's meat and kibble. Only then did I realize I, too, was hungry for more than brownies and banana bread.

Refilling the cooker with alcohol, I melted another batch of snow and used it to thaw two pouches of Kate's wondrous "Cowboy" potatoes—a fried onion, hash brown combo, topped off by a few strips of bacon.

Next to the dogs, grease is a musher's best friend.

❖ ❖ ❖

Gwen still led several teams at Stewart River. The twelve swift dogs pulling her sled easily beat Bill's nine into Dawson City. Then came the scratches by Dieter Dolif and Tony Blanford, the starting time adjustment, followed by last-minute notification about a thirty-minute penalty for her difficulty locating that promotional packet way back in Carmacks.

Mind you, Gwen *did not* understand that penalty. She may have misplaced the dumb packet, but she found it later. The way she read the rules, nothing but her official arrival time at that early checkpoint should have been affected. Whatever. It wasn't worth fighting about.

Actually, she didn't mind staying that extra thirty minutes. Her lousy handlers had put her behind schedule. She'd warned them they wouldn't have time to sleep in Dawson. Gwen learned that much handling for someone else several years before. But neither Ken, her boyfriend, nor her brother Kevin, had believed it. She awoke to discover chores as vital as drying her down jacket—undone.

It helped knowing that Bill, too, faced a penalty delay. His own late-morning departure was knocked back a full hour because of the dog he shipped home from Stepping Stone. That's what the guy said. Gwen was glad to hear it, because it meant Bill had the Red Lantern. He could *have* that distinction. Gwen felt fortunate to be leaving town ahead of *somebody*.

Bill heard different. As far as he knew, service of his Stepping Stone penalty was to be deferred until later. He had his team harnessed and was ready to pull the snowhook when Mel, the race judge from Dawson, joined him at the campground.

"You didn't get the message?" asked Mel, explaining that Bill had another hour to kill.

"I'm all hooked up," the musher protested. "Let me go now."

The judge relented. Afterward, he told Gwen she, too, could take the penalty later.

"Screw that," she said. "I'm already ten minutes into it."

She won her point, but then it dawned on her: *Bill's gone. That means no one is behind me!* Gwen Holdman faced the Yukon River alone. *Rude awakening!*

Overloaded with supplies, including a soupy meal for the dogs sloshing inside her cooler, Gwen's sled proved nigh impossible to control threading the rough ice. She flipped repeatedly and, each time, struggled picking that sled up. She finally lightened the load by feeding her dogs early that afternoon.

Gwen figured to catch Bill before sundown. Between her tumbles and the subsequent drifts, the Quest's Red Lantern driver was still running alone when the trail vanished near dusk. It was light yet for picking out marker reflectors. Gwen wasted the better part of an hour scouting sections on foot, pulling her team on course, only to lose the trail mere yards later.

The wind rose, hurling loose snow at Gwen. "Well, you lost the trail on the Yukon," she calmly told herself. "But you're not really lost. You know where the trail goes."

The snow turned powdery and deep. Each wading step became a struggle out on the river, so vast and utterly indifferent to the progress of a lone woman and her string of dogs.

"Oh my God," Gwen whispered, her self-control ebbing. "I'm slowed down and they're all gaining distance on me."

Darkness brought a reprieve, disclosing a gleaming reflector in the distance. Gwen hauled her leaders to the promised path, which proved tangible. *Thank God.* Blessed with firm footing, her dogs took off.

Approaching an overland portage, the trail climbed a short steep bank. Gwen's leaders topped the slope and were into the trees when the sled jammed near the bottom. Confused by the resistance, her lead dogs halted, freezing the balance of the team on the slope. Gwen was shocked. She and Ken lived in the hills north of Fairbanks. Her sled dogs ate hills for lunch. She never imagined they would quit on a tiny hill.

Gwen scrambled up the bank and yanked her leaders by the neckline. The dogs didn't understand their master's frantic motions. Fast training runs, even those towing a heavy sled, hadn't prepared the dogs for pooling their energy to break a massive load free, the sort of skill considered fundamental when dog teams hauled mail and other freight on this same trail in days gone by. For all Gwen's leaders knew, their master had set a snow hook.

Gwen unloaded her sled, a hassle costing more than just time: The musher's confidence in the team was badly shaken.

Bill Steyer, dissecting his team's troubles through personal experience running marathons, concluded that his pacing was at fault. Six hours on, six off—that was the coach's new drill. Karma blessed the strategy when the initial six-hour run from Dawson placed Bill's team camping in a sheltered forest portage. He'd been there two hours when Gwen caught up.

"I'm here for four more hours," Bill said, noting her stress as he explained his schedule. "Why don't you stop and we'll run together."

Not far back, Cor had tipped Gwen that his trapline cabin was warmed up and waiting for a trail-weary lass such as she. From her recollections of the Percy De Wolfe, Gwen believed it was located just ahead on the same portage. Besides, thought Gwen as she begged off, she hadn't forgiven Bill for the many annoyances on the trail to Dawson. "I really want to get to that cabin," she said, leaving him there clutching that weighty, though intangible, Red Lantern.

The overland trail looked almost familiar, but not quite. Dodging the spruce trees encroaching upon this freshly cut portage, Gwen was too busy to figure it out. Not until she popped onto the Yukon did Gwen realize her mistake: Cor's cabin was at the *other end* of this portage. Somehow she'd missed it.

Now what do I do? Gwen fanned the river with her powerful lithium-battery headlamp. She shuddered reading a message etched in the Yukon's corpse-white mask: *Don't even think of think about stopping here.*

I awoke shivering—the most reliable means of rousing a bone-tired musher. Relinquishing my miserable perch atop the sled bag, I tossed the dogs a piece of fish, replaced boots on Khan, Danger, Hobbes, Cyclone, and Scrim—the dogs prone to developing splits between their toes and pads—and away we went.

The Walkman had become cold while I was napping. Again Stevie

Ray Vaughan paid the price. I switched off the tape player. The chill in my bones was enough to keep me dancing tonight.

It was dark on the Yukon. The trail was tricky enough to demand use of my headlamp, but I switched it off whenever I turned to check for signs of pursuit. No reason to give the posse extra encouragement, and I knew, absolutely knew, that Gwen and Bill had their teams on the march, sniffing our tracks, just itching to overtake us. I had quit kidding myself about the others: Rusty's group simply couldn't be at Cor's all this time.

It came as no surprise when I saw a distant light bobbing along what had to be the rough ice lining the far side of the river. "We've got company, boys," I said. "Get up. Get up, Khan."

We barreled into a slough. I didn't bother checking the map; Fortymile had to be close.

The headlight, incredibly bright to my eyes, was gaining on us. So rapidly, in fact, that I relaxed. "Got to be a freaking snowmachine. Got to be," I told myself, chuckling. "Nobody's dogs are that fast."

Gwen thought her mind was playing tricks. Out of the corner of her eye she'd see a flicker of light, then nothing at all. And suddenly there it was again. She *did* see something ahead in the slough. She called her dogs up.

Khan had the whole crew loping. It wasn't enough. The way that other team came on, blazing headlamp overrunning us with shadows, it felt as if I was riding my old Yamaha 350cc two-stroke with a semi bearing down. A few yards short of entering the woods, I hit the brakes and turned to face the blinding light driving those impossibly fast dogs. "You want to go ahead?"

"Oh, no," Gwen sang pleasantly. "We should be close. You've led all this way. Why don't you take us in."

"You got it," I said, ridiculously delighted by her gesture. "Let's go home! Let's go home, Khan." The sled struck the riverbank before I was ready and flipped, burying my face and chest in the snow. Burning with embarrassment, I jerked the sled upright and charged up the little hill.

Broken buildings heralded our entrance into Fortymile. Once the largest gold-mining settlement on the Yukon, all that was left now were a few mossy structures, caving under the burdens of snow. Khan followed a blazing line of trail markers into a clearing, which erupted with barking. Dog teams, too many to count, were parked helter-skelter between brush, wood piles, and odd heaps of snow-covered clutter. A glorious glow of hospitality radiated from a small cabin's window.

"We've been waiting for you, Brian," called Sam, a photographer from the *News-Miner*. He guided the team to a parking spot close to the cabin.

"Who's still here?"

"Everybody," Sam said, grinning as he shared my joy.

The owner of Fortymile cabin, Sebastian, got up to greet me, pointed out warm water waiting on his stove, then retreated to his bunk, tip-toeing over bodies half wrapped in sleeping bags. We'd missed out on the party. I could live with that.

Leaving a meal soaking in the cooker, I returned outside and joined Gwen by her sled. "Listen," I said, "we've caught these guys, and I think we should try and hang with them. You know, follow them out. If we can get a few hours rest, that's what I'm going to do. You should, too."

Gwen was kneeling by her sled, examining a crack in one of Mackler's spring mounts. Below the bright light strapped to her frosty fur hat, her blue eyes were red-rimmed. Her lips pursed as she listened. "Thanks for telling me what you're doing, but I *need* to stay here," she said, sounding apologetic. "We came all the way from Dawson."

❖ ❖ ❖

GWEN'S JOURNAL   Feb. 17, Sebastian's Cabin

Run to Fortymile kicked everyone's butt. Trail was blown shut. Have caught a pack ahead of me. Ran 12 hours almost straight through. Hope the dogs will recover. Rubbed them down well and they all ate, but it was a tough run on all of us. We are all like sardines on the floor of Sebastian's cabin. Will leave with the rest if possible, don't want to be last and easier to travel in a group. Wind has died down, but storm is rumored to be coming. I'm just thankful to have the Yukon and its jumble and drifts behind me for a while.

❖ ❖ ❖

The cabin door burst open. A knight clad in dusty white armor stood framed against the steamy night air. "I need some help here," Bill said urgently. "I'm not stopping, and you guys are blocking the trail."

Guilt yanked me from dreamland. I knew I shouldn't have parked in the center of the trail. *You hated it when people did that to you on the Iditarod.* I'd allowed Sam's well-intentioned assistance to overrule my better judgment. Time to pay the price.

"Give me a minute," I told Bill, peeling myself off the cabin floor, where I had collapsed between Brenda and some other snoring mummy.

Bill explained his schedule as I helped him get his dogs past mine. "Stick with it," I mumbled. "Good for you."

Inside the cabin, Thomas Tetz was rooting through the gear dangling above the warm stove, retrieving dried gloves and other prized possessions. Other members of Rusty's group were stirring, stretching, and cursing life as they gathered themselves for another joust with dog-eared destiny. My watch read 3:20 A.M. Another twenty minutes or so, and my dogs would have four hours here. It would take me that long to get ready. *It's now or never.*

Clutching my parka with one arm and hastily filled Thermos in the other, I paused near the door, reluctant to leave. I'd been too tired to notice much of anything when I arrived. It was a cramped, but cozy place, with a hammock stung in the back and ringed with shelves chock full of mechanical parts, books, spices, and other items you'd go a long way to replace.

Dirty plates were scattered across the main table and counters. I dipped my fingers in the last remains of a casserole, it was tasty but cold. Nothing worth grazing had escaped Rusty's hungry band. *C'est la vie.* The door swung open as someone else left. An icy slap of air cleared my head. "It's show time," I announced, lurching out into the crystal-sharp night.

The German took off first. Feets and Danger were leaping in wheel, exhaustion forgotten in the excitement ripping through the clearing.

Khan snorted impatiently. I freed the slipknot anchoring us to a tree and he bolted sideways, pouncing on the snacks and other supplies Walter had piled alongside his sled. "You asshole, Khan," I cried, hauling the big dog back to the trail. On the second try, he lunged for the door swinging open as another musher stepped outside. "No! No! Khan!"

Boss dog looked sheepish as I again pulled him over to the trail. Seeing Rusty charge after Tetz, Khan howled to give chase. "All right," I said, pulling the hook.

We pursued Rusty through the woods and down onto the cake-smooth Fortymile River. I felt pleased. Bill had leaped ahead, but his schedule dictated another camp before long. Meanwhile, I'd just passed Brenda, Keith, and Walter, or at least joined them, since everybody was spilling out of Sebastian's cabin now.

Except for Gwen. The last I'd seen she was hugging her sleeping bag, seemingly unaware of the boots passing over her body. I imagined she sensed the exodus. I would have. I hoped she knew what she was doing. Her team looked stupendous running mine down, but then it sounded like she'd made a fairly desperate push. I wondered if I'd see her again.

An unusual kink in Luther's stride caught my attention. Clumps of white snowed on his rear pads. Snowballs! In the rush to follow Tetz out, I'd only bootied a few dogs. The omission forced me to break off the chase.

Brenda overtook us while I was cleaning feet.

"See you up the trail, Brian."

I waved and redoubled my efforts. Another musher was closing fast. We took off again, moving well, but the other team kept coming.

"Looking good, Keith," I shouted, watching his formidable brutes race past. It wasn't just the size of the dogs that impressed me: Keith still had thirteen pulling his damn sled. No wonder he mowed us down.

I fell in behind him. My old Iditarod team wouldn't have even needed prompting to cling to such an easy target. But Keith's team simply walked away from lumbering Khan. Brenda's headlamp was already out of sight. "Christ," I muttered, "we're not even drafting off these guys."

We needed a lineup change. I moved Cyclone up front. He and Khan hadn't been getting along, but I knew the little leader enjoyed chasing. Maybe we could hitch a ride when Walter caught up, which I suspected wouldn't take long.

Walter lingered another two hours at Fortymile. Rosy light was peaking over the blue-shadowed canyon walls before he showed up behind us. McKee's little leader went berserk as Walter's team flashed by. Suddenly I had a dog team!

Nose buried in Walter's runner spray, Cyclone hauled Khan on a merry chase. "Get up! Get up!" I cried, reveling in the little dog's performance rounding a thrilling series of bends, and saluting the peaks sunning themselves high above.

And suddenly he sat down. "Whattaydoing Cyke?" I spluttered, spearing the brake to avoid a tangle. "C'mon, Cyke!" But he calmly watched Walter's team vanish around the next bend.

"So what was that about?" I said, shifting Cyclone back inside the team.

He panted happily, lips gaping in what resembled a damn grin.

Walter, meanwhile, breathed a sigh of relief. He hadn't expected such a hard chase—not from me. For a moment, he had even considered pulling over, figuring the pursuit was bound to start distracting Hera and Anise. Fortunately, that wasn't necessary. *But what happened back there?* Walter knew several of his females were in heat. Could that account for it? Or was O'Donoghue's team faster than it appeared?

Following our ten-minute run for the ages, Khan fell into the pace of a box turtle stalking a tasty slug. Here on a river as flat as the Fortymile a team like Walter's might reasonably average ten miles per hour. My GPS registered 5.8. Our destination, a cabin owned by Dave Likins, a miner and former Quest musher, was approximately forty-five miles. The math was discouraging.

Feets didn't slip or anything, but he suddenly began limping, arching that long back with each tender step. "Oh, no," I said, rushing toward him.

I couldn't locate any painful spots and when I finished checking him over, Feets playfully rolled in the snow. Stumped, I snacked the dogs and then hit the trail again, hoping I'd witnessed the effects of a cramp or some other fleeting malady.

Feets held his tug line taut—what a good dog—but the limp was unmistakable. Each lurch felt like a stake piercing my heart.

My ambitions had soared pretty high catching those teams last night. They shriveled now. If I had to drop Feets, one of my hardest workers, this team was down to a measly eight dogs. *And we haven't even reached Eagle!* Hell, I wasn't even sure we were clear of Canada yet. The border fell somewhere along this river, but no one put up fences in this corner of the wild.

Feets kept pulling, laboriously, courageously, throwing his entire body into it.

Watching him, I felt unworthy.

All the way from Dawson, I'd been cheating Feets and his fine comrades out of their deserved rest, grinding them down in the pursuit of teams faster than mine. *I was racing, right? Racing to ruin.*

"New policy, guys," I announced. "Effective immediately. We run no more than we rest. Got that?"

Ears perked. A few heads turned my direction, but their eyes quickly returned to the trail. The boss was babbling again. Who had patience for that?

❖ ❖ ❖

GWEN'S JOURNAL   Feb. 17, Fortymile River

I just started to get my period. Holy shit. Must be the stress since it wasn't due anytime soon and I'm not prepared for it. Dogs tired, left after 6 hours at 40 mile. Joey limping. Leaders burned out. Need sleep. Beautiful country, but hard to enjoy it. Bill is behind me, but everyone else is ahead.

One Man's Race: O'Donoghue's Quest Scrapbook

▲▲ Take four hundred pounds of dry kibble, divide it into three-pound baggies, toss in a scoop of fat and you'll have a hint of the nightmare that is food drop.

▲▶ As the first to draw for starting position at the banquet, we were free to escape the drawn-out affair.

▲ Why is it everything fits until the night before the race?

▲▲ Kate's sister, Margjy, checks out the booty ritual the morning of the start.

▲ The dogs and I were ready to roll.

► I was so engrossed in the final inspection I never noticed Fulda's army.

▲ Seeing Rory at Braeburn, the hours of effort melted away.

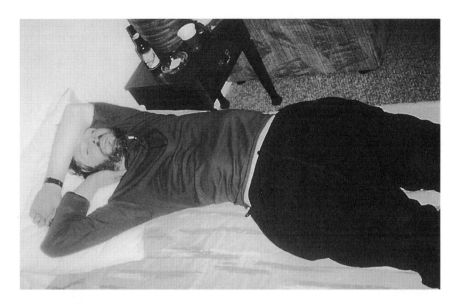

▲ Dawson City payoff.

▲▲ Jack Studer, on the right, bends Mowry's ear outside Braeburn Lodge.

▲▲ As in winters of old, the sternwheeler S.S. *Keno* can only watch as dog teams exit Dawson.

▲ From Dawson City, it's back to the wild for dogs and driver.

◄ Brenda Mackey confers with Rusty before departing Likins' Cabin.

▲ Likins' cabin rests on a century-old claim staked prior to the Klondike gold rush.

▲▲ A musher with lead dog trouble.

▲ Luther's gruesome eye filled me with remorse.

▶ The trapper's cozy cabin would have been just the thing on a cold day.

▶ Frosted beaver suits Gwen Holdman.
▼ Kahn surveys the jumbled ice while Gwen threads a nasty Yukon section.
▶▶ Gwen stretches out for a Quest siesta.

▲ Welcome to the kitchen.

▶ Approaching Eagle, the Yukon is bracketed by cliffs.

◄◄ Glare ice and open leads are among the hazards of running the Yukon.

◄ Personalized greetings brightened the fire hall in Circle.

▼ My conquerors of the Yukon enjoyed fresh straw in Circle City.

◄◄ Searchlight cleans her feet.

▲ Kate's beaming face was the best reward waiting in Circle.

◄ Tails were high as the dogs hit the trail from Circle, two hundred and fifty miles from thefinish line.

▲▲ Little Cyclone, nursing sore toes, looked ready to nest in Central.

▲ By Central, my dogs learned to sleep through the booty ritual.

►▲ A quick snack before Eagle Summit.

► A dog truck winds its way across Eagle Summit.

►► Recollections of other teams descending the summit in years past heightened my dread.

◄▲ Few landmarks and a myriad of crisscrossing trails further complicate the descent off Eagle Summit.

◄ Reuniting with Kate and Rory behind Angel Creek Lodge, anything seemed possible.

▲ Toting the booby prize again. The Mowth swore it was no record.

CABIN FEVER

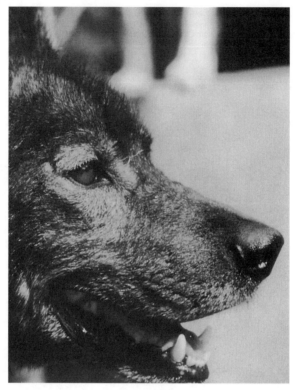

9

CYCLONE

I was looking for a personal message in the cartoons adorning the walls of David Likins' outhouse when Gwen made the team's plight official. Being a reporter conditioned to pay attention to such things, I noted the exact time—4:40 P.M., February 17—she mushed past the cabin without stopping, depositing the Red Lantern in my bare-assed possession.

From the barking down on the river, I assumed Walter was still in the vicinity. But his team's presence was a fluke byproduct of the musher's easy-does-it traveling schedule. He could spot Rusty's group an hour or two and catch them when he pleased.

My former Iditarod team had that kind of speed. Mowry proved that in 1992 when he took essentially the same dogs from my Red Lantern crew, including Harley and Rainy for leaders, and came from behind to crack the Quest's top ten.

My position in the latter half of the 1991 Iditarod, bringing up the end of an eleven-team convoy, stemmed from confidence. As the convoy ground through storm after storm, I was resting longer than the teams immediately ahead, figuring to rocket past a few others down the stretch. I hoped to pass them right on Front Street. At least, that's the way I imagined the game might play out—before I stupidly forgot my parka in the bathroom at Golovin—another Kodak moment on a crapper.

The present situation didn't support finish-line fantasies. "They all walked away from us last night," I cried bitterly. "Just *walked* away!"

I'd just parked when Rusty, showing his usual concern, came over to see why it took me so long.

"My team's strong on the hills," I told him, "but you guys are *all* faster. Maybe it will equalize out by the end, but the chase is over for now."

Heading up to the cabin, I figured to at least have fun ribbing Dave Likins, a resident placer miner working a claim known as Maiden Bench. You wouldn't know it from the miner's modest log-cabin spread overlooking the river, but his claim dates back to 1887, the second year of the Fortymile gold rush. Dave wasn't home. I had to settle for asking his girlfriend Theresa to pass on a message.

"Tell Dave I'm working on a story about EPA's investigation of his failure to obtain a canine discharge permit. You know, protecting the Fortymile from urinary and fecal contamination," I said, pointing to the Quest teams camped on the river out front. "Tell Dave I'm going to need a comment."

"What?" said Theresa. Then she got it: Dave's tiny suction dredge operation drew constant scrutiny from bureaucrats egged on by American Rivers and other national environmental groups, who depict the activities of mom-and-pop miners on the Fortymile, a federally designated Wild and Scenic River, as an abomination. Well, the river's a wild one. It's as scenic as they come, but placer mining remains a legal part of the landscape, as Likins and other claim holders are proud to point out.

"A canine discharge permit!" said Theresa, beaming. "Let me write that down. Dave will get a kick out of it."

Two plates of Theresa's sourdough pancakes kept me in good humor as Rusty, Brenda, Keith, and Tetz packed to go. Bill, sticking with his schedule, had already leapfrogged ahead. Only Gwen was still then on the way.

Rusty made a point of wishing me luck, and so did Brenda, with whom I swapped tapes.

I had resolved to stay no less than seven and a half hours, the length of the last run from Sebastian's cabin. That left me with two hours to kill after Rusty's group departed. I passed the time talking with Theresa. She had followed a National Park Service job to the Yukon, where she fell in love with the hot-headed miner, broadening her views about life in the wilderness, where government isn't always viewed as lending a helping hand.

Sundown found me down on the river awakening my furry friends with chunks of chicken and whitefish. While the dogs gnawed and stretched, I loaded new batteries in the GPS and the Walkman, slipped on a fresh pair of gloves, adjusted my headlamp, and then I crouched with my hand on the hook.

"On your feet," I called softly. The dogs snapped the gang line taut as they strained forward in anticipation. "All right, Khan!"

The whole team moved out smartly, and Feets wasn't limping at all!

❖ ❖ ❖

GWEN'S JOURNAL   Feb. 17, O'Brien's Lodge

This day seems to never end. I'm at O'Brien's Creek Lodge, 35 miles from Eagle. Quite a slog to get here. Hootch seems to be the only leader I have right now. I have to constantly rotate dogs. Jojo is limping hard. Amberlin led most of the way here. Dogs are very tired and I have to push to keep

them moving. We ran 5 hours to get here. Only Brian is behind me as the others all decided to go ahead with no rest before I got here. I cannot afford to skimp on rest anymore although I hate to cross the summit alone. Sounds rough. But at this point this has almost ceased to be a race and become a survival exercise for me. I just want to finish, but I have been pushed close to my limit today. I wish I were a dog in the team so someone could take care of me! I'm not eating or drinking enough. Dogs eating well, but look terrible. I feel like I'm trudging along behind a 4-dog team for all the power I've got. We average 5 mph. Will stay here 8 hours. We all need the rest as I have been cutting breaks short. The summit has been rough, the trail hard to find. Will almost certainly take 7 hours to cross. Hopefully I can travel with Brian if he stops here. He was at Likins last I saw him. I think I need some good sleep because right now I'm very bummed. I keep thinking of Schandelmeier saying that the dogs will look like shit in Eagle, then they will pick up again later. I sure hope so or else we may be out here a month. I feel a lot of pressure to keep up with these guys ahead of me, but they are always just a little too far ahead.

❖ ❖ ❖

Hobbes dug in her heels, sending Searchlight and Cyclone spilling over top of her.

It was that hazy hard-to-see period after dusk and before stars lit the backcountry sky. We had been trotting down the center of the Fortymile at a satisfying clip when the pileup occurred. I jammed on the brake and barely avoided Cinder and Luther in wheel. The sled came to rest with the brush bow spearing a tangled ball of dogs, but I hardly noticed that. Was it moose? Open water? *Something* had spooked Hobbesey.

Her eyes were wide as I dragged her back into position alongside Khan. He acted more irritated than anything. Sled dogs generally react en masse. The appearance of a rabbit, a tiny vole underfoot, or a raven flapping overhead, will electrify an entire team. Aside from Hobbes, however, none of my dogs acted concerned. Feets, my wounded warrior, was twisting on his back contentedly.

Hobbes gazed into the darkness, hackles raised, back ramrod straight. "Wuff, wuff," she growled softly, nervously.

"What do you see Hobbesey?" I said, rubbing her neck and scanning the dark river basin. *Very odd.*

I pulled the hook, but we didn't get far; Hobbes again caused the team to bunch up.

"Wuff, wuff," she spat, sounding more apprehensive than aggressive. Her manner was giving me the creeps, but I tried not to let on.

"C'mon, Hobbes, you big scaredy cat," I chided her, lining out the crew once more.

Hobbes remained tense. When she quit after a few steps, I demoted her to wheel, where the other dogs overpowered her protests. We rolled on.

The answer to the mystery gradually took shape.

Long before my eyes registered anything, Hobbes had apparently detected the distant silhouette of the Taylor Highway's Fortymile Bridge. I don't know why she decided this particular bridge looked menacing, but approaching the dark span her body language erased any doubts about the connection: My burly girl's tail drooped, her ears flattened and she slunk low to the ground. It reminded me of a cartoon mouse tip-toeing past a sleeping kitty.

"Poor Hobbesey," I whispered fondly.

Just past the bridge the trail climbed off the river. Springing back to size, Hobbes pulled frantically until the demon was safely behind us.

Two hours after leaving Eagle, Lee rounded a bend and found Nadeau stopped in a slough. He hadn't planned for this. Lee much preferred the stalker's role, which played into his decision to stay an additional hour at the old schoolhouse the evening of February 15, though light snow was forecast.

The veteran's schedule called for next resting at Trout Creek, another twenty miles or so ahead. Lee initiated a pass, but paused long enough to tell his rival about the cabin, figuring it would be to his advantage to keep Nadeau in sight. *If I can lure him into there, get another free break, then we'll be leaving together.*

Nadeau nodded, inscrutable as ever.

Lee's team charged ahead—catapulting the musher from Denali Park into the Yukon Quest lead for the first time in seven years. The thrill, if it could be described as that, was short lived. Now that they were in front, his dogs had to work harder breaking a new path. He hadn't realized the fresh powder was nearly belly deep. That explained the ease in which he caught the Nadeau; leading the race was a costly thrill here.

The drifts eased not long afterward. So it hadn't cost too much, Lee judged, directing his leaders off the river to the cabin at Trout Creek. Inside, he was pleased to find a local trapper had a fire going. The L.A. reporter was also ensconced within, angling for insights from the Quest's new frontrunner. Lee, ever the cerebral musher, cautioned against jumping to conclusions, but he acknowledged his team was in a good position to dictate the pace.

Sticking with his schedule, Lee fed his dogs and took care of other chores. One hour passed, then another, with no sign of the Ghost, whose failure to appear undercut Lee's complacency by the minute. *Is he just sitting back there or has he gone on?*

Dogs began barking, suggesting the answer was at hand. But no headlamp came into view in the yard fronting the cabin, or the river below, and the team eventually quieted.

Overcome by curiosity, Bruce Lee got up and took a walk. At the Quest Trail's junction with the cabin, he found a fresh set of runner tails continuing up the dark Yukon.

"OK," Lee observed to himself, staring at the evidence of the Ghost's passage, "now what is he doing?"

❖ ❖ ❖

Nadeau and Lee exploded the old game board. Savvy racers belatedly adjusted, bypassing traditional rest stops like Likins' in favor of longer point-to-point runs. The Mowth didn't figure that out until he paused to change socks at O'Brien's, a place that wasn't usually even open. He wasn't surprised to hear that he was three hours behind Nelson, Dalton, and those others. But he was startled to hear most of those teams took long breaks at the lodge. *I'm off schedule*, he realized.

Leaving Dawson he'd been right in the thick of things. That's when the wind began blowing. The fifty-mile run to Fortymile took Mowry eight hours, which the veteran considered a miserable showing for a team coming off a thirty-six-hour break. And it took a lot out of his dogs.

Worried that Alf was shouldering too much of the load, Mowry paired Laverne with him to cross American Summit. She didn't like that windy mess one bit, but her master insisted. Checking her over in Eagle a few hours later, vets detected an irregular heartbeat. It might have been bullshit, but Laverne was headed home. That reduced Mowry's string to nine. *And it's my fault*, he berated himself. *She's not a real lead dog. You screwed up.*

The only good news was in the rear-view mirror. The closest pursuit, hot-shot rookie Aliy Zirkle, was a solid ten hours behind leaving Dawson. And she must have been hammered on the river, because Aliy was way late to Fortymile.

The Mowth kept expecting to pass Nelson up. But somehow that ol' Louie kept that worn-looking bunch *on the move*. The pattern was repeated in Eagle, on February 16, where the villager from Kotzebue pulled into town four hours ahead of Mowry, rested through the heat of the day, then exited holding a two-hour advantage.

Mowry wasn't too worried. He couldn't help but notice the vets at Eagle were *all over* Nelson. He'd never hold that team together through another five hundred miles. The Mowth's complacency vanished when he confronted the fresh snow washing over the Yukon. Three miles from Eagle, the six-time Quest finisher was in a state of near panic. *Slow as we're going, the dogs are going to quit, or it's going to take us forever.*

Ripping open his sled bag, Mowry cast off thirty pounds of meat to lighten his load.

❖   ❖   ❖

The Quest Trail followed a snowmachiner's groove straight down the unplowed Taylor Highway. Mileage markers made it easy to measure our progress as the trail twisted, climbed, and fell, hugging the sides of canyons carved by creeks with names such as Buck, American, and O'Brien. All had been named by the prospectors who probed and panned these hills searching for the source of the bewitching flakes tumbling down the bed of the Fortymile.

"Where is that damn lodge?" I wished I'd paid better attention driving to Eagle last summer. My mind had been on the newspaper assignment ahead, an undefined feature story about author John McPhee's return to Eagle, the town he made famous in the pages of *Coming Into the Country*. All I could picture was the lodge's location in a dark, boggy area, more likely to attract mosquitoes than tourists.

Eagle is a dry town, so I had pulled in at O'Brien's to buy beer. The price of the transaction—eighteen dollars for a twelve-pack of Kokanee, usually a cheap Canadian brand—kept the memory vivid.

The guy selling the beer mentioned he was the son of the lodge's new owners. His folks had only recently moved to Alaska. "They're planning on keeping it open through the winter," he said.

Even on that weekend in July, the height of the Taylor's annual RV invasion, O'Brien's had an isolated feel. "This is their first winter up here?" I said. "Your folks are pretty brave."

"Or crazy," the man said, laughing. "They're looking forward to it."

Tonight I hadn't planned on stopping more than a few minutes—just long enough to fill my cooler with hot water, assuming it was available. I was aiming for a place called Liberty, located at the base of the long climb to American Summit, where Rusty's group had talked about stopping. I was probably kidding myself, but I clung to the hope we might yet catch a team or two there.

The topo map fooled me. O'Brien's was a good eighteen miles, not the ten I reckoned, from our last stop at Likins'. And buzzing to Eagle in Kate's little Toyota last summer, I overlooked the many hills that now slowed my dog team to a crawl.

Tonight's trip stretched to three hard hours before Khan and his mates trotted into the lights bathing the lodge parking lot. By then, I accepted that he and the crew could use a full meal and a couple hours of rest before continuing toward American's 3,420-foot ridge.

It was about 10:00 P.M. Gwen's team was snoozing near one of many large pieces of rusty mining equipment decoratively arranged outside the lodge. Shadows cast by the lodge's harsh lights magnified the relics, giving O'Brien's the feel of an alien zoo, an illusion complemented by the lodge's clattering generator.

The bar door swung open and a tall broad-shouldered man came out to greet me. "We've got water waiting inside," he said in an accent that placed him somewhere from the Southwest.

"Hot water?"

"Hot as we can get it on the stove."

"That's great," I said. "I was hoping you might have a beer, too."

"Oh, we've got plenty of beer," he said, grinning under his mustache.

I mentioned my summer visit. Art Reeves introduced himself as the lodge's new owner. "So is your son still around?" I said, making conversation.

I learned the son was long gone, along with Reeves' wife. The country wasn't for everyone, he said. I agreed.

"I love it here," the lodge owner added. "You couldn't *pay* me to leave."

Another brother had moved up from the Lower 48, along with his wife. The three of them were waiting when I joined Gwen inside the bar.

The woman sounded sad that the parade of mushers was coming to an end. "I've never seen anything like this race," Arlene Reeves said. "It's kinda exciting."

Gwen had taken over the bar's interior. Her parka, bibs, neck warmers, gloves, and other pieces of gear dangled on all sides of the lodge's big wood stove, every flat surface of which supported buckets or pans of melting snow.

"So," she asked sweetly, "are you ready to start traveling together?"

Funny she should ask. Toting the Red Lantern the past few hours I'd been giving that a lot of thought, weighing the prospect against memories of a certain day in Rohn on the Iditarod Trail.

A bonfire had been roaring that day, shooting sparks dangerously high in the spruce towering over the Iditarod's checkpoint cabin in

Rohn. Race volunteers, eager to break camp, were heaping armloads of used booties and other trash on the fire, driving those flames ever higher.

Rohn was then most popular place for taking Iditarod's mandatory twenty-four-hour layover. The solitude of the forest camp, protected by its remote location from intrusive media and curious village children, was considered perfect for resting dogs and mushers. Or so I'd been told.

They pulled down the musher's tent before I finished using it. Not that I could have napped worth a damn in the din of the snowmachines screaming past, ferrying loads of gear to the airstrip. My entire stay was filled with apprehension. The luck of the draw had catapulted me into the lofty position of leading Iditarod's seventy-five-team field out of Anchorage. Rohn marked the payback: Adjusted starting times coming off the layover now thrust me into last place, trailing even those few teams I beat into Rohn by an hour or more.

The checkpoint's impending closure felt like a gate shutting behind me, sealing off any chance of retreat. In the hours that followed I twice broke my sled, splintered the reflector of my lone headlamp, lost the trail several times and, finally, found my bid to catch the teams closest to mine snuffed by a blizzard.

Nothing so dramatic confronted me at O'Brien's, but I hadn't shaken the effects of the morning's demoralizing march to Likins' cabin, which had demonstrated I would be lucky to hang with anyone leaving Eagle.

And therein sprung my dread, for Eagle marked the Quest Trail's return to the Yukon River. I doubted any of the other rookies fully appreciated the god-awful possibilities inherent in mushing two hundred miles between supply drops on that shape-shifting beast. You couldn't pack enough food to go the distance through a real Yukon storm—not breaking your own trail, you couldn't. That was the situation the day God told my friend Barry Lee to call it quits on the Iditarod. Three of us traveling together spent more than thirty-six hours slogging through the seventy miles separating Grayling from the next checkpoint. Poor Barry, following a few hours later, never had a chance out there alone.

"Oh, I'll travel with you," I told Gwen. "All the way up the river if you'd like."

My new partner confided that she thought Bill Steyer had made a mistake.

"He was supposed to wait for me," she said. "I know Bill's dogs needed rest and he was planning to stay here. I guess those other guys talked him into coming along."

So Bill cut his rest to chase the pack. That was interesting. It was essentially the same move I tried seventy miles back, when I chased Rusty out of Sebastian's cabin. *Does he have the dogs to pull it off? I doubt that, but I won't fault him for trying.*

Taking a seat on one of the bar stools, I popped open a can of beer and dined on a spicy roll of moose sausage, which I'd been packing as an "emergency ration" since Whitehorse. The lodge owner sat down alongside me and chattered about expanding O'Brien's tourist trade and building a new bunkhouse for mushers.

"I need to talk to the Quest," he said. "There wasn't any time this year, but we'd like to make this more of an official stop."

"You know, this is great the way it is," I said, nodding at Gwen, who lay on the floor, blissfully curled in her sleeping bag. "All anybody really wants is water and a warm place to sleep."

Reeves frowned. His grand vision didn't include crashing on the bar's bare floor and a stove cluttered with pans of melting snow. He launched into an explanation about problems with his well, or maybe he was in the process of drilling one. Tired and flush from the unfamiliar heat, I wasn't tracking too clearly. The lodge owner assured me everything would be better by the time I arrived next year.

"If I'm back on the Quest Trail it will be as a reporter," I said, chuckling. "I'm not doing it this way again."

He didn't seem to hear. His mind was back on the lodge's potential, which was getting bigger by the minute.

I rolled out my own sleeping bag and grabbed three hours of rest. The lodge owner's brother was fiddling with the stove when Gwen and I stirred. He asked if we were hungry. "Now that you mention it," I said.

Arlene laid out cold cuts. Learning I was a reporter, the brother, a chunky, gray-bearded man who looked quite a bit older than his wife, let it be known that his life story would make for a great book. He alluded to past deeds as a Navy Seal, his career as a covert operative. He was, he said, a man who knows what it means to kill. One of Tom Clancy's characters was either based on him, or conducted similar missions—the distinction wasn't quite clear to me. I did catch that The Government had used this guy and spit him out. Spit him out! And that this new life in Alaska, free of telephones and deadly obligations, had come in the nick of time.

Between bites of my sandwich, I offered vague comments about governmental idiocy, then gathered my gear and fled. Safely outside, I turned to Gwen. "Did you catch any of that?"

"What *was* he talking about?"

"I'd say this place has got a serious epidemic of cabin fever."

Gwen and I had planned to leave by 3:30 A.M. We were only an hour behind schedule when the lights of the lodge faded behind us. We were bound for the tree line, the last sheltered spot before the long haul across American's bare summit ridge.

Sawatzky had told me I couldn't miss it. We found Walter camped at that last tree stand. Dawn was breaking and the ridge ahead of him looked remarkably calm. I took him for an idiot—ignoring the gift represented by a clear, peaceful summit.

I was being unfair.

"We tried the summit last night and didn't make it," said Walter, his eyes frighteningly wide. Walter Palkovitch, forty-seven, had twice scaled Mount McKinley, North America's tallest peak. He'd spent nights dangling on sheer walls, buffeted by avalanching snow. He hadn't been deterred by the wind that rose to meet his team on American's ridge. After the long, boring climb up the mountain, his leaders, Hera and Anise, actually seemed invigorated by the sudden climate shift.

Walter's dogs made good progress at first, knifing through the loose snow shooting sideways across the trail. But that changed as Hera and Anise became disoriented. While the leaders never turned backward, Walter sensed mounting wildness in their directional choices.

Darkness combined with the barrage of dancing, shooting, churning snow made visibility too poor to offer much help his position on the sled. At last, he saw no choice but to shut down before the team blundered off the mountain.

Inside his sled bag, Walter wasn't comfortable, but he didn't feel threatened. It was the dogs he worried about. Most had acquired new blankets of snow covering their tightly curled forms, but the musher could tell they weren't getting any rest. *This is pointless*, he told himself. *How are they supposed to work tomorrow?*

His thoughts turned to our brief exchange the previous afternoon at Likins' place, our only real conversation the entire race. It had to do with Dave Sawatzky's advice about the summit.

The last night before leaving Fairbanks—more than two weeks ago now—Sawatzky and I had talked about where and when to travel light. For American Summit, the Quest veteran recommended dumping everything non-essential, including my last ounce of food, before launching across the long, exposed passage. That sounded risky to me.

"What if I get stuck up there in a storm?"

"Whatever you do," Sawatzky said, his voice dropping even lower than usual, "don't stop up there. Do NOT stop up there, Brian. I'm telling you, do WHATEVER it takes to get across. You do NOT want to get caught up there.

"If you do get stuck," he added after a pause, "retreat to the tree line. Even if the wind is howling and blowing on top, it stops when you enter those trees and you're not losing much altitude."

After ninety restless minutes, Sawatzky's advice taunted Walter into turning around.

Hera and Anise were eager to go. *Well, they think this is a good idea,* noted Walter, who vowed to drive them as long as it took to gain satisfactory shelter.

It wasn't far at all. Winds ceased the instant Walter reached the trees. His dogs, tense only moments before, shook themselves off and settled cozily on the ground. Ten hours had passed. Walter was fixing his sleepy dogs a breakfast soup when Gwen and I paused before entering the ridge.

"It was unbelievable," Walter said, "just like Sawatzky told you—out there it was blowing like mad, and here it was perfect calm."

What were the odds I might pass along that tip mere hours before it was needed? It had to be more than chance. Had to be.

While the men were talking, Gwen snacked her dogs, then jotted down a quick journal entry: *Feb. 18: 6:30 A.M. Preparing for assault on summit. 25 miles from Eagle.*

A serene summit beckoned. Gwen packed away her journal and again asked if I thought my dogs would lead over the mountain.

"I've got Khan," I said smugly, nodding toward the Savage One, who was baying and whining, begging to pillage and destroy.

Leaving the trees, the trail continued along the unplowed road, but you couldn't detect it through the drifts. The wind was light, but it's potential was apparent in the odd shapes sculpted on the slope before us.

Down at the lodge, I had discussed the upcoming miles with Reeves, who often made the run in his snowmachine. Using a napkin he sketched the route, which wound along the left edge of American's ridge top, shading the areas most prone to drifts. The worst stretch, he said, waited just past the first curve.

"The drifts can be real deep, but it's not real long. So if you run into trouble—keep going."

We hardly started across the ridge before Khan lost the trail. Up ahead, I could see an alley of faint fragmented tracks, perhaps six feet wide. But the big leader grew frustrated as he broke through, sinking to his shoulders in a series of unblemished mounds separating us from those clues. Ignoring my commands, Khan began pivoting the team from side to side, searching for better footing.

"Maybe I should try," shouted Gwen, unnerved by my poor start.

"No way," I said, irked she had such little faith. "Were not even close to that yet."

Dragging Khan back on course, I sunk to my knees in powder. Regaining the sled before he strayed anew was a struggle. The effort firmed my resolve to explore all options, including playing lead dog myself, hauling the dogs with a rope tied to my waist, before letting my inexperienced partner go ahead on this tricky summit. My dogs weren't verging on quitting. Khan was confused, that's all.

The first option was Hobbes. Schandelmeier's former pup, for all her nervous tricks, had showed she wasn't scared of drifts on the Yukon. How would she fare on a windy mountaintop? *Only one way to tell.*

Hobbes had an immediate impact, nudging Khan toward the scratches carved by previous teams. We made decent progress rounding the first curve, where the powder deepened. I kept urging Hobbes onward and, as the lodge-owner promised, the team soon reached better footing. *So far, so good.*

The slope of the trail became ever steeper. I had to flip the sled on one runner to avoid fishtailing downward. The sky was overcast now and the wind picked up. The neck line connecting Khan with Hobbes stretched tight as the younger dog pulled the old veteran uphill, away from the buried road, along tracks faintly etched in the slope's wind-hardened surface cover. Visibility worsened amid blowing snow. I could see my leaders, but the world beyond was merging into churning white. "Good girl, Hobbes. Go ahead! Go ahead, Khan," I shouted, keeping pressure on, driving them.

It wasn't cold, but I had stripped down to my vest during the climb to avoid sweating. Now the wind was getting to me. Freshwaters' kuspuk was stowed in the top pocket of my sled bag for easy access. Yanking it out, I attempted to slip it on without stopping. The team entered another steep side-hill section before I got the kuspuk over my head. Thrusting it under one arm, I again muscled the sled on one runner. This took both hands and the garment slipped free.

"Damn," I cried, but the deed was done and it was crucial to keep moving. *Freshwaters will understand.*

The wind whipped the dogs' fur and flailed the small bushes lining on the steep slope below us. Something about Cyclone, who I had running in mid-team today, drew my attention. The little guy looked tentative. Erratic. Suddenly, he threw himself to the left, straining to pull the team *downhill.*

"No, Cyclone! NO!" I shouted, hardly believing what I was seeing. McKee's son-of-a-bitch was trying to dive off the mountain.

Khan and Hobbes slowed to check out the commotion. "GO AHEAD!" I screamed. The team shot forward, hauling along the traitor, who continued trying to yank us downhill.

Emerging from the wind tunnel, I stopped the team and pounced on Cyclone. I could have killed him barehanded. I settled for hurling him upslope, and yelling: "Bad dog. Bad, bad dog." Then I bit him on one ear.

He squealed and cowered.

"NEVER! NEVER do that again."

The wind had ebbed, but that meant little. Somewhere the seamless white expanse held a liquor store marking the halfway point of this summit crossing. From there, Reeves promised, I'd find the trail easy to follow due to the heavy traffic generated by Eagle's closest booze outlet. But we weren't there yet.

I looked back at Gwen. She waved the kuspuk, which she had snatched from the wind. Our partnership had paid its first dividend.

I didn't know it, but Gwen was also grabbing any chance she could to straighten, or replant markers, wanting to give Walter every chance to follow.

We came across a wide circle trampled in the snow. Several teams had camped, and not long ago judging from the drifts. It had to be Rusty's group. *They must have been trapped up here.* I chewed my lip pondering the implications.

SUMMIT STORM

10

KHAN

Amy Wright had several sick dogs. Chenee was the worst off. The little girl was so weak, the musher packed her out of O'Brien's Lodge. Crossing American Summit, Amy suddenly found herself in a real windstorm. Before long, her leaders quit and the rest of the pups stalled, hugging the mountain in fear.

If it hadn't been for Expo, her husband's old leader, Amy might still be stuck up here. When all else failed, she turned the team around and placed her husband's old Quest dog in lead. Grasping her intent, Expo hauled the frightened youngsters back off the ridge and down the mountain.

By the time they reached the lodge, Amy was exhausted and feverish. Gobbling aspirin, she used the lodge radio-phone and called Peter back in Dawson to arrange a rescue plane. He tried to talk her out of it, but Amy was certain. *Her* Quest was *finished*. She was scratching.

Reeves broke the news that planes large enough to haul a dog team couldn't land anywhere near his lodge. If Amy wanted to bow out, she'd have to mush to the nearest open road connection.

Amy, a plucky, practical woman, called her husband back. "If I've got to run them out to the road, I might as well go over the summit."

Her team had been resting some five hours when Bill showed up. He planned to stay a while. But he hardly finished stripping off booties when Tetz pulled in for a quick pit stop, with Keith, Rusty, and Brenda close behind.

The group urged Bill and Amy to join them in a convoy over the summit. Amy figured she had nothing to lose and packed as fast as she could.

Bill's decision was tougher. The group was on a different traveling schedule. His poor dogs were coming off a long march and deserved a break.

Brenda's comment proved persuasive: "You don't want to do the mountain alone."

Tetz and Keith went first, pledging to wait for the others at the foot of the climb. Rusty hung back to give Bill and Amy more time to get ready. Brenda took advantage of the delay to dash inside the lodge for a drink of water. She could have used a meal, but there just wasn't time.

Daylight was ebbing when Rusty, Bill, and Brenda joined the pair waiting at the Liberty Fork bridge. For Rusty and the others, who had been traveling together some two hundred miles by this point, it went without saying: They were waiting for Amy.

Bill, the new recruit, wanted to keep moving.

Rusty found his attitude offensive. Brenda, likewise. *There's no sense in encouraging Amy to come*, she reasoned, *then leaving her an hour behind.*

They didn't understand: Bill's dogs were so tired, he feared they'd quit unless he kept them rolling. Being unwilling to lead, however, he was in no position to force the issue. Amy showed up, rendering the whole discussion moot.

The convoy hit the summit ridge at dusk. It was foggy as Tetz led onto the exposed ridge, but conditions quickly turned windy. The trail became increasingly difficult to follow; the few markers standing were mostly buried, or tilted at crazy angles. If there was a guardrail marking the highway's edge, it was lost in the drifts rippling and growing before the mushers' eyes.

Tetz's team foundered. Keith took over. His dogs, too, buckled in the wind, now howling across the convoy's path. Keith methodically switched leaders, searching for better combinations, finding none that would continue more than a few feet. The effort and strain of trudging to the front to change leaders drained the musher physically and emotionally.

Tetz again forged ahead. This time he got off the sled and broke trail for the dogs on foot, plowing through waist-deep snow until he could go no farther.

The mushers had barely started upon the six-mile-long ridge when dogs throughout the convoy started rebelling. Bill's dove for shelter with each pause, becoming more and more resistant to his commands. Tetz, again waiting his turn behind Keith, saw his own leaders suddenly turn around.

Camaro, an old female leader in Brenda's team, picked that stormy setting to blossom in full heat. Squabbles and attempted breedings kept Brenda too busy to pay much attention to the storm, then a powerful gust bowled over Camaro and lead-dog partner Lilly. The frightened pair circled back toward their mistress. Rusty left his own team to help straighten out the resulting mess.

Afterward Brenda knelt in front of her team. Hugging Camaro and Lilly to her chest, she shielded her poor girls from the scary wind and the attentions of their hormone-drunk comrades.

She was in that position when Keith approached with news that he and Tetz were admitting defeat. "We're going to camp," he said.

"You're going to stop here?" cried Brenda, shocked.

"I'm not making my dogs camp in this. This is how dogs die on the coast," she said, recalling her father's stories about Iditarod mushers pinned down on the windy Bering Sea.

Like most drivers in the race, Brenda had a full set of Fulda dog coats. Now that she needed them, however, Brenda realized those coats were soaked with sweat. She was to blame for that, having skipped earlier chances to dry them out. The only protection within reach was escape. Brenda turned her team around and retreated toward what she remembered was a calmer spot. Rusty and Amy followed.

Bill tried to retreat, but his tired dogs wouldn't move. "Hey, there's no point," he told Keith and Tetz. "Let's just dig in."

Plowing a trench with his legs, Bill thrust his dogs into it.

Brenda found the calm spot she remembered. It was little more than a dip in the trail, but the angle of the surrounding slope deflected the wind somewhat. Instincts took over. The sled dogs pawed for shelter. Rusty emptied his sled and climbed inside. It wasn't comfortable. He got out, flipped his sled on its side and hunkered down with his back to the wind. That was slightly better.

Before she could fit inside, Amy had to evict poor Chenee. She tenderly wrapped the sick dog in two coats and placed her on the lee side of her sled. It wasn't much, but it was the best she could do.

While the storm howled outside, Amy raged within. Her husband had talked her into this. What made Peter so sure she could make it through? He didn't know how sick her dogs were. He wasn't the one stalled on the summit for the second time.

"This is fucking miserable," Amy muttered. "This is so stupid. I can't *believe* I'm here."

Nearby, Brenda also cursed away at the situation. Each of the women gradually became aware of the other's ranting, heard themselves in the complaints, and together burst out laughing, sharing a flicker of warmth in the storm.

Before long, however, Brenda felt dreamy and weak. The sourdough pancakes available at Likins' cabin hadn't appealed to the Quest's youngest musher. She passed them up, figuring she'd make it to Eagle on the snack food in her sled, but the stash ran out. Making matters worse, Brenda had worked up a sweat climbing the mountain.

Now she began shivering.

At the front of the convoy, Tetz was too anxious to sit still. Leaving his team, the tireless German struck out on foot and located markers as far as a mile ahead of the teams. If the storm provided an opening, he knew where to go.

An hour or two after the teams first dug in, Tetz returned to inspect conditions near Brenda's trio. He saw that the young woman was shivering and hadn't even pulled out her sleeping bag! Hauling Brenda to her feet, Tetz forced her to accompany him back to the upper camp.

Entering the upper camp Brenda dimly noted the wind whipsawing Keith's ruff and hood. The next thing she knew Tetz was thrusting a cup of warm tea into her hands. "Can I make you some soup?" he asked, sounding almost maternal.

Five hours passed before Tetz judged the wind was slackening. He dispatched Brenda, who by that time seemed to be reasonably alert, with orders to get Amy and Rusty moving.

Brenda stumbled down the trail to her sled, stretched out on top of it and, without a word to her companions, fell asleep.

Thirty minutes later, an angry Tetz burst into the lower camp demanding to know why his orders weren't being followed. Realizing what she'd done, Brenda felt embarrassed, then guilty for letting him down. *He's the only one even trying to save us,* she thought.

Rusty was surprised at the convoy leader's urgency. The weather hadn't improved much, if at all. "I thought we were going to wait until it really died down," he said.

It was a little past 4:00 A.M. when members of the convoy lurched into motion for the second time. Tetz and Keith took turns in front. Together they pushed maybe a quarter-mile before bogging down.

Slumped over his sled, Keith watched Tetz pull his dogs forward for yet another try. "This is getting bad, *real* bad."

Bill's outlook was entirely different. Refreshed by his nap, he had decided this storm was a blessing in disguise. For the first time in hundreds of miles, the musher reckoned, his team was on schedule with these others.

Tetz and Keith appeared stuck. Bill signaled that he was ready to try. Ordering Beaver and King forward, he passed the other teams and broke trail, but only for a few yards.

Rusty noticed that his own team was acting feisty and cheerful.

"If Bill's dogs quit," he told Keith. "I'm going to pass all of you guys and let's see what happens."

When the moment came, Rusty surged past the mired teams. His lead dogs, Gator and Kid, were hitting their stride when the trail vanished under billowy drifts. The pair plunged into the soft snow, then paused, looking tentative. "OK, guys," Rusty called encouragingly. "Let's go, guys. Let's go."

He had to sweet talk his dogs through about thirty feet of powder before they gained better footing and confidence. From that point, Kid and Gator picked up momentum until Rusty's team was nearly loping across the ridge.

The wind whipped light snow at Rusty from ever-changing angles. Though his overall visibility was limited, the convoy leader was able to track other teams from the string of glowing headlamps bobbing along the ridge. Except for Bill, whose dogs kept pace, riding the heels of the lead team, the others kept falling behind.

Whenever the gap widened to the point of concern, Rusty halted to allow teams to catch up. These pauses carried an element of risk, but Rusty Hagan had faith in his lead dogs. And he knew the teams trailing his would all move faster if he kept them close.

Amy remained unaware of the maneuvering up front. With all the snow blasting her face, the driver of the convoy's last team was just glad to catch occasional glimpses of headlamps up ahead.

The moment he began descending off the ridge, Rusty stopped and set his hook.

Bill rolled up from behind. "What are you doing?"

"I'm waiting here until everybody is off," Rusty declared. "I'm not going into Eagle and leave somebody on this hill."

Bill countered that it was unsafe to park in the thin snow covering the road. Snow hooks couldn't be trusted on this surface, he said.

Rusty heard him out, but his hook, fabricated, and sharpened in his own shop back in North Pole, was holding fine. He wasn't budging.

It wasn't that Bill wanted to strand people. The thought never crossed his mind. Bill's attention focused on what was best for his own dogs and that was to keep moving.

Keith arrived ahead of Brenda and Amy. When the women made it, he ran over and hugged them.

"Thank you so much," cried Amy, who mistakenly thought her arms were around that German, Thomas Tetz, who impressed the life-long Alaskan as about the strongest man she'd ever met.

Her mistake was understandable: Mushers were all so thickly encrusted with snow, it was tough to tell anyone apart.

My dogs took one look at the campsite and had brain farts, losing their minds in the presence of these unexpected smells. Hobbes, Feets, and Cinder were the worst offenders, but they had plenty of company digging for the turds and snack bits scattered during the group's extended stay. Only Khan appeared willing to listen, and he was under-mined by the slackers sharing the gang line.

The scene reminded me of the Unalakleet village dump, where I once lost control of a garbage-chomping Iditarod team. The situation wasn't really comparable, but the memory of it drove me from the sled screaming and hauling dogs by their collars, by their harness, the gang line, whatever it took, until we were clear. Afterward, I cursed the mushers responsible for baiting these summit traps.

Clouds were streaming across the ridge as Gwen and I neared the liquor store. Before us, a wide snowmachine highway beckoned. "Go ahead, Khan," I commanded.

Hobbes neck lined passing the store and would have stopped com-pletely if Khan hadn't dragged her past. She wasn't scared or tired. It seemed that with the day's big challenge over, Hobbes simply wasn't interested in leading anymore.

I had a cure for that.

"Let's go home," I called, signaling that we were nearing a check-point or camp, neither of which was true.

The team surged as my hungry girl dashed for the promised dinner pail.

"Let's go home! Let's go home!" I sang, spurring the dogs into a false-hope lope.

I kept up the deception for miles, until we were off the ridge and well into the descent. Gwen was nipping our heels the whole way. Hobbes was beginning to act suspicious when I finally stopped and doled out the last of our snacks.

Gwen parked nearby and brought over Freshwaters' kuspuk.

"It's dangerous traveling behind you," she said, laughing.

We discussed the passage over a cup of warm Gatorade.

"That was about perfect," I said. "Tough enough for a thrill, but nothing we couldn't handle."

Gwen couldn't get over Khan and Hobbes. "I'm really impressed with your dogs."

That puffed me up.

Walter had scrapped his breakfast menu and chased us over the summit. He had closed within sight of Gwen at the liquor store and now moved to pass us.

"I thought I left you with the Red Lantern back there," I joked, waving Walter forward.

"You can have it back. I've got a whole string of them at home," he shouted, referring to an ornamental set of lantern lights decorating his cabin in Two Rivers.

Gwen also took the opportunity to go ahead. Her dogs were faster than mine, I couldn't pretend otherwise. Still, it was disappointing to again land in last place after my dogs performed so well crossing the summit.

Hobbes was staring at me, expectant. A measly chunk of whitefish wasn't what she expected for being a good girl. She wasn't going to be happy when we hit the trail without the promised meal.

I shifted her to wheel. Hobbes promptly squatted. Her lips were tight and she looked displeased.

Cyclone, traitor of the day, couldn't be trusted to lead anywhere. Searchlight, another possibility, lay on the road, curled tightly, one eye following my every move. "I don't think so," I whispered.

Am I imagining it? Or is the whole team pissed at me?

Not Khan. The old dog was on his feet whining. Teams were getting away, he seemed to be saying. He didn't need, or want, any help to correct that affront. "OK," I said, "the job is still yours, big guy."

He was primed. The instant tension relaxed in the gang line, telegraphing the snow hook's release, Khan hurled himself forward with an excited grunt, yanking Search and Luther to their feet. My heart quickened. After five hundred miles, the old dog's get-up-and-go remained magnificent. I dared imagined that he might actually sustain a lope. It was downhill to Eagle. The trail was hard packed from snowmachiners. But Khan soon reverted to a marching gait.

"Good dogs," I said, lying.

My gloom lifted when we overtook Gwen. She was having trouble with her leaders and waved me ahead. "Cool," I whispered, savoring the moment.

Khan marched smartly on by. Once in front, however, our pace remained pitiful.

With Gwen's leaders nudging my heels, we slowly, slowly wove down the Taylor Highway into town. Several times I spun around on the runners and asked Gwen if she didn't want to pass. Each time she declined. Being polite, I guess.

Five months' pregnant and battling the flu, Kate tried not to let on how blue she felt as she and Rory saw me off from Dawson. Afterward, she stood for quite a while on the riverbank, bouncing Rory in the backpack and watching the big white river gradually swallow me up.

Trudging back through the campground she bumped into Patti Mackey.

Roland, the defending champ's toddler, was still sick and wouldn't take his medicine. The clan's motorhome had already departed, leaving the mother and her wailing son living out of a pickup cab. Brenda, meanwhile, had left behind her own broken dog truck for her mom to somehow ferry back to Alaska.

"Do you want to get in and just drive around with us for a while?" Patti asked, after spilling out her tale of woe.

Kate begged off, fearful Rory might catch Roland's bug. But Patti's distress haunted her afterward. *Here's a woman who's done a million Iditarods with her husband and she's a wreck.*

Freshwaters took charge of breaking down the camp. The biggest challenge was finding space on other Fairbanks-bound trucks for the excess meats and other supplies I left behind at Dawson and previous checkpoints.

Though Kate's dad was ultimately headed for Juneau, he offered to detour about fifteen hundred miles and drive his weary daughter home. But Kate sensed Rory was restless and likely to become difficult if the road trip didn't end soon. My wife also figured she could use a few days breathing room in Fairbanks before rejoining the team as handler on the home leg checkpoints. A quick flight home was the obvious solution.

So Kate, Rory, and her dad piled into his Ford Explorer and drove to Whitehorse, the region's major flight hub. Kate, who hadn't packed for the trip with flying home in mind, found herself toting massive baggage, including her father's borrowed winter gear. The sheer quantity caused Air North Canada, which uses small commuter planes, to slap on penalty charges, greatly inflating the cost of the tickets.

We'd raised about $13,000 for the race from relatives on both coasts and dozens of friends, including $1,000 from O'Donoghue and O'Donoghue, my father's old law office in Washington, D.C. Kate slaved to bring in another $1,219 through a spaghetti feed, featuring her family's labor-intensive traditional recipe. We thought we were set.

But dog food for the season ran $5,500. Gear needed to train and outfit the race team cost $3,470, with another $800 for the Quest entry fee. I spent $1,550 leasing or purchasing dogs, a fraction of the investment at most kennels, but then we picked up Hobbes, Feets, Luther, Martin, and N.C. for free. Vet bills for the bunch totaled nearly $1,400, including roughly $400 of surgery extracting a rock plugging Searchlight's gut early in the season.

Those bills accrued prior to the race. Kate suspected the road trip expenses were way out of control. Fortunately, my wife didn't have the figures; she was already stressing and the hole was much deeper than she thought. Hotels and the truck crew support had pushed the total cost of my race past $17,000.

Kate couldn't believe it when they told her the flight was routed back through Dawson. *That long drive—for nothing!*

The flight departed so early she had no chance to give Rory a decent breakfast, but he merrily subsisted on crackers and juice. He was sitting on Kate's lap, playing contentedly, when an odd look crossed his face. "Mommy," Rory said plaintively. Before Kate could react the toddler hurled, soaking their clothes, coats, fur hats, and gloves with puke.

A man seated behind Kate handed her a napkin.

She could have screamed.

The plane touched down in Mayo, a small village, where passengers all had to get out. Drenched to the skin, Kate stood outside in the snow, hugging Rory to her chest, and begging the pilot to find the satchel with her dry clothes. It took him *forever!*

Kate almost slipped on snow entering the village's tiny air-service building, which doubled as Air North's waiting room. My wife avoided making eye contact with any of the other passengers; if anyone looked sympathetic, she knew she'd burst into tears. Changing Rory in the bathroom, Kate began sobbing. Before long, Rory was wailing, too. He reached up uncertainly from the floor to touch his Mommy's tears.

You don't want to traumatize the child, thought Kate, recovering her composure.

In Dawson, Kate and Rory had to get off the plane again. Again, it was freezing cold. She found Judy Steyer, Bill's wife, waiting inside the building.

"What are you doing here?" asked Judy, who knew Kate left town the day before.

The women commiserated on the flight back to Fairbanks, where Judy drove Kate to her car and waited patiently while the vehicle warmed up—little kindnesses hugely appreciated by a pregnant woman near her breaking point.

In the morning she got the call about Freshwaters rolling the dog truck.

❖ ❖ ❖

"It vas unbeeleev-able," Thomas Tetz declared, wearily rising from a bench seat in Eagle's old one-room schoolhouse. "Snow up to heeere," the German added, pointing to his waist. "Ve had to vade through it to make a path for de dogs. Unbeeeleev-able!"

"Yeah," I said, "now you have a *hint* of what a Yukon River storm's like."

After years of pecking away at a laptop at these same checkpoint tables, it was fun trading summit stories with fellow racers. Clearly, the guys ahead of us got the worst of it. Tetz was about the only one who didn't look run over. Keith was a zombie. Amy, Brenda, and Rusty looked whipped. Bill's eyes were bloodshot and sunken. He was annoyed at my suggesting they screwed up by stopping on top.

"So what would you have done?"

"I don't know, tie a rope to my waist or something. Like Swenson did on Iditarod," I said. "All I know is—you don't camp on a mountain-top. You guys are lucky it wasn't worse."

"It wasn't like we had a choice," Bill said. "You had to be there."

The competition was shaken. Excuse me for enjoying it, but their brutal night was our bonanza. "I'm glad none of them got frostbit," I told Gwen after the others left the table. "But if it took something out of their teams, great. This could be the great equalizer."

Indeed, from the moment Khan trotted under the banner waving alongside the old schoolhouse, Eagle was everything I could have wished.

Water for the dogs was waiting inside the checkpoint. Clumps of steaming harnesses, dog coats, parkas, snow pants, hats, you name it, ringed the old barrel stove, dangling from the center of sagging ropes. All nine teams traveling in the rear of the Quest's field, the infamous "back pack," were sharing the quarters. A bowl of moose stew? A plates of enchiladas? Hot chocolate, Tang or cider? Attentive volunteers kept it coming.

Marcus, the booty man, set up shop in an adjacent horse stall to outfit each team in the latest foot fashions. "Pretty much you can have whatever you want," he said, opening sacks of new booties for my selection.

Afterward, Marcus pulled out a notebook and assisted Florida, the greyhound vet. She examined each dog in my team, dictating observations about their condition. Such scrutiny from vets generally made me nervous—one always feared the discovery of an unsuspected ailment in a key dog. But Florida, a disarming southern gal, put me at ease. "These dogs are something else," she said cheerfully, confessing her growing appreciation for our amazing northern athletes.

Florida quickly diagnosed Cyclone's puzzling aversion to loping. "He's got sore toes on both his front paws," she said after manipulating his wrists. "I don't think it's any reason to drop him, but there's your explanation," she said.

She traced Feets' fleeting limp to a tendon bruised above his right wrist and demonstrated a useful massage treatment. "You keep doing that every time you stop," Florida said, "and this big dog of yours will be pulling at the finish line."

While I was relieved to hear Feets' injury wasn't serious, Circle City was a hundred and eighty miles upriver, leaving me wary of miracle cures.

"This isn't a greyhound track," I said. "Feets is a big boy. If I make a mistake, I'm stuck hauling him a long damn way."

"Tell you what," she said. "If this dog doesn't make it, I'll buy you a beer at the finish banquet."

"You sound pretty sure of yourself."

"Is it a bet?" the vet said, her eyes sparkling.

"Guess I can't lose, can I?"

"You got that right," Florida declared, strolling back to the schoolhouse with me.

When I returned a few hours later to fetch my maps, the dogs hardly acknowledged my presence, sprawled in utter repose on their sun-baked straw beds.

Their lethargy contrasted sharply with Walter's maniacs, who greeted my approach with machine-gun barking.

"Walter, these dogs are *supposed* to be tired," I told the other musher, who was fixing his team a meal. "I'm pretty sure it's a rule. You're going to get in trouble if you don't quit resting so much."

We bantered about the summit for a few minutes. Then I got serious. "You know, Walter," I said, "you're driving the team the rest of us all want, dogs that are fast and happy. You must be doing something right."

Gwen, like Brenda before her, pulled into Eagle in need of repairs to her sled. Race judge Ty Duggar allowed a local volunteer to do the work. But the women had to stand by and assist. It cost Gwen a chunk of sleep, but it was worth it to finally patch the cracked block supporting her runner spring.

Afterward, she fretted about Jojo. The dog she'd considered her best leader entering the race really wasn't contributing. Gwen had twelve dogs. Trimming down by one would make it easier to run a single leader, something I'd been suggesting she might try. She filled out the paperwork to ship Jojo home, listing "sore feet" as the reason for dropping him.

Gwen faced one last, self-inflicted chore.

John McWhorter had already alerted radio listeners to her challenge: "Most drivers sent three or four bags to the Eagle food drop, Gwen sent twelve." The musher dubbed "Miss Kitchen Sink" had to sort through that mountain of material and squeeze items she deemed crucial in her sled.

I napped through the late afternoon, with a plan to get started by 7:00 P.M. When I returned outside to pack, I found Gwen's campsite was in total disarray.

"Brian, you *have* to wait for me," she pleaded.

Instead of putting on booties, I returned inside the checkpoint to patch some harnesses recently chewed by Hobbesey and Danger.

"I'm glad to hear you guys are traveling together," the race judge said, joining me at the table.

"Hey, Gwen starts slow, but she rockets past me every time," I said. "Besides, I've seen what the Yukon can do. There's strength in numbers."

Duggar nodded. "Well, we're glad she's not going to be out there alone."

He and I talked about the booty fiasco early in the race, and the consternation caused by my protest. "It got their attention," the judge said, chuckling.

"What's happening with Zirkle?" I asked, referring to the musher who had arrived in Eagle the previous day with a dead dog, the only fatality of this year's race.

Aliy's dog had collapsed, he said, then appeared to recover while riding in her sled. She eventually put the dog back in her team, with fatal results.

The musher was allowed to continue pending the results of a necropsy. At this point, the judge added, there was no reason to believe she mistreated the dog in any way, so it was unlikely Aliy faced a major penalty. "She seemed pretty broken up about it," he said.

The incident had me second-guessing my own moves following Danger's near demise the first night of the race. *What did I really know about his condition when I stuck him back in the team? Oh, but for the grace of God!*

I turned the conversation to something I'd heard back at Stepping Stone. Local volunteers claimed that one of the mushers ahead of me, a team still in the race, hadn't ever come through. They suggested the driver took advantage of a shortcut, shaving an hour or more off the run to Stewart River.

"No one signs in at Stepping Stone, so it was just a theory," I said. "But those folks were pretty certain and were going to alert headquarters. Anything come of it?"

"There's not much we can do about things like that," Duggar said wearily. "We're probably wouldn't even investigate—unless another driver makes an official complaint."

"Just asking," I said. We left it at that.

Knowing Gwen, I had pretended to be in a big rush. It worked almost too well: She finished packing while I was off bullshitting with the judge. Suddenly, I was the one playing catch up.

Gwen was pretty good about it, gloating only mildly as I gave Feets a hasty massage, then scrambled to place booties on Khan and select others.

The checker and Duggar were on hand, ribbing me, as I failed to get out of Dodge within the specified hour of signing out, a lapse making me liable for a time penalty.

The checker told me not to worry. "At this point in the race," she said, "things get a little more informal."

❖ ❖ ❖

It's said that Eagle City owes its existence to a stampeder infuriated by the Canadian justice system.

Old Man Martin, upon release from several weeks of wood-cutting for a minor infraction "against the peace and dignity of the crown," reportedly said to his partners, the Hudson brothers, "Yuh know what this country needs more 'n anything else? It needs a good hell-roarin' git-up and git-thar American town, and I'm going to start one if you two jaspars will back me up."

Alaska Life magazine published that account, penned by Cash Darrel, back in 1946. The accuracy of it remains unknown, according to historian Elva Scott. But her interviews with old-timers lend credence to the notion that Eagle began as a tent camp populated by miners who were hostile to Canadian laws and taxes.

If true, miners were trading one form of government for another. In 1899, the U.S. Army constructed Fort Egbert bordering town. A year later Judge James Wickersham showed up and established the first federal court in Alaska's Interior.

Eagle's prominence as a government center faded as new strikes lured gold-seekers farther north. The town's reputation persisted as a sort of outpost in the wilderness.

Vietnam and the generational conflict of the late 1960s and early 1970s triggered a new stampede of self-reliant souls to the road's end on the banks of the Yukon. Dick Cook was one of those "river people," as Eagle residents called them, drawn by the desire to find a simpler life, closer to nature.

"I wanted to get away from paying taxes to support something I didn't believe in," he told author John McPhee, "to get away from a place you can't be sure of anything you hear or anything you read. Doctors rip you off down there. There's not an honest lawyer in the Lower 48. The only honest people left are in jail."

The Yukon wilderness is a harsh school. Newcomers intent on living off the land are sorely tested acquiring the skills to survive before winter entombs their illusions. Cook, a former real estate appraiser from Ohio, was one of the few who thrived in the forest beyond town.

"In all the terrain that is more or less focused on the post office at Eagle," McPhee wrote in 1979, "[Cook] is the most experienced, the best person to be sought out by anyone determined to much beyond the outermost tip of the set society. He knows the woods, the animals, sleds, traps, furs, dogs, frozen rivers, and swift water. He is the sachem figure."

Cook served as McPhee's philosopher-guide when the author explored the Yukon's social currents in the late 1970s, a turbulent period following the construction of the trans-Alaska pipeline.

One of the pipeline's many side effects was new formality in Alaska land ownership. Discovery of oil on the North Slope spurred Congress to enact a sweeping settlement of Alaska Native claims, providing a land entitlement of forty-four million acres. President Carter signed authorization for massive new federal parklands in Alaska, including the Yukon-Charley Rivers National Park and Preserve. Such changes brought the free-spirited river people under increasing pressure from land owners, public and private, hostile to the idea of latter-day Tarzans building cabins wherever they pleased.

Over time, legal harassment, primarily from the National Park Service, led many of the river folk to abandon their forest camps. Others simply retreated to more settled lives in Eagle, or fled the Yukon entirely, having gained new appreciation for the urban amenities they once spurned.

Cook, now in his late sixties, stayed on.

I chanced to meet him the previous summer when he canoed into Eagle to visit with McPhee. Rail thin and balding with a ratty, gray beard, Cook, in person, bore little kinship to the Great White Hunter I pictured reading *Coming into the Country*. The man seemed more fond of discussing his garden than expounding upon survivalist philosophy.

Our conversation eventually turned to sled dogs. Cook mentioned that his trapline kennel bloodlines had become racier thanks to dogs acquired from Quest friends. The trail passed right by his cabin, located about twenty-eight miles down river from Eagle. Mushers were always welcome.

I filed that information away.

Eight months later, as Gwen and I mushed past the starlit cliff north of Eagle, I had the location of Cook's cabin penciled on my map. Given the nagging injuries to Feets and Cyclone, I proposed breaking the ninety-mile run to Biederman's cabin into three pieces, which suggested a visit to Cook was in order.

"Oh, I like that idea," said Gwen, who doubted any of her leaders were up to a forty- or fifty-mile run. "Besides, meeting guys like that is one of the best things about the Quest."

Back at Likins' cabin, I had asked Theresa if she had any dealings with Cook during her tenure with the Park Service. Not exactly, she said, but she recalled that federal employees navigating the river in those days were warned to give his cabin wide berth; the agency didn't want to give Cook any cause for opening fire.

During a subsequent snack stop, I jokingly mentioned Theresa's story. Gwen was brooding about it, 1:30 A.M., February 19, when she came upon a footpath just past the mouth of the Tatonduk River, which she suspected connected with Cook's cabin.

"Brian, where the *hell* are you?" She felt hugely exposed on the river, with who-knows-what lurking in the thick forest above. She heard dogs barking in the woods, a whole team of dogs from the howling. Gwen took that as a further indication this was the right place, which was anything but comforting.

"I'm not going up there and get shot," Gwen muttered, eyeing the footpath's entrance into the woods.

By the time I caught up, Gwen was pretty worked up. "You see if you can find him," she demanded. "I'll stay here and take care of the dogs."

I followed the well-trodden path past a dozen or more yapping sled dogs to what appeared to be a root cellar, fronted by a heavy, slanting door. Having nothing to lose—I knocked.

I heard activity inside. A moment later a skinny old man in a tattered robe peered out.

"Mr. Cook, I presume?"

He stared hard for a moment, then broke into a broad smile. "C'mon in," he cackled, "it's not often I get company here. Oh, Quest mushers used to stop, but everybody's in too much of a hurry these days."

"There's another musher down on the river, a girl, let me go get her."

"Fine, fine," he said. "I'll get my shoes."

Cook remembered me all right. "I thought you were going to send me a copy of that story," he said, fixing a pot of tea.

He had me on that. It was one of those promises reporters make in good faith, then forget under pressure of the next deadline.

"Well, I saw the story, no thanks to you," he said, observing that it came out all right.

Asked about his dogs, Cook's eyes brightened. He was in the process, he said, of putting together a team for the Percy De Wolfe, but hadn't had much luck training them, lacking both the time *and* a sled. "A tree fell on my last one," he said sadly.

The cellar reminded me of a Lower East Side shanty. It was a chilly hovel with a small wood stove, dusty floorboards, and cluttered with odd boots, gloves, and other odds and ends that had seen better days, but might yet prove useful. "You knew my cabin burned down, didn't you?" he said, somewhat apologetically. "Two years ago. Burned to the ground. I'm planning on rebuilding, but haven't had the money, or the time.

"In the eyes of many of my friends," Cook said with stiff formality, "the greatest loss was my journal." The work, thousands of pages in length, had contained decades of field observations concerning animals, plants, and other aspects of nature encountered in the surrounding wild. He described the contents of his lost notebooks in a voice stripped of animation, as if reciting a coroner's report about a friend's autopsy, a message of finality I found more terrifying for its calm delivery.

Though he'd apparently lost his life's work in that fire, Cook's passion for studying the world around him remained keen. That was evident listening to his story about an unusually solitary raven. Over time the woodsman forged a relationship with the bird, who visited him each morning. The pups were then very young and one day Cook noticed the raven fooling with one of them, landing, hopping, and flying away, repeating the maneuver again and again.

"It had me stumped, but then I finally realized what was happening," Cook said, his eyes daring us to guess. "That raven was trying to teach it to fly! The bird couldn't understand why the pup wasn't getting it."

Gwen nodded off as the hermit and I continued talking about sled designs, tricks for staying warm, the forces shaping the current Yukon ice, all manner of subjects appropriate for a river lord's close study. In the morning, Cook resumed his nature lecture as he fixed us steaming plates of honest-to-God blue potatoes—grown in his own garden—and filled my thermos with freshly brewed tea.

The monologue, authoritative and fascinating, continued up until the moment I pulled the snow hook and waived good-bye. I left Dick Cook, clad in a thin coat and oversized shoes, standing on his footpath, a hardy weed springing from a crack in the Yukon's great white pavement.

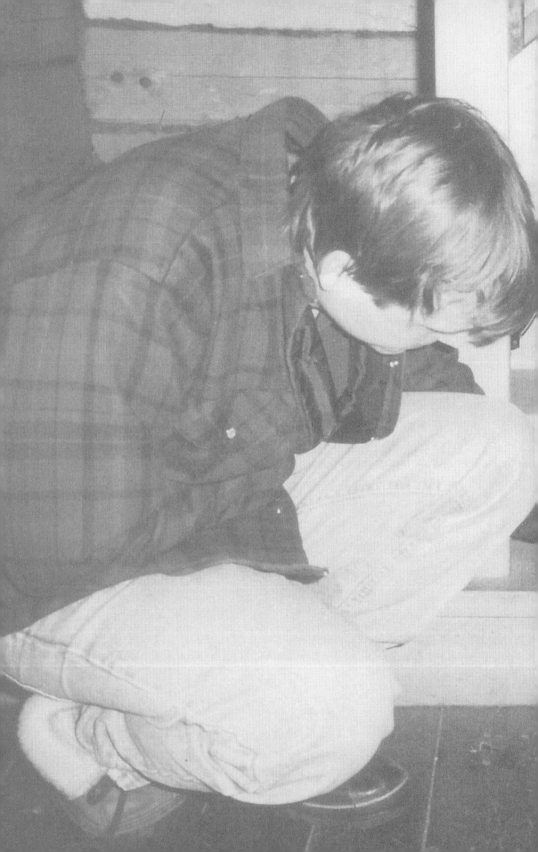

IN SHAMBLES

11

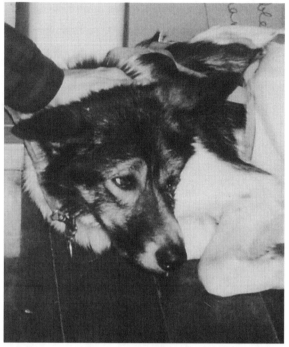

LUTHER

The settlement at Nation River pre-dated the Klondike gold rush by at least a decade. But where towns like Dawson and Eagle flowered in the tumultuous stampede that followed, the camp at Nation, like Fortymile, gradually withered.

The map showed Nation was about thirty miles northwest of Cook's cabin, the right distance for our second camp. Folks in Eagle told me we'd probably be welcome by a couple residing in a cabin at the old town site. Before we left him, however, Cook set me straight.

"How are you going to get across the river? The trail runs on the north bank and that's always a dangerous place to cross."

When we got to Nation—after hours of leaning off the sled's uphill runner to counter the sloping shelf ice—I saw just what Cook meant: Between the Quest Trail and a cluster of cabins visible on the far bank, the river held clumps of extremely rough ice framed by unusually smooth strips of snow. Given Cook's warning, the creamy skin radiated menace, its unblemished complexion, so rare in this area, hinted at fresh ice covering recent holes.

I shivered at the glaring reminder of my inexperience. *When in doubt, stick to the damn markers.*

"What do you say, guys? Want to pass on this one?"

But Khan wasted nary a glance on the distant cabins. His nose reminded me of the wobbly point of a spear in flight, relentlessly sailing toward impact.

A few miles farther, the trail entered a slough. A local trapper driving six or seven dogs rounded the bend and met us head-on. "Gee," he cried, sending his leader bounding off the trail into deep snow, where the dog obediently plowed a new groove. Another small dog team followed. On command, it peeled off the main trail and joined the other, which had stopped a few yards across from Gwen and me.

"With leaders like that, you guys should be the ones in the Quest," I said.

The musher grinned at the compliment. "Oh, these are just trapline dogs."

"They look pretty good to me."

The guy shared what he knew about the trail and gave us directions to an unfinished shelter cabin, about seven miles ahead. "It's small and hasn't got much inside except for a stove," he said. "But there's plenty of wood. You could stretch out for a few hours."

We didn't know anything about each other. Yet, having crossed paths driving dog teams on the Yukon, I left those trappers feeling a bond of shared experience.

We found the cabin with no trouble. With the temperature holding at fifteen below on a sunny afternoon, there was no need to use it. Gwen and I camped four hours out, swapping her chocolate for my Gatorade, while our dogs lazily recharged.

That evening I was leading when the trail crossed from the mouth of the Kandik River to the Yukon's south bank, weaving and bobbing through hellacious ice. Biederman's was so close I smelled the wood stove. At least, I thought I did and that was reason enough to dance on the runners. Having the Neville Brothers blasting through the headphones merely enhanced things.

Gwen, traveling close behind, was fiddling with her headlamp cord when folks at the cabin, which overlooks the river from a bluff, shined a snowmachine light our direction. Her dogs went ballistic. Off balance, Gwen couldn't find her brake and the team careened between icy boulders. She caught her knee on one. "Oh, my God!" Gwen gasped in pain.

She clung on weakly. Her sled bounced off yet another big ice chunk, which smacked that same leg in passing.

"Brian! Brian!" Gwen shouted, toppling from her sled.

I never heard her.

On her hands and knees in the snow, the musher watched her team floating away. Her sled, taking a mad bounce, landed just so, wedging

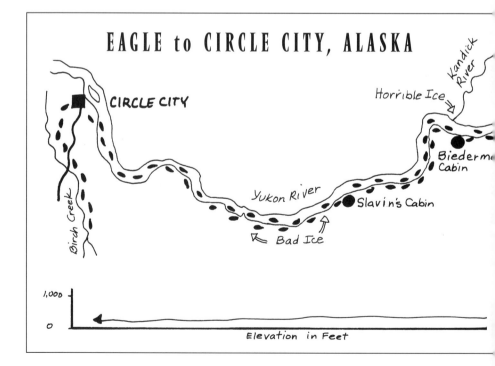

EAGLE to CIRCLE CITY, ALASKA

CIRCLE CITY

Birch Creek

Yukon River

Bad Ice

Slavin's Cabin

Horrible Ice

Kandick River

Biederman Cabin

1,000

0

Elevation in Feet

itself between several boulders. The gift drew Gwen to her feet and, forgetting her injury, she ran to reclaim her team.

Nadeau was dictating the pace in a manner that obscured the strength of his team. Lee was reminded of that when he again caught the frontrunner resting his dogs a few hours past Trout Creek. One *could* read that as further indication the big Siberians were faltering. That fit with the notion that Nadeau was marching his dogs, cutting his team's rest to preserve an eroding advantage. But both assumptions were dangerous.

Nadeau had those seasoned soldiers pulling his sled. Whatever their speed, they were capable of covering great distances without an extended rest. Lee decided that it was *possible* the wily Ghost had simply switched tactics. He seemed to be resting each time he gained a slight advantage, then shadowing Lee's next move.

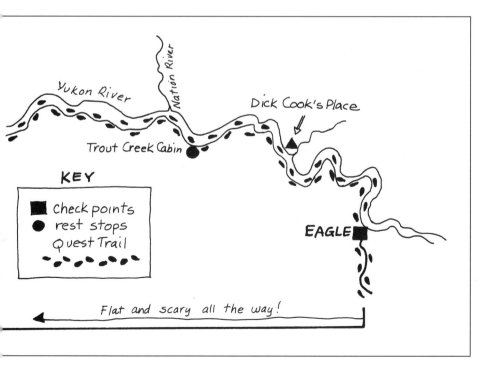

Could it be Nadeau was husbanding those iron dogs of his until he was close enough to drive, say, the final ninety miles into Circle? Take that one step further. Could the rookie be scheming to suck *him* into a grueling chase on this final leg of the Yukon, one calculated to crush the spirits of his rival's young dogs? *I have to have that doubt,* Lee realized. *I have to think that because I have to remember what Charlie Boulding did.*

"Let's play a trump card," Lee whispered, passing up Biederman's.

The veteran resolved to push another twenty miles to Slavin's, a National Park Service cabin, roughly sixty miles from Circle. *One of two things will happen,* Lee thought. *Either Nadeau can stop at Biederman's because he has to, which totally gives me control of this game. Or he can chase me to Slavin's—but he can't keep going all the way to Circle.*

Nadeau trailed Lee into Biederman's by an hour and eased off the pressure, camping there nearly six hours. Quest volunteers staffing the remote cabin radioed the development to headquarters, where it signaled to most observers the onset of the rookie's long-predicted collapse.

Freshwaters knew that he was hurting for sleep. But the truck was loaded and he was itching get on the road from Dawson while he still had daylight. He had things to take care of back in Fairbanks before a planned hunting trip.

He didn't get far before he caught himself nodding off. Freshwaters began looking for a place to pull over. Miles later, he was still looking for a suitable opening in the low berms flanking the Klondike Highway. *This is dangerous. A person could fall asleep and go off the road.*

My handler awoke in time to grasp that the truck was committed for the ditch. He took it head-on, plowing about eighty feet through low brush before finally stopping. "Pretty soft landing," Freshwaters coolly observed, inspecting the smashed mirrors and dented passenger door. "Could have been a lot worse."

Ninety minutes later, he had cut down, perhaps, a hundred bushes, shoveled the necessary snow and assembled the ropes and cables needed to drag my dog truck to safety, as soon as the right vehicle came along. Freshwaters had one in mind. He'd left Keith Kirkvold's handler back in Dawson catching a nap in the musher's converted school bus. Mark Freshwaters watched for him now, staking out the highway with an intensity he usually reserved for hunting.

Two days later, he was in Dawson getting the truck's alignment corrected, with Kate's father's help, when the local Quest office received the times out of Fortymile cabin. The unofficial report showed that I not only caught Rusty's group there, but left ahead of everyone but Tetz. "Well, good for Brian," Freshwaters declared.

Back in Fairbanks, Bill McKee got a similar kick studying the printout from the Quest's Web page. He was also glad to see Brenda hanging in there with her small team. In their last call, McKee's wife, Sandy, who was handling dogs for Brenda, filled Bill in on the team's many setbacks, including the baffling hunger strike that led Brenda to drop Star.

He never expected that. *We give away Searchlight to Brian thinking she didn't have what it takes. And she's still in the race. We keep her sister, Star, thinking she's the best of the litter and she doesn't even make it to Dawson. That's dogs for you.*

Shaking his head, my neighbor returned to analyzing the out times.

"Speaking of the leaders," observed the studio host of KUAC radio's Quest show on February 17. "We've got Bruce Lee running out in front of everybody else at this point. He's expected into Circle, like any moment."

Lee had been resting at Slavin's for several hours when he heard his dogs bark. Sure enough, he found fresh tracks waiting outside, indicating Nadeau had come and gone, probably aiming to take the ninety-mile run in a single shot. *Gutsy move. But that's what we were expecting.* Noting the time, Lee coolly figured he could give his dogs another two hours rest and still catch Nadeau entering Circle, which was the plan all along.

Six hours later, the first light was breaking as Lee neared Circle City. His eyes were strained from scanning the broad river for signs of the frontrunner's headlamp. A sinking feeling gripped the veteran. "Dang it, he does have more speed!"

Nadeau had mushed alone into Circle City at 8:21 on the morning of February 17. No one had seen him coming; the cunning rookie was running without a headlamp.

Only moments later, Lee's team swung into view out on the Yukon. He arrived sixteen minutes behind the frontrunner, having covered the sixty miles from Slavin's a good deal faster.

Back at Biederman's cabin, radio reports concerning the pair's arrival at Circle sparked speculation among the second pack of Quest mushers.

"When do you think we'll catch them?" Paddy Santucci asked Rick Mackey.

The defending champ laughed. "Don't you get it?" he said. "We won't even see them before the finish line. We're all racing for third place now."

Nadeau, fielding questions translated by his wife in Circle, also sized up the race as a two-way duel to the finish.

"If I were not in this race, it would be easier for Lee, and it is the same for me," he told reporters. He granted that Lee held the edge in speed, but didn't seem worried. "His dogs travel faster, but they have to stop longer."

Bruce Lee, meanwhile, couldn't believe the winks and smirks directed at him from people who ought to know better. *We're not in Carmacks anymore, where everybody was saying: 'Are you worried about these guys?' We're smelling the finish line and he's still moving OK. His dogs just ate really well,* Lee thought ruefully. *People are discrediting Nadeau and they should look at what he's doing. He's feeding different, running different, trying a different strategy. I applaud him for it. He may crash and burn, but he's still in first or second place, guys.*

Asked why he *allowed* Nadeau to again seize the lead, the weary veteran made a stab at educating these self-appointed experts. "You just can't ever forget what the *dogs need,*" Lee declared, sounding drunk with fatigue. "They're not machines. They're *living animals.* They're *living creatures.* The hardest part of mushing is knowing what your dogs need."

None of the reporters tipped to the glaring weakness in Lee's own team. His young leaders, in particular Hawk and two-year-old Canvas, had so far managed to fill the gap created by the injury to Miles the second night of the race. But that didn't mean any of them were ready to lead over Eagle Summit.

Lee, being a forthright soul, would have elaborated on the loss had any of the reporters asked, but the team's performance apparently had them fooled. So be it. That meant Nadeau was in the dark, too.

Instead, Bruce Lee gently reminded the media that his name wasn't inscribed on the Quest trophy waiting in Fairbanks. *"That's* a pretty incredibly *tough* dog team," he said of the Ghost's outfit. "I'm going to stick to my schedule and let the chips fall where they may. But he can do some *really* extended hard runs."

The musher's voice faded. "I know I'm faster," Lee added after a pause, "but it doesn't mean that I will be, and it doesn't make him less of a threat."

❖ ❖ ❖

The old Kotzebue musher, Louis Nelson, kept dancing away. His dogs looked frail, but they beat Mowry's barking beauties into Trout Creek, Biederman's, then Circle City, expanding the villager's lead from one hour to three on that last leg.

The Mowth held the last position in the money, fifteenth place, worth a total of $1,500. That paycheck mounted to $1,800 if he could just slip past Louie. Three hundred bucks might not seem like much, but he had a kid on the way. Every dollar counted.

Studying the checkpoint times in Circle, Mowry noticed a familiar name directly under his own. So Larry Carroll was gunning for him again. He recalled Carroll mounted quite the chase as a rookie in 1997, coming from way back in the field to place twelfth, some six hours and $800 shy of The Mowth's tenth-place, $3,300 finish.

It was academic. This year Carroll was sixteen hours behind Mowry leaving Dawson, seventeen hours behind out of Eagle, with the gap unchanged at Biederman's.

It came as a shock when Carroll mushed off the Yukon River before Mowry got out of Circle. Still, it wasn't like Big Larry was breathing down his neck, not with more than thirteen hours separating them. Nelson was the one who had to be feeling his nuts in the vise.

❖ ❖ ❖

GWEN'S JOURNAL   Feb. 20, 1:50 a.m. Biederman's Cabin

Feel like hell — like I've been run over flat. Slept 3 hours but cabin was
very warm. Too warm. Feels good to be outside again. Nice place, nice
people. They say jumble ice ahead isn't as bad as we'd heard. Got Taco
running in lead again last night. Team looked better again. Realization: we
won't make the banquet. Chase very tired and possibly limping although
vet Turner can't find anything. Ruffy still sore on left shoulder and wrist
but not getting any worse . . . Feel like I'm getting the flu or something.

❖ ❖ ❖

Though Doc May had warned me against it, he knew I was bound
to try Danger in lead. So he'd suggested giving the situation a lot of
thought. "You'll want to be someplace with no turns, absolutely no
choices to make," he said. "I don't know, out in the middle of the
Yukon, maybe."

Gwen was leading out of Biederman's. All I needed was a chaser up
front. Danger filled that role in training, leading teams driven by handlers that I recruited for tagalong missions.

On those training runs, I usually paired Danger with Cyclone, but I
hadn't forgiven Mr. Sore Toes for his stunts on American Summit. Speed
being the whole point of this evening's gamble, neither Khan, nor
Hobbes was fast enough to share lead duties with May's psycho. *Nope,*
if Danger's gonna lead tonight, it has to be solo. As Gwen lined her team out,
I placed Danger dog in Khan's usual spot and waited to see what
might happen.

We flew.

For the first time since Gwen and I partnered up, my team stayed
glued to her heels, dipping and dodging through the ice fields, rolling
down the side of the river. A couple times Danger was so close to overrunning the team in front, I paused and spotted Gwen a few hundred
yards. Each time, Danger streaked after that bobbing light, muscles

rippling, tongue flapping, reminiscent of a greyhound crossbred with the Incredible Hulk.

Clinging to the sled, I felt as if I was in a free-fall. Fatigue weighed more heavily than at any moment prior in the race. I tried nibbling on brownies and candy, sipping Gatorade, slapping myself—the usual tricks. Nothing helped. Paws blurred before me and I verged on a blackout.

It made no sense. We had stayed six hours at Biederman's Cabin.

"You tell your friend Mowry he lost his bet," the cabin owner had said, handing me a cold beer as soon as I sat down to enjoy the feast prepared by local volunteers. "Tim swore we'd drink all the beer before you got here. Well, goddamn it, this proves him wrong!"

The man grinned. "He shamed us into saving you some."

A thin sled dog was asleep in the corner, breathing slowly. "We've finally got her drinking again," said the veterinarian, a New Englander, noticing my interest.

"Whose dog?"

"Brenda's."

"Wow," I said, "she can't have many left."

Someone pulled out the list. "Looks like she left here with seven dogs. One more than the minimum."

The cabin was so warm my face burned. The room was so bright I had trouble finding space on the bench by the kitchen's grandly set table. A spirited discussion was underway, but my internal batteries were fading. Downing a second bowl of stew, chased by one last gulp of cool beer, I thanked the hosts and staggered off to the bunkroom. I hung up my Carhartt bib overalls, fleece outer shirts, gloves, and neck warmers on a manmade spider web overhanging a big barrel stove. Only then, having completed all known chores, did I surrender to the bodacious chunk of foam beckoning from the floor.

At precisely 2:00 A.M. on February 20, my wristwatch, beeping and shrieking, summoned me back from what felt like a coma. Hair matted and glued from dried sweat, eyes sunken, I staggered into the kitchen, drawing hoots from the volunteers.

"Say the word and we've got another beer with your name on it."

They confessed the suds stockpile was greater than Mowry imagined.

"Oh, I'll go for the Tang," I said.

I was sipping a third cup of the orange-powdered brew, when Gwen joined us in the kitchen. "I can't believe we slept two hours," she blurted, examining her watch. "It feels more like two minutes."

It wasn't until I was outside with the dogs, breathing in the cool night air, that my head cleared. "That cabin is too damn hot," I told Gwen.

"You can say that again," she said. "I'm surprised we woke up. I could have slept another twelve hours in there."

Amen to that. Still, two hours is practically a sleep-in for a rough, tough sled-dog racer. "Keep telling yourself that," I muttered, snapping back into the present out on the Yukon.

In truth, I'd never been so tired on a dog sled. Several times I simply blinked out, awakening as the handlebar slipping from my fingers, somehow recovering in a terrified whiplash save.

"Gwen's right ahead," I told myself, "if I fall off Danger will plow right into her."

You hope.

After two hours of dashing along the Yukon with the magnificence of a falling star, Danger dog dove off the trail, burying himself in the bordering powder. Taken by surprise, I damn near ran over the wheel dogs before I found the brake.

The team was stopped on a flat, featureless stretch. Brilliant stars added a glorious shimmer to the surroundings. Gwen's headlamp was floating away. I pulled Danger out of the powder and petted him. His whiskers gleamed with crystal makeup. The dang fool wagged his tail.

Running to my sled, I pulled the hook. We surged forward about twenty feet, before Danger peeled off to one side and began rolling in the snow. I tried again. This time Psycho Dog ran ten feet and sat down, sending Search and Luther charging over him.

"Well, it was fun while it lasted," I said, unclipping Danger from lead.

Gwen's headlamp light crested a mound in the distance and blinked out. I shifted Khan to the front of the line. The big leader began whining.

He pawed the trail. Used his nose to shovel snow angrily. He rose on his hind legs and shadowboxed the night. I smiled: *Behold the Mighty Khan!*

I pulled the hook and Khan shot forward, growling contentedly, pride and intensity showing in each energetic step. Yet, compared to Danger's thrilling pace, we were plodding. A quick check of the GPS showed Khan was registering a steady 7.5 miles per hour—for him, that was tearing down the trail.

Danger, banished to wheel, was a dog reborn, bounding forward powerfully, practically carrying the sled on his back. "You hairy screwball," I said, scowling.

❖ ❖ ❖

Walter Palkovitch did his chasing the night before. He was last in line as the Party Pack—his new name for Rusty's detested bunch—neared Slavin's Cabin. Mushers were told we could expect a meal and a warm bunk at Slavin's courtesy of the National Park Service, which controlled the surrounding Yukon-Charley Rivers National Park and Preserve. Walter was betting the six of the teams ahead of his wouldn't be able to resist. And *that* would be ideal, because trail conditions were fast and Walter's dogs were looking good; the time had arrived to drive them and ditch that rude crowd.

The clearing fronting Slavin's was jam-packed with resting dog teams, so crowded, in fact, that Hera and Anise slammed on the brakes. Walter was angry. *This isn't part of the game. You don't park in the middle of the trail and go in and have soup!*

He got off his sled and surveyed the situation. He found what appeared to be a trail leading back down to the Yukon on the far side of the campers. But there weren't any Quest markers. That tore it, because it meant Walter had no choice but to ask for directions, tipping the others that he wasn't sticking around.

Seething, he headed inside the cabin.

"Is that trail over there the 'out' trail?" Walter said, directing the question at the first non-musher he saw.

"Do you want some coffee?" the ranger said.

"No," Walter snapped angrily. "I want to get out of here."

Walter squandered ten or fifteen minutes pulling his dogs past those other teams. None of those mushers, he couldn't help but note, lifted a finger to help. They were ensconced inside the cabin, contentedly spooning who-knows-what from identical Styrofoam cups. The uniformity of their behavior appalled him. Group think at its worst, judged Walter, who could conceive of no justification for stopping here, a mere three hours from the Party Pack's last camp. The group mind had spoken and none of the sheep dared question it.

Bill offered a case in point. He alone, Walter noticed, hadn't been eating. He was dressed in his wind garments, obviously itching to get back on the trail, but prevented from doing so by his dependency on the collective imperative. *You don't have individual thought anymore,* Walter mused as he continued down the river. *Group think is very powerful. People who make decisions in groups very seldom change them.*

Bill would have argued that assessment. His inertia wasn't mental. He didn't have any leaders left. Oh, he had a few that strung the team out, but none of them were dependable. Hanging with the group gave his team others to chase, which Bill presently considered essential.

A black crack, perhaps four inches wide, yawned beneath one of my runners. As I jerked the sled to one side, I heard a distinct whimper. Scanning the dogs with my headlamp, I noticed Cinder was running on three legs. "Damn."

I stopped the team and ran to him. He was holding his right rear foot off the ice. Nothing seemed wrong with the paw, so I massaged his hindquarter. After a bit, he tenderly set the foot down. We'd just crossed several broad plates of ice, sporting numerous cracks. Cinder must have caught his foot on that last one. One bad step in seven hundred miles.

"Could be worse," I observed, rubbing Cinder's neck. "The foot's not broken and *you're* not Khan."

We proceeded. Cinder ran three-legged at first, then gradually settled into a more normal, if limping, gait. The injury hadn't affected his workmanlike attitude. "Good boy, Cinder! Good boy!" I called, admiring his tight tug line. If the limp didn't worsen, he might make though the seventy miles to Circle City. With any luck, he might even finish the race.

Near dawn we entered jumble ice covering the river as far as I could see. Trail breakers skirted the worst of it, plowing through waist-high bushes of small willows, no big deal for a snowmachine, but nasty work for dogs. I winced watching Khan crash through the sticks, which whipped backwards into each trailing dog. The blows caused Luther, Searchlight, and a few others to duck and weave, but they kept moving forward, perhaps drawn by the scent of previous teams, perhaps drawing inspiration from each other.

And how would you do? The unspoken question shamed me anew. *Never, never as well, I'll admit that much.*

The rough ice lining the Yukon's south bank eventually flattened and we escaped the punishing thickets.

"Whooa," I said in a voice hardly above a whisper. The dogs stopped on a dime. I laughed. "I see you've mastered that one."

I tossed out chunks of whitefish. Then I walked forward to Khan and worked my way down the chain, rubbing ears, playing with everybody. Luther, running in the team's center ranks, hadn't touched his fish. He sat there quivering. At my approach, he slowly raised his head.

"Aw, God!" I cried, dropping to my knees and staring. "What happened, Luther? Jesus, what happened to you?"

A mass of yellow-green gore coated the hair below his left eye socket, which must have been speared in that recent thicket. I gently cupped his snout, training my headlamp on the injury. "Luther," I said, "where's your eyeball, buddy? Oh, Luther, you poor, poor boy. I'm so sorry."

I moved to gingerly load my injured doggie. Luther wouldn't have it. Eye gouged and all, he struggled to remain with his teammates. "Whatever you want," I said, reluctant to force anything upon him and feeling a bit faint myself.

Switching around several other dogs I placed Luther across from Cinder on the right side of the gang line, figuring his good eye might best serve him there. As an afterthought, I popped a Cephelexin broad-spectrum antibiotic capsule into Luther's mouth, stroking his throat until he swallowed it. "I don't know what else I can do for you, guy. Hang in there."

Luther fell to work as if nothing happened. Cinder's tug was also tight despite his traveling on three legs more often than not. The sight choked me up. *They're doing this for me and I don't deserve it.* I suddenly longed to hold Kate and Rory, who was growing up so fast. I was missing so much. *And for what? What are we doing out here?*

Running Hootch solo seemed to be the answer to Gwen's prayers. The short-legged, long-backed leader acted delighted with the new-found freedom, just romping up the river. Hootch was still flying as the trail left the river proper on a winding passage through sandbars and sloughs, then briefly jumped overland to Coal Creek. Whipped by her powerful hounds, Gwen made the passage in thrilling fashion, hugging corners within inches of disaster. She completed the run feeling jazzed! "We're going to catch those guys," she declared, stamping her hook into the snow outside Slavin's cabin.

For the first time in the entire race, she didn't bother stripping off booties. She merely doled out snacks and made for the two-story 1930s-era cabin, figuring to grab a quick bite to eat. "Brian should be here any minute and we're not staying long, forty-five minutes, maybe an hour, max," Gwen told Kevin Fox, a Park Service ranger, with whom she was pleased to discover she had lot of friends in common.

She was wolfing down a bowl of federal chili, washed down by hot chocolate, when my team arrived.

Leaving booties on the dogs for a quick pit stop had been my idea, one borrowed from Sawatzky, which I shared with Gwen during our last trail break. But there I was plucking off booties and casting them aside like a wild man. "Uh, oh," Gwen muttered, watching from the widow. "This *isn't* good."

Gwen had developed this image of me as a calm, upbeat musher. She didn't know the person scattering gear outside Slavin's Cabin.

"Brian," she said gently, joining me outside, "are you OK? Is every-thing all right?"

"No, it's not OK," I shouted, flapping my arms. "Luther just poked his eye out! Cinder's only got three legs!"

Gwen hastily examined Luther. She saw right away that the young dog hadn't lost his eye. Though gobs of fluid oozed from a puncture wound below the socket, it didn't look *that* bad. Not as bad as I apparently thought.

Watching me stamp around, deranged by worry and fatigue, vowing to stay six hours, eight hours, as long as it took to save my team, it occurred to Gwen that dogs were the least of the team's troubles. *Brian's freaking!*

With that realization, my tirade struck her as hilarious. "I've got something you could put on that eye," she said soothingly, leaving to fetch the salve before her mounting mirth bubbled over.

Quest Rule No. 18 states: "At no time during the race may a driver house dogs in a heated shelter." The idea is that any dog in need of such care probably ought to be dropped from the race, an admirable goal, perhaps, but I didn't see where it helped Luther, miles from assistance on the Yukon.

"Screw the rules," I told Gwen, releasing Luther from the gang line. "I'm bringing him inside."

The ranger brought me a pot of warm water hot water and I cleaned the wound.

"I really think he'll be all right," said Gwen, helping me apply ophthalmic ointment.

"Oh, yeah? I don't see any eyeball in there." After a pause, I added: "I can't believe you brought eye medicine? I swear, Gwen, your sled is the warehouse. How do you fit it all in?"

My poor maimed doggie was amazingly stoic and accepted treatment without so much as a whimper. Afterward Luther curled in a tight ball and slept.

Returning outside, I massaged Cinder's bum leg, hip to toes, with Krestensen's juice, which I also dabbed on Cyclone's sore toes and used rubbing down Scrim. She hadn't displayed any injury, but seemed stiff towards the end of the last run. Feets was, by then, waiting for me, holding his hind legs open in anticipation of the tendon massage a la Florida.

Searchlight looked disappointed when I passed by without wrapping her wrist; Florida had pronounced that cured. "You miss the attention, don't you?" I said, dropping down to stroke her belly until her tail began wagging.

To hear me chatting, one might think it was one big picnic. It was an act. Between the wraps and medicinal smells, half my team looked like escapees from a hospital ward. Six of my nine dogs had some degree of injury, leaving me depressed as hell and wondering how we were ever going to make Fairbanks—two mountains and three hundred and fifty miles away.

I stumbled through the usual feeding ritual, returned inside, where I drained a cup of hot chocolate, then stepped over Luther, climbed the ladder to the cabin's loft and fell into a bunk.

Mid-morning light streamed through the cabin windows. Downstairs, Gwen felt the tugs of what promised to be a beautiful day on the trail. I hadn't asked her to stay. I'd simply announced I was taking six here. *Brian's frazzled*, Gwen recognized, applying her catch-all term for a personal crisis.

She had tried to cheer me up, persuade me to keep moving—until she realized where I was coming from, that injuries might leave me driving as few as six dogs at Circle City, two hundred and fifty miles from the finish line, a hundred miles short of Eagle Summit. The implications were sobering: *Brian could end up scratching.*

Gwen had eleven solid dogs. She'd survived those terrible opening days, when she mainly wanted to avoid being the first racer to quit. Her confidence in the dogs and herself had grown over the miles. She couldn't imagine anything stopping her now.

Gwen wasn't bound to stay at Slavin's. She knew that. Had there been anyone else behind us, anyone at all, she would leave right now.

Gwen recalled the pressure of mushing out of Dawson in last place. She hadn't forgotten the terrors of her solo runs on the Yukon and the Fortymile.

"I'd want someone to travel with," Gwen declared, hearing a decision in the words. She knew in her heart that she was making the right move, if not as a sled-dog racer, certainly as the person she aimed to be.

Four hours later, refreshed from the nap and encouraged by the re-emergence of Luther's eyeball, I led him back outside. The other dogs stretched and barked happily. The whole crew acted frisky, even Luther, whose tail was wagging as he sniffed Searchlight's crotch.

They were like children, and I feared for them. We had so far to go. These dogs of mine simply had *no* idea.

Following Gwen out onto the Yukon, I watched for the slightest indication of limps, stiffness, slack lines, signs of any of the many infirmities probable among my ailing crew.

What I saw surprised me.

All nine tails were high, something I'd seen only once before in the entire race. "Ye of little faith," I whispered.

Despite all the injuries, my strategic errors, and training shortcomings, this dog team of mine remained happy. Come what may, they had the momentum of honest dogs.

PREY

12

SEARCHLIGHT

Pulling into Circle City, Walter felt pretty chipper.

"Where are those other guys?" the checker asked.

"Well," Walter said, "you know it depends on how much soup they ate. I hope it's two hours worth. Because if it is," he said, grinning, "I'll never see them again."

But Walter's move at Slavin's had spurred a general exodus. Rusty, Tetz, Brenda, Bill, Keith, and Amy spilled from the cabin like angry ants. Nearly all of the teams took a turn leading on the sixty-mile trail to Circle.

Lemon and Beaver, another four-year-old male, had emerged as Bill's main pacesetters. But their shuffling performance was nothing to brag about. Lemon was the main offender, of course, seizing upon the slightest excuse to stop. Entering the second half of the run into Circle, his master's patience ran out.

"The hell with it," Bill said, shifting the erratic pooch back inside the team. "Beaver," he declared, "you're running single lead."

The effect was electrifying. Free of distractions, Beaver leaped forward like an F-16 kicking on the after-burner.

Running at the tail end of the convoy, Amy glimpsed Bill's sudden surge. It wasn't until the river widened that she got a good look. She was impressed at the way that black dog stretched the team out.

Beaver's joyous tear lasted into Circle, where Bill officially mushed the nineteenth Quest team off the Yukon at 10:55 A.M., February 20, slightly more than a half hour behind Walter. Within fifteen minutes, all five other members of Rusty's group joined Bill and Walter in the field adjacent to the local fire hall.

When she finished her chores, Amy sought Bill out.

"If you can leave us, you should just do it," said Amy, whose upbringing as a racer kept her focused on the larger game.

Bill, riding high on Beaver's recent show, was enthused, but he wasn't so keen about cutting loose alone.

The dogs slept through the afternoon, while drivers drifted between the cafe at the Yukon Trading Post and the bunkroom set up in the local fire hall. Most caught at least a catnap. The exception was Brenda, whose packing efficiency hadn't improved over seven hundred and fifty miles of practice.

Watching the tired teen fumble with her sled, Bill grew impatient. "We should just leave the girl," he told Rusty. "She's not ready to go."

Rusty declined. The good-natured musher just didn't see any point in rushing, not at this stage. None of them had a shot at the top fifteen, the cash-prize spots. His goal was finishing, period. He looked forward to doing so with Brenda, Keith, Tetz, and Amy, true comrades in what amounted to the greatest adventure of Rusty Hagan's life.

He tipped Brenda regarding Bill's suggestion. She was incensed; it confirmed everything she suspected about Bill's sneaky attitude.

Brenda hadn't slept a wink at Circle. But when Walter and Bill pulled their hooks late that afternoon, the defending champ's daughter was ready and chased the pair out of the checkpoint. Anger had awakened that Mackey blood.

❖　❖　❖

Three days earlier, Andre Nadeau's team hadn't shown any cracks preparing for that same run. Looking sharp as ever, all ten rose on command after six hours of rest and marched out of Circle City.

Lee also was down to ten dogs. But his last run had been twenty miles shorter, and he rested an extra hour before resuming the duel to decide the 1998 Yukon Quest.

The flat, hard trail down Birch Creek offered a track perfectly suited to demonstrate whose team was faster. Lee's young lopers caught Nadeau before the bridge, roughly twenty miles from Circle, and streaked away. That felt pretty good to Bruce Lee, whose confidence had suffered when he failed to overtake Nadeau during that final Yukon run. *Believe in your strategy. Believe in your dogs.*

It was seventy-five miles to Central. Lee accepted that his rival's team was capable of chewing up the distance in a single run. His dogs *could* do it, but that was asking a lot, possibly too much, from unseasoned leaders about to face the challenge of their lives in Eagle Summit. He decided to run long enough to build a buffer, then stop for a brief nap and feeding.

Perhaps an hour later, Lee parked and quickly fed his dogs the meal already prepared in his cooler. After it was consumed, the veteran unpacked his cooker and spread pans and a few bags in the snow, giving the appearance he just made camp. *Maybe he'll think that, but I'll already be done.*

It took Nadeau what seemed like a long time to catch up. He mushed right past Lee's team, then stopped a few yards ahead. Throwing open his sled bag, the rookie fished out snacks and doled them out to his dogs. Less than an hour later, he boarded the runners and took off.

Watching the Ghost disappear around the next bend, Lee agonized.

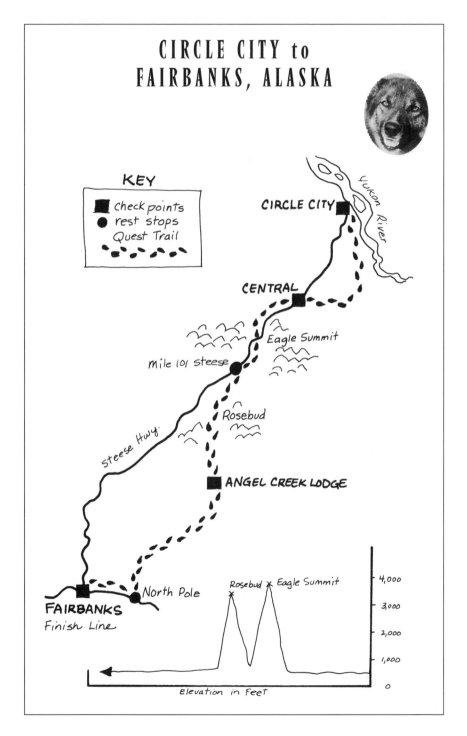

CIRCLE CITY to FAIRBANKS, ALASKA

KEY

■ check points
● rest stops
Quest Trail

Yukon River

CIRCLE CITY

CENTRAL

Eagle Summit

Mile 101 steese

Rosebud

Steese Hwy.

■ ANGEL CREEK LODGE

North Pole

FAIRBANKS
Finish Line

Rosebud ✗ Eagle Summit

4,000

3,000

2,000

1,000

0

Elevation in Feet

How long can I stay? How long can I give him at Central and make up the time before Angel Creek?

Lee stayed a while, but nowhere near as long as he would have wished. This Nadeau was far too dangerous to let roam unchecked. The veteran only rounded several bends in the twisting creek when, lo and behold, he came upon him camping. Like his own ruse with the cooker, Nadeau's snack routine had been a ploy. *He wasn't making a break,* Lee realized. *He's trying to make me screw up my schedule.*

The trail dipped, rose, and zagged on the fractured river, where we were traversing ice formations resembling the smashed cells of a broken honeycomb. Bouncing from one icy boulder to the next mere yards ahead of Khan, Gwen flipped her sled three times in the length of a football field. Each time she picked herself up, jerked the sled upright, and ordered Hootch forward, never letting on about her aching knee.

Watching from behind, I doubted I'd be so quick to get up. *You've got to give it to her, man. The girl is way tougher than she looks.*

Of course, she wouldn't have such trouble if her sled wasn't loaded to the point of bursting. "That's Gwen," I whispered, smiling at the sight of her wrestling that ungainly load.

The afternoon sun cast long shadows off the jagged blocks. Hootch, still running solo, led his teammates up and over a fold in the river, briefly disappearing from view. Cresting the rise, Gwen heard a funny bark. The team bunched behind Hootch, who'd stumbled upon a dark mound at the bottom of the bowl. "Oh, shit," Gwen cried, seeing a huge moose lurch to its feet.

With a startled glance, the moose used its spindly legs and clambered over the boulders.

"Did you see that?!" Gwen shouted as I caught up.

"See what?"

"A moose! It was right here. My dogs ran right over it."

My full attention had been on the sled. I scanned the river ahead. It was broad daylight and I didn't see any moose, but this crazy ice could conceal anything.

❖ ❖ ❖

Big Larry crashed the party in Central. At that point, Mowry's lead over the lumbering driver from Willow was slashed to four slim hours, while Nelson's edge had expanded to eight. The Mowth inwardly quaked: *What were you thinking stopping on Birch Creek for three hours!*

He'd been thinking about Eagle Summit. Wondering if Alf might revert to form. Wondering what, if anything, he might do if that happened, because Mowry needed that paycheck waiting on the other side of the mountain. The loan he'd taken out to run this race loomed large.

And suddenly so did Carroll.

All this time he'd been focused on getting past Eagle Summit, possibly bumping Nelson down a notch in the process. Now Mowry faced a threat greater than the mountain itself. He could miss out on the money entirely.

And there wasn't much he could do except sweat it out. He lingered in Central two hours past Carroll's entrance, giving his dogs a solid six before tackling the mountain that his only lead dog had quit on twice last year. *And we weren't even to the steep ridge,* Mowry recalled, watching Alf set the pace leaving Crabb's Corner Cafe.

Big Larry was on the trail three hours later. Hunting season had opened on the Yukon Quest Trail.

❖ ❖ ❖

The plane dipped one wing as it made a second pass.

"You think they're looking for us?" asked Gwen, who was resting her dogs behind mine in a slough forty miles shy of Circle.

"It sure looks like it," I said. "And that's pretty decent of them—this *is* the Quest."

Four hours and an interminably slow twenty miles later, I was leading through another slough, when we came upon a hand-written sign. "Circle, 21 miles, " the sign proclaimed, with an arrow pointing straight ahead. A second arrow pointed to the left: "Warm cabin, 100 yards."

"What do you think?" I yelled toward Gwen's blinding headlamp.

"What do *you* think?"

No one was home at Dill's Cabin. But the door was open and a worn ax was resting against neatly stacked firewood, which just begged to be split. By the time we finished tending the dogs, the cabin was toasty. Gwen was writing in her journal as I slipped into my sleeping bag. "What do you say I set the watch for 2:15 A.M.?" I suggested. "Get us on the trail by 3 at the absolute latest."

"That sounds good," she cooed.

The green numerals read closer to 5:00 A.M. when leg cramps summoned me from the dead.

"Gwen! Gwen!" I said, shaking her. "We got to get up. I must have screwed up setting the alarm. It never went off."

The shapely blonde lounging in polypro skivvies wore a guilty smile.

"I heard it," she said meekly. "I *tried* to wake you. I even kicked you. Then I thought, well, if he's that tired maybe we should sleep a little longer."

We packed so fast I didn't bother collecting my discarded booties. Bad as I felt about the mess, it was nothing compared to the guilt from oversleeping. Assuming that pilot reported our position, folks in Circle, poor Kate in particular, probably expected us hours and hours ago. *You know she waited up all night.* "Get up, Khan," I shouted. "Get up!"

Though Khan had them loping, Gwen left us in nothing flat. "Oh well," I muttered dourly, "She can at least pass the word that I'm on the way."

The rangers at Slavin's had warned us that a snowmachiner broke through the ice just outside Circle. Sunrise was setting the snow ablaze as I came upon crisscrossed markers, flagging the hole. A new skin of ice had formed, resealing the river. I shivered as we passed on the side.

Out in the center of the Yukon, a long cloud of reddish fog signaled water rushing through an open lead. It was twenty-five below. I felt like a mouse racing for the hole in the molding, praying the house cat wouldn't pounce.

Ahead I saw a handful of cabins and small buildings. "Let's go home, Khan. Let's go home!"

Minutes before 8:00 A.M. on February 21, Gwen, whom I hadn't seen for hours, popped off the river ahead climbing the boat launch. Only five minutes behind, Khan charged through patches of brush toward the same cut in the riverbank.

"Welcome to Circle," called Kate, snapping a picture.

"Hi, Babe!" I croaked. "We made it."

Kate looked perky standing there, billowy parka concealing the life brewing within. Had I not been dog-tired I might have seen through my wife's determined mask, glimpsed the toll of sleepless night spent envisioning the Yukon opening beneath my sled, and her guilt over leaving Rory in the care of friends for the first time in his young life. But Kate had resolved to be the good soldier through these last miles to the finish line. She wasn't even going to let me in on the hassles her father and Freshwaters underwent patching together the truck in Whitehorse. *Thank God, Mark wasn't hurt. That would have been too much.*

As it was, my back ached. My neck was so stiff that it felt artificial. Cinder and Scrim, likewise, were both limping as we turned down the hard-packed roadway. But their tails were high, and I was loving life. After nearly two weeks of quiet terror, the Yukon River was behind us for good!

Swank, the vet from West Virginia, was waiting at the checkpoint outside the village fire station. "Understand you've got a problem?"

"Man, I'm glad to see you. I've got a dog with an awful-looking eye," I said, gesturing toward Luther, "and I was sure you guys were long gone."

"We got the word from the park ranger," Swank said, giving Luther a quick once-over. Apparently satisfied with what he saw, the vet glanced at me, a grin spreading across his face. "Oh, this isn't that bad. Nothing like we heard," he said, pausing. "We heard it was *your* eye that got poked out."

❖ ❖ ❖

"Try three miles an hour," Dick Hutchinson announced from his counter stool in the Yukon Trading Post's cafe.

"No way," I said from the table I shared with Kate. "We were moving closer to five or six, sometimes seven miles an hour."

"Dan saw you yesterday forty miles out. It took you more than fifteen hours to get here. You do the math," said Hutch, owner-operator of Circle City's telephone and fuel companies, whose floor I've often slept on covering past Quests. "No, I'm wrong," he said, grinning evilly, "your true speed is probably closer to *two* miles an hour."

"Only if you count rests and everything else."

"All part of traveling speed," observed Hutch.

He was really enjoying himself. I racked my sleep-deprived brain for a comeback, but the facts confounded me. *Two or three miles an hour, that's God-awful.*

Hutch and the owners of the Trading Post, Virginia and Dan, shared a good chuckle at my obvious distress. It wasn't mean-spirited. These folks were all long-time supporters of the Quest, one of the village's biggest events of the winter. Dan was the pilot who had flown out to find Gwen and me. Virginia had my breakfast bacon sizzling on her grill. If these three wanted to poke fun at the Quest's last-place driver, they were entitled.

Still, after the solitude of the Yukon, it sure felt as if everybody was on my case.

Freshwaters had gone hunting. Watching me fumble through the dog chores, Kate fought the urge to shove me aside and take care of them herself. The tension was mutual.

"I want you to try really hard not to come in last," she said as we returned from the cafe.

"Babe, I'm doing everything I can. But Gwen's got a *hellacious* dog team."

"Promise me you'll try."

"Like I haven't been, so far?"

Gwen was getting similar pep talks. Her entourage had expanded with the arrival of her mother, Erica, a polished European now residing in Chicago. Gwen found it amusing that her mother, brother, and boyfriend were acting so worried. *You kept going when other people scratched and look how far we've come. It's going to happen,* Gwen thought, *you're going to finish!*

The rules allowed for replacing gear in places like Circle, where all mushers have equal opportunity to purchase the items commercially.

Back at the Trading Post, I had asked Dan if anyone in town had dog harnesses for sale.

"You have a chewer, huh?"

"A couple of them."

He arranged for a woman to meet me at the campsite. She sold me three worn harnesses for fifteen dollars, an excellent deal. Hobbes and Danger were each sporting one as Khan steered his eight comrades down the road out of Circle.

Luther, Cinder, and Scrim remained in the team, pulling diligently. My decision to take them was blessed by Swank, the West Virginia vet. The wound below Luther's eye was clearly on the mend, he said, noting Gwen's ophthalmic ointment had worked wonders. His examination indicated the limps exhibited by Cinder and Scrim stemmed from soft-tissue shoulder injuries that might yet heal with frequent massages and Krestensen's juice. "I'd take them as far as Central and reevaluate," the vet had said, referring to the flat seventy-five-mile passage before we embarked upon Eagle Summit.

Before we parted, I reminded Swank of his question back in Carmacks.

"You wanted to know which race is tougher."

"And?"

"The Quest, hands down," I said, chuckling. "Iditarod has stiffer competition, but the Quest Trail is vastly harder, it's not just the mountains. It's the Yukon River itself. Iditarod only has about a hundred and thirty miles on the Yukon, the Quest stays on the river closer to four hundred miles. You're fighting that side-hill stuff all the way."

"Well, it's behind you now," he said.

"You got that right."

Gwen remained behind packing when I left Circle, early afternoon on February 21, on five and a half hours of rest. "Just point me at finish line," I shouted to Kate. "We've got the lead."

"I love you," she called, waving from a small berm. She looked so alone standing there.

The Quest Trail followed Circle's main street to the edge of town, took a hard left on another road, then peeled into the brush. That last turn was poorly marked. *Maybe Gwen will get lost.* I felt a little guilty for even thinking it, but it was our best chance to pull this out for Kate.

Less than an hour out of Circle, Panda and Hootch led Gwen's team powering past. "Get up, Khan," I said, spurring the old warrior into chasing her. He picked up the pace, but we continued to lose ground. Bushes crowding the trail soon swallowed Gwen's team. Khan settled into truck mode, registering 6.1 miles per hour on the GPS.

Gwen was making camp outside Carl Cochrane's cabin when I caught up. Cochrane, a lean, bright-eyed fellow with a steel-gray mustache, came out to say hello then set to work melting snow on his big stove. When we finished the dog chores, he invited us inside his finely crafted cabin. The interior was cramped, but richly decorated with realistic whittlings, hand-painted decoys and other pieces of handiwork that have proven big sellers with tourists, now that Cochrane, sixty-seven, no longer has sled dogs and traplines to tend.

Playing the name game over hardtack crackers and peanut butter, I learned that Cochrane, a life-long bachelor, was for a time pretty serious with the late Pat Oakes, a local historian on whose couch I often crashed during reporting forays to Central. "I guess Pat realized I was too far gone in my ways," the old trapper said, chuckling.

Pat left her mark all right. Years before settling in the area, Pat was a schoolteacher in the southeast Alaska town of Douglas. Kate's mom was in her class. *Talk about a small world.*

The stove hissed. Cochrane left to work in his shop, and Gwen and I napped.

The thermometer dangling outside Cochrane's cabin read sixteen below when we first arrived. I forgot to check it before we left that night. From the burning sensation on my cheeks, which remain sensitive from past frostbite, I figured it was twenty-below and probably dropping. We rolled out onto Birch Creek, where the brilliant, starry firmament offered further indication of a plunge. *You're supposed to get cold, dammit. This is the Quest!*

Past midnight, the northern lights erupted. No vague green

shimmers for us. Our passage was heralded by bursting, pulsing, red and yellow flares, lighting up the cosmos with random artistry. Suggestive shapes pulled at my thoughts: A turtle flowed into an eagle, which became an Indian Head nickel. *Been a while since I saw one of those. Whatever happened to my coin collection?*

Rounding a bend I came upon Gwen. She'd parked to observe the show. Race officials assumed the blonde was an airhead, an image that her packing routine did nothing to refute. They would have been astonished by Gwen's studies in physics and her past work at Poker Flats, the University of Alaska's rocket range.

Watching the lights ablaze above Birch Creek, Gwen reflected on a past project using a Lidar Laser to study the aurora's effects on the planet's sodium layer. Where I saw morphing turtles, Gwen noted the effect of solar wind pushing tonight's aurora farther into the atmosphere than usual, causing the red-hued reaction with oxygen atoms.

It wasn't the brightest display she'd seen—obviously the particle energy wasn't real high—but Gwen read intricate forces at work in the shifting dark patches, which only hinted at the turbulence molding tonight's aurora. *The solar wind is really slamming into the ionosphere. Causing it to change and adjust.*

"So what do you think of the lights tonight?" Gwen said as I joined her. "Pretty neat, huh?"

We split a mug of warm Gatorade and moved on, each of us gladdened by the presence of a witness, though we drew such different meanings from the cosmic bonfire.

The aurora was ebbing when I nearly lost the sled on a curve. "Getting a little stiff there," I muttered, fanning my arms one at a time to get some blood pumping. My left foot, the one in the boot I didn't replace, was getting really cold. So were my hands. *Been a while since you drank or ate anything. Let's not get stupid here.*

Hypothermia creeps up on a guy. Feeling bone cold is an early-warning sign. Ignore that and pretty soon a mental fog seeps in, blinding you to what's happening until the chills hit. By then, you're in serious need of assistance. *It's cold enough to get in trouble tonight.*

Gwen's headlamp floated away as I hit the brakes. Tucking my thermos under one arm, I walked up front, petting dogs all the way. Then I squatted on the creek ahead of Khan, sipping an unpleasantly cool cup of Gatorade.

We had to be pushing thirty below tonight. Returning to the sled, I went over my options. I could fire up the cooker and melt snow, fixing myself another hot meal and steaming hot juice for the thermos. *That'll eat up an hour! It's not like you're dying.*

I settled for changing my socks and gloves, popping new chemical warmers in both my boots and mitts. As a final piece of armor, I slipped Freshwaters' loose kuspuk over top of the Fulda parka. I was wrapped tight as a mummy, but the warmth was delicious.

"On your feet," I called. The crew shook themselves and obeyed. Stopping in this cold hole hadn't been their idea.

Gwen was surprised when I failed to catch up during her next snack stop. Afterward, she kept glancing backward for my light, but her dogs were flying, acting more excited, in fact, than their master had seen in a long, long time. An odd rustling sound penetrated Gwen's fur hat. She scanned the creek but didn't see anything. "Oh, you're just scaring yourself. Mellow out."

There it was again.

She studied the creek behind her team. Nothing. Then a movement up on the bank drew Gwen's attention and she saw them: Two wolves were pacing the team.

"Oh, shit!" cried Gwen, feeling extremely alone.

Abandoning any thoughts of waiting, Gwen Holdman called up her dogs. Though faintly aware of the cold, she paid no mind to it. She was preoccupied by the image of wolves swooping down upon her poor doggies. Gwen drove hard all the way up Birch Creek. She kept those dogs loping until her team was free of the trees, free of the brush, clear out in the center of vast Medicine Lake, where nothing could take her by surprise.

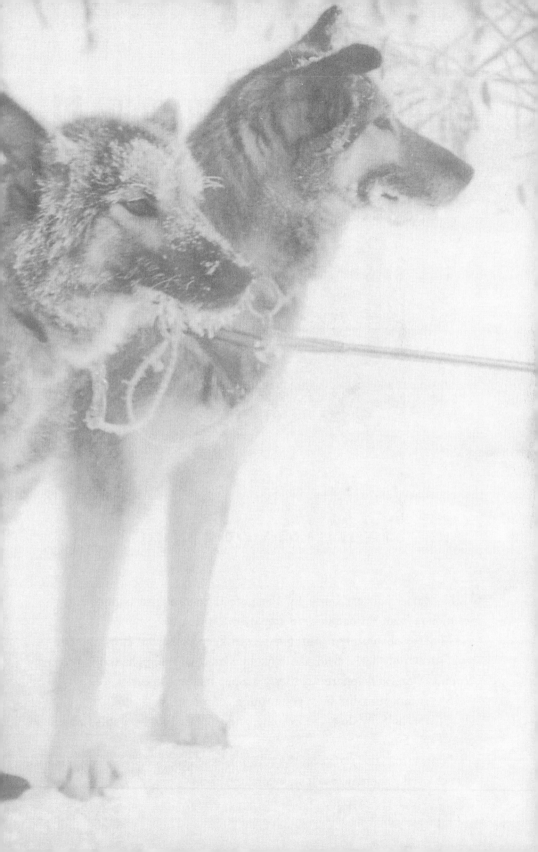

IN THE MOUNTAIN'S SHADOW 13

DANGER AND SCRIMSHAW IN HARNESS

Old Marie cornered me by the cafe. She and the other Quest volunteers from Fairbanks were preparing to pull out.

"There's absolutely nothing that will keep you from finishing the race," declared Marie, who had stayed up most of the night waiting for Gwen and me, and apparently thought a pep talk was in order.

She meant well, but her presumption set me off.

"Marie, half my dogs are limping, and the last I knew, I still had to cross Eagle Summit."

"Conditions are *perfect* on the summit," she snapped. "The mushers who crossed yesterday said it was calm and clear."

Marie was proclaiming some other theory about all dog teams possessing roughly the same speed when I left to find Kate's room in the lodge behind Crabb's Corner Cafe. Staggering toward that oasis, I inwardly fumed at the volunteer's smug certainties. Nearly two hundred miles separated us from the Quest finish line in Fairbanks. Nothing could be taken for granted. Nothing.

Kate, too, had been up all night waiting, tortured by the cafe's cigarette smoke, which she found more bothersome than usual in her pregnant state, and a certain loudmouth seated at the bar. He kept spouting off about the *real reason* Brian and Gwen were traveling so slow. Kate knew it wasn't true, but it hurt her to hear me accused of such awful things.

When she couldn't take it anymore, Kate drove out to a spot overlooking the trail near Circle Hot Springs Resort, about eight miles from Central. She got out of the truck and was thrilled to hear a dog team coming through the woods. It was Gwen. Her dogs dashed off the trail toward Kate, missing the turn before halting in a tangle.

"Brian should be right behind me," Gwen said, cheerfully realigning her team.

The encounter raised my wife's hopes, but an hour later she was still waiting.

Leaving Birch Creek, the trail wound through heavy thickets, most of it taller than my six-foot, two-inch frame. Odd arcs of light sporadically flashed across the sky ahead. *Gwen's looking for me.*

Out on Medicine Lake, I realized the sweeping light more likely was an aviation beacon.

We had to be getting close to the resort erected on the site of a former tent camp, where miners passed the winter soaking in steamy pools. In the 1930s the clientele changed when an entrepreneur erected a majestic three-story hotel overlooking the springs.

The old building retains the bearing of an aging grande dame. The steaming Olympic-sized outdoor pool also remains a big draw, particularly in the dead of winter when bathers have fun making ice sculptures in each other's hair.

Rory was conceived in one of the resort's cabins. I was daydreaming about that weekend, and another night when Kate and I found ourselves alone in that outdoor pool, when Khan abruptly slowed, acting unusually hesitant. "Go ahead! Go ahead, Khan!" I yelled angrily.

Too late, I saw that what I took as trail markers were reflections from glass globes poking through a snow-covered airstrip. Khan marched down the taxi strip into a parking area, where the trail abruptly ended, and he wrapped the team around a small plane. "Christ," I said, stomping in the hook, "this night's never going to end."

On the outskirts of Central, some ten miles ahead, Gwen was having trouble deciphering the Quest Trail from intersecting snowmachine routes. She mushed into an icy parking lot. Her brake had nothing to bite and the team barreled straight through the open door of Central's power plant building. "Oh no," Gwen gasped as her dogs piled inside the industrial facility. "How am I ever going to get them out of here?"

Inside our truck, Kate could hardly keep her eyes open. Worried that she might fall asleep and miss me completely, she put the truck in gear and slowly motored back to the cafe.

Jim Crabb met me under the Quest banner outside his cafe. "What took you so long?" he shouted, grinning as he handed me the check-in sheet. Kate felt lost in the crowd pouring out of the cafe.

She wanted to hug the dogs, her original babies. That wasn't permitted, of course. She wasn't allowed to do anything but watch as I bedded them down. It seemed to Kate that I was doing a poor job of it. She pointed out that several dogs still had booties on. "And I think Cyclone needs more straw," she said.

"I've told you before," I snapped, "I wait until they've settled down— then I spread the rest of the bale. Otherwise they won't use it."

Kate fled to her room, where the tears just wouldn't stop.

❖   ❖   ❖

A back rub restored Kate's spirits. Afterward, I collapsed in her arms—one distinct advantage of wagging the Quest's tail so far removed from probing race officials. I might have slept a week had she not shaken me from my dreams ninety minutes later. That too was technically illegal, but who was keeping track?

Feeling restored, we ducked into the cafe for a feast topped off by my free musher's steak. I was packing, about 2:00 P.M. on February 22, when Crabb came to see how I was doing. "So tell me about the trail over the summit," I said.

"Just follow the tripods," the checker said. "There's only one trail this year. No way you can miss it."

"It's pretty narrow on top, isn't it? I've always heard it's easy to come down on the wrong side."

Crabb snorted. "It's narrow all right. But there's only one trail this year. Just stay on it."

Gwen was still packing when I pulled the hook.

Khan lowered his head and threw himself forward with a gruff bark. The other members of the team shuffled along behind. "And once again they charged ahead with blinding speed," I shouted, drawing a laugh from Kate and the other spectators.

The trail threaded through the trees of Central Park, a little RV park across from Crabb's Corner, then continued along the Steese Highway, the sole road connecting the Circle mining district with other parts of the Interior.

Hard-packed snow covered the two-lane rural highway, providing a decent sledding surface. But confusion eroded Khan's work ethic. He veered from side to side searching for the true path. Our speed, such as it was, further degenerated as each dog had to pee, shit, or sniff prior deposits of the same.

Forward progress in a long-distance race, however ugly, is an accomplishment to be cherished. Markers lined the berm on the left side of the road. Our speed was pitiful, but we were on course.

The trail finally left the road and Khan bent to business. Alas, the shoulder-high brush offered no protection from the sun. The dogs' enthusiasm melted under the warm lick. I sought to cheer them up with a quick stop for whitefish. Khan polished off his snack, grabbed a few bites of snow, then resumed his place at the front of the gang line, whining to go. I felt pretty good about that—until we took off again and the GPS registered 5.4 miles per hour.

An hour after leaving Central, I heard Gwen's freight train coming.

"Be my guest," I shouted, bowing from the runners. This section of the trail was narrow. Hootch balked. Planting the hook, I pulled Gwen's leader past my sled, breaking a wider path through the soft snow. I stood protectively in the middle of the team, ready to intervene if a tangle were to develop. But her dogs, by now well acquainted with mine, exchanged a few friendly sniffs and moved on.

I ran back to the sled, hopeful of shaking off the lethargy with a Hell's Bells chase. Khan barked, lunged, and the charge was on.

"Get up, get up," I called, mixing the verbal cues with kisses and kicking behind the sled. The only trick held back was my "let's go home" command; I had to save something for Eagle Summit.

Brush lining the trail thickened. I lost sight of Gwen's dogs, her sled, and, last of all, the back of her green parka floating through the thickets. Once again, Khan and his eight mates on the gang line gradually fell off the pace. Before long, we were moving slightly faster than I generally walk.

The brush ceased as we passed between broad, white mounds, gleaming in the midday sun. It was another gold mining camp. The machinery, glimpsed through thick cloaks of snow, appeared of fairly recent vintage. Winding through what I presumed was piles of either tailings or rock slated for processing, I was struck by the contrast between the Quest's image as a solitary wilderness trek and these repeated excursions through industrial sites.

Covering public meetings, I've heard people attack small mining operations such as this as desecrations of the land. Folks holding that perspective would undoubtedly take offense at the rusting machinery and rotting shacks scattered along the Fortymile, the swath cut through the forests by Scroggy Creek and other old mining roads, and those vast ruins outside Dawson City.

I honor these few scattered footprints, most of which I imagine were left by regular Joes seeking fortune.

My father was forty-eight, at the height of his profession as a labor attorney, when he suffered a stroke that left him paralyzed on one side, incapable of speech, and yet acutely aware of his surroundings. Sitting up with him one night, ten weeks later, my father wanted to tell me something. We played the guessing game that had become his sole means of communication. That night it made him angry, frustrated and, eventually, quite sad, because I just didn't get it. He died before dawn.

Six years later, I boxed up the contents of my efficiency apartment on the Lower East Side to fill a reporter's job at the *Frontiersman* in Alaska. Since then I've gazed out across the world from Denali's lofty base camp, chased oil spills and wildfires, clutched the stick—and a puke bag—executing a roll in a F-16, and collected tales from Alaska Native elders.

Few reporters have mined a richer vein. In the process, I struck El Dorado meeting Kate.

I'm hoping to stretch out our days together, but I never forget that it's all a race. And I'll never blame anyone for grasping opportunities to leave a personal mark on this indifferent world.

In the low-hanging afternoon sun, my dogs underwent what I call the multiplier effect—each acquiring a high-stepping shadow. I pulled out Kate's camera and snapped off a few frames, documenting the odd twists that placed this former urban dweller driving a dog team on the Yukon Quest Trail. *Is life stranger than fiction or what?*

Taller mounds loomed on the horizon. Those barren peaks marked the approaching showdown.

Cinder squatted to shit, which caused the team to bunch up. "Cinder," I shouted, "cut that OUT!" The other dogs dragged him forward, skipping on his heels as he unloaded tiny chunks of poop. Afterward he glanced over his shoulder at me, flashing what I took to be a peeved expression. He had a point: It was late in the game to be demanding change in a behavior pattern I'd tolerated the entire season. *It's your nerves*, I realized. *The summit's getting to you.*

Cinder was still favoring his right leg paw on and off. His sagging tug line was getting harder to ignore. *That's my error. Should have cut him loose in Central.*

Scrim's performance was more encouraging. Her limp was barely detectable. Ears perked attentively, tug line taught, *she* was still into it, pulling her weight. *Just get me over that mountain, girl. Get me over that mountain and it's home sweet home for you both.*

The mining camp gave way to a frozen marsh. Khan handled the ice without flinching. Luther, as I'd come to expect, shied from each glassy contact, but didn't fight the pressure of the gang line. For my part, I alternated between tapping the brakes for control on the straight sections, then leaning sideways as I rode out the slippery turns.

The ice was firm, but showed the unevenness characteristic of repeated flooding. I dodged the occasional white patches I took to be fragile panes. Occasionally, the surface was wet and I tensed, half expecting to break through.

The trail veered left crossing one of the wider overflow sections. The sled careened across the ice to the right, directly toward an open hole.

My feet remained on the runners as the sled splashed down, sinking from the rear. "Go ahead! Go ahead," I shouted and the dogs popped the sled out. *Thank God for bunny boots.* Though my bottom laces were soaked, not a drop penetrated the military boots' thick rubber lining.

Ten miles out of Central, the trail turned toward the highway. Kate stood at the corner, beaming. Gwen's team was parked up near the road crossing, flanked by well-wishers.

"She's already been here about thirty minutes," Kate said. "She wants you to lead over the summit."

We had, perhaps, another ten miles to the summit. I'd heard there was a cabin located just below the tree line. "I'm planning on giving the dogs a real break there," I told Gwen. "I want to change gear, you know, get ready for the summit.

"Why don't you meet me there?" I suggested. "We're just crawling today. No reason for you to putter along behind us."

We descended into a heavily mined valley. Hundreds of Fulda booties littered the last dip before the trail began climbed along an unplowed road. I wasn't the only one dreading the upcoming passage.

❖ ❖ ❖

When the group's neat freak, Thomas Tetz, stripped off booties to enhance traction and didn't bother to pack them out, Brenda and the rest immediately followed suit. The rookies were too preoccupied with the mountain to observe customary niceties.

Bill and Walter, who had paired up in Central, were roughly mid-way up the first hump when Brenda saw them in the distance. It appeared that Bill was passing Walter's team on the bare slope. That looked ominous.

Walter had trained his leaders to pull on the run. That was their style even moving up an incline. Climbing Eagle Summit required a slower, harder-pulling gait. Hera and Anise didn't like it one bit. The pair quit, stalling Walter's team in a most inhospitable spot.

"How about if I try?" Bill said.

He got his dogs around Walter's, a difficult maneuver, and both teams continued toward the saddle leading to the final summit wall. The second pitch was tougher. "Can you push my sled?" Bill shouted, rushing forward to take his leaders in hand.

Walter found the sled so heavy it was all he could do to hold it in place. "Bill," he cried, "you're missing it here. What have you got in this thing?"

Packing a generous load of emergency food, a well-advised precaution for most trail sections, was potentially disastrous on the Quest's steepest mountain passage. "I can't believe your dogs made it this far," cried Walter, whose own sled was stripped of everything but snacks and mandatory gear.

Before he and Walter made it into the pass, Bill had to stop and hand carry most of his freight up the last wall. Bill was leading on the descent when Lemon balked, perhaps a third of the way down the mountain. Walter, grateful for Bill's heroics on the ascent, held his own team back, giving the other musher room to work out the problem.

Brenda climbed the mountain sandwiched between Keith and Rusty. Her own progress was hampered by Sky's attempts to mount Camaro every time the teams ahead paused. Yelling kept the randy male in line, but the war of wills threatened to get out of hand.

Cresting the mountain, Brenda was taken by the spectacle of the setting sun engulfing the dog team directly ahead. *I wish I had my camera,* she thought, following Keith's fiery path across the summit.

Tetz was still leading as the convoy teams commenced their back-to-back descent.

Handlers and friends were watching from the distant highway as the Quest teams cascaded down the brilliantly lit summit. It was a glorious moment for those present, one repaying all the effort, all the sacrifices made to put those dog teams and valiant drivers on the trail. Walter's wife, Keith's girlfriend, and several others linked arms and danced. "We want champagne! We want champagne!" they sang, kicking up their boots like chorus girls.

Observing the flood, Walter fled past Bill, whose dogs remained blocking the trail.

Tetz saw the obstruction and did his best to slow down. Keith nearly collided with him before veering off to one side. Brenda, whose sled was all but empty, bounced hard on the slope tussocks and flipped. She was dragging behind her sled when Rusty, who had been troubled by his own poorly angled brake the entire race, lost control of his team, which was then last in line.

Helpless to prevent it, Rusty rode that sled bouncing right over one of Brenda's leaders.

The teen, still dragging, heard Camaro's sickening yelp. *Oh no!*

The teams separated, carving new parallel tracks down the mountain's white skin.

In the shadows cloaking the valley floor, Walter stopped to dig out his headlamp. Keith loped past without formally requesting the trail. That annoyed Walter, but he was used to the other musher's rudeness in that regard from repeated encounters during training. *Keith gets off on passing.*

Tetz was next. Walter waved him on, then dashed forward to clear a tangle.

Rusty attempted to follow suit. Walter, fed up with the ill treatment from these people, blocked his path, shouting: "You guys are really weird."

"What are you talking about?" Rusty said.

"What are *you* doing?" Walter countered.

"I'm passing you," Rusty declared.

Being run over didn't seem to affect Camaro, but Brenda knew all sorts of sprains, or worse, might yet reveal themselves in her best lead dog. She passed Bill in time to catch the argument at the bottom of the mountain.

"I'm not even stopped," she heard Walter tell Rusty.

The guy was standing by his leaders and claimed his team wasn't stopped. It cracked Brenda up. Sky seized the chance to jump Camaro. "Wait till we get to 101," Brenda told the male as she broke up the mating attempt. "Then you can have her."

Bill caught up during the traffic jam.

"I'm really sorry, Brenda. I'm really sorry."

Brenda's smile died. She heard Bill all right, but didn't grant him so much as a word. *If Camaro is injured, it's Bill's fault*, she decided, too angry to discuss it.

Walter sent his team forward, cutting Rusty off.

The move outraged the other musher; Walter's antics threatened to entangle both teams. "I want you to stop!" Rusty shouted from behind. "I want to talk to you right now!"

Walter did nothing of the sort. Who was Hagan to order him around? *What does he want? To shake my hand? Maybe kiss me?* Ignoring Rusty's demands, he focused on catching Keith and Tetz. The Quest had a dog drop at Mile 101 Steese Highway. Upon reaching the camp, Rusty pulled up alongside Walter's team, set his hook, then stepped in front of the other musher.

"I'm really really mad at you."

"Get your headlamp out of my face," Walter shot back.

It occurred to Rusty that he could punch Walter right now and the musher would never even see it coming. He pictured himself flattening that nose.

"Why didn't you stop out there?" he demanded

Walter feigned disinterest.

Rusty couldn't believe the other driver's flip attitude. The son-of-a-bitch didn't appreciate his anger. He began stripping off his parka.

"What are you doing?"

"I'm really pissed off at you. You're a real jerk," said Rusty Hagan, who meant to have it out.

A veterinarian intervened. "I believe I better take a look at a few dogs here," he said.

Turning away, Rusty noticed Nancy Palkovitch standing nearby and felt a twinge of guilt. *It isn't right to dress a man down like that, not in front of his wife.*

The confrontation came as a complete shock to the women. Walter's wife and Keith's girlfriend, dance partners only minutes ago, found themselves sobbing.

Brenda missed the fireworks; she had her own show to watch. Her team was hardly parked before Sky again leaped upon Camaro. *Wow,* the musher thought, *he knows what I said to him.*

The teen was tending other chores when a well-meaning spectator rushed over.

"You have some dogs tangled up."

Brenda Mackey laughed harder than she had in days.

An hour had passed since I left the highway. Gazing up at the summit, I could make out the notch cradling the old Winter Trail to Fairbanks. I didn't see any clouds or blurs that might indicate wind sweeping the pass. That was about all that looked good about the towering, barren slope.

I kept expecting to find Gwen waiting beyond each turn. The few cabins I did see were tightly boarded up, or in ruins. None showed tracks of visits from previous Quest teams.

Then the last trees parted to reveal Gwen's team parked just beyond a patch of shrubs about halfway up the slope. *Is the cabin way up there?* I couldn't tell in the flat afternoon light, but what else would Gwen be doing up there?

"Go ahead," I urged Khan. He continued up the mountain for several hundred yards then paused, confused by the hard, wavy drifts. "Damn," I muttered, suddenly grasping that there wasn't any cabin in those scrubby bushes ahead. Somehow we had missed it, and I had just driven my tired dogs past the last vestige of shelter, blundering into the final assault on Eagle Summit.

This is not good. We're not ready for this! I considered turning around to regroup. But I could see Gwen, just past the second tripod, waving to us. She sure picked a god-awful place to stop. Was she sticking to the plan and waiting for me? Or had her dogs quit on her? I felt obliged to press ahead.

"All right," I cried. "All right, Khan. Go ahead!"

He was willing, but couldn't read the wind-raked trail. The team meandered left, then right, growing more disorderly with each new arc.

I stopped and moved up Hobbes to share the lead duty. We needed my burly girl's gifted nose for trails.

With Hobbes pointing the way, we quickly gained several dozen yards, then faltered.

"Let's go home," I shouted, cashing in my best chip. Hearing the magic words, Hobbes, Feets, and several others snapped their tug lines taught. But the power of my ruse was weakening. "Let's go home. Let's go home," I called out cheerfully. Each repetition inspired less of a response.

Other teams had taken a half-dozen alternative paths up this hill. Hobbes, like Khan, began drifting from side to side, searching for the trail offering the best footing. Several times I had to get off the sled and drag my leaders back toward the tripods.

The drifts were deeper back on American, but the route across that summit was essentially flat. Here the dogs were punching through snow six to eight inches deep on a serious hill. We didn't budge unless I pushed the sled. Before long, I staggered to a halt, wheezing.

Resting my head on the handlebar I heard my heart beating like a base drum. And I felt sweat raining from my armpits under the heavy parka. "This should NOT BE HAPPENING," I shouted. "YOU ARE AN IDIOT!"

I sensed mutiny building as we gained the first tripod. Either I initiated a break here, or that decision might be taken away. I tied off the leaders on the tripod's closest leg and, shucking my steaming parka, rummaged through the sled for a bag of white fish. I avoided looking up the hill at Gwen. *The girl's to blame. She can goddamn wait.*

Ears perked and heads rose at the sound of the plastic bag. That was encouraging. I had cheated the team's rest at Central, then pushed them four hours through the heat of the day. Yet their fatigue appeared mainly spiritual.

While the dogs wolfed down their savory tidbits, I slipped on Freshwaters' kuspuk, tightening the cuffs against the light gusts licking this slope. The sun had slipped behind the mountain. It hadn't started to cool off, but I knew that could change quickly. These mild conditions were a gift to be seized.

We couldn't stay long. The snow hook, planted backward and uphill, was tenuously supporting the sled's weight. My current wheel dogs, Danger and Cyclone, had scratched out holes in the hillside, where they curled like they planned to stay a while. Sled dogs aren't stupid: all of them would be digging in soon. This team was likely to quit on me unless we made better progress.

I disconnected my tie-down rope from the gang line and knotted it around my waist. Then I pried loose the snow hook. Cyclone slipped backward under pressure from the sled before struggling to his feet. Danger, showing off his strength, adopted a rigid stance, resisting the slippage. *So far, so good.* I climbed to the tripod and freed Khan from it, tying the neckline he shared with Hobbesey to the rope on my waist.

I glanced up to see if Gwen had observed my tactic, which she, or any other musher, could only read as a sign of desperation. But her team had vanished into the saddle up slope. "Good for you, girl," I whispered.

Neither Gwen, nor I, knew it, but a handful of folks were attempting to track our assault on the mountain. Our handlers had continued up the Steese Highway seeking the best vantage for watching our teams top the summit. Kate, driving the first vehicle, was nearing the pass when she encountered sizable drifts rippling across the roadway.

"I *hate* this truck," my wife cried. "Two-wheel drive should be illegal in Alaska. I just know we're going to get stuck."

She somehow found the invisible pavement and burst through the low white wall, closely trailed by Gwen's motor escort. The trucks continued to the survival shelter located along Eagle Summit's inhospitable crest. A car was parked on the side of the road. Not far away a man in a red Fulda parka was hiking off across the ridge. He was toting a big camera tripod.

"Looks like he knows where he's headed," observed Ken, Gwen's boyfriend, resolving to follow that photographer. He ran up to Kate's truck and asked if she wanted to join in.

Kate was tempted. Covering previous Quests, she'd seen press photographers strike out on the same route. But the snow looked deep and she recalled hearing the hike was difficult. "I better not," she said, thinking about the baby.

Daylight was ebbing. The view to the southeast, where Gwen and I would be crossing, was obscured in flat white haze. Kate thought she might have to backtrack a mile or two to find a better spot. She floated the idea to Gwen's mom.

"I'm not driving through that again," blurted Erica, whose Midwestern sensibilities remained shaken by the last passage.

The issue was settled by the arrival of summit-savvy Jim Crabb in his powerful four-wheel-drive Suburban. "No reason to go back unless you want to get stuck," he told Kate, grinning. "It's the wrong way. The place for watching mushers is Mile 105. C'mon, I'll show you."

Khan looked skeptical. What was I doing in his position at the head of the team?

"Ready," I called, striving to project confidence I didn't feel. The dogs straightened and, on cue, threw themselves at the hill, apparently pleased to see the boss finally pulling his weight.

Hobbes enjoyed the new game and headed after me. Half-stumbling, half-crawling up the powdery hillside, I somehow managed to keep the rope in front of her nose, signaling the desired path. She and the team marched right up.

I entered the saddle at dusk and beheld the mountain's real test. On the far side of this little basin, the Quest Trail rose another two hundred yards or more on a tremendously steep angle leading to the 3,600-foot elevation pass. Gwen was nowhere in sight. *She's home free*, I realized, envious.

Crabb, a veteran Quest summit spectator, brought a pair of powerful binoculars. Training them on the key ridge, he frowned.

Recent snowmachiners, media mostly, had cut dozens of new tracks in and around his carefully marked trail. The effect this was having on dog teams was obvious from the numerous paths taken down the mountain on less than ideal, if not dangerous, routes. Crabb could only assume the confusion was also repeated on the summit's backside, where straying from his packed trail during the climb could land the best of dog teams in serious trouble. "Those snowmachiners shouldn't have done that," he said gravely.

Kate borrowed the binoculars and had the summit under direct surveillance when the first headlamp appeared. It was supposed to be mine, because Gwen had said she wanted our team to lead over the summit. Strain as she might Kate couldn't make out any details about the dogs or the musher. Even the color of the sled bag was lost in the murky failing light. The headlamp itself was quite bright. She was amazed how fast it bobbed down the mountain. "Oh, my God," said Kate, witnessing what had to be a plummeting ride.

Doubts about the identity of the musher grew as Kate and Erica waited and waited for a second headlamp. Gwen, driving what all believed was the faster team, should have been right on my heels. That headlamp was another clue. Gwen used powerful lithium batteries, while I relied on cheap alkalines.

Minutes stretched to the better part of an hour. Kate's certainty grew that Gwen was wearing the bright headlamp floating across the valley floor. Having covered the Quest the year that Cowboy Smith's dogs crashed on the hidden side of yonder abyss, she knew a lot could go wrong. *Oh Babe*, she thought, praying for another light, *please, please make it over.*

Exertion was making my eyes water, rendering my damn contacts all but useless. I could make out a half-dozen different trails entering the barren bowl, those were interlaced with dozens more snowmachine tracks. The whole area was blanketed in shadowy blue light, making it tough to ferret out the few tripods and markers left after the earlier onslaughts of traffic. I switched on my headlamp, but the beam failed to light even the lone marker standing a few feet in front of Khan. A layer of wind-blown snow or frost covered the stick, blocking the marker's reflective tape.

Which way do we go?

Khan and Hobbes seemed anxious to begin. I let them decide. The pair took aim at a heavily traveled path feeding into the center of the basin. Before long we were locked in the actual climb.

"Go ahead. Go ahead," I rasped, gulping breaths and pushing the sled from below. Way, way above us in the faltering light, I saw a tripod silhouetted against the navy blue sky. The pitch leading to it was incredible to behold. *Imagine this thing in bad weather.* The thought made me shiver; I'd heard about Lee.

SUMMIT PLUMMET

14

HOBBES

Bruce Lee appeared invincible four days earlier in Central, where he beat Nadeau to town with eighty minutes to spare. More telling, the rookie stayed behind when the veteran struck out for Eagle Summit at 11:30 A.M. on February 18, after seven hours' rest.

Lee read the Ghost's restraint as a concession: *It looks like Nadeau's gracefully accepting second.* He applauded his rival's good judgment. *He's racing in unknown territory. Starting to drop a few dogs. All of the sudden he's realizing he's got to rest. That's being very realistic. He's protecting position.*

Conditions were calm and mild as Lee began the climb late that afternoon. The team was past the tree line, well into the first slope, when the musher noticed one of his leaders glancing down the mountain. *I ought to get whoever did that out of lead—right now.*

But the dogs were moving steadily. Stopping carried its own risk. Near the first tripod, both leaders veered off on a traversing path. Lee stopped and straightened the team out. Afterward, the front pair took a few steps and paused, facing slightly downhill. That decided it. Lee quickly changed leaders.

"OK, let's go," he called.

Nobody moved.

"I can't believe this," Lee muttered. Concealing his concern, he strolled the gang line, petting his dogs. When he again ordered them forward, the team took two, maybe three steps, then halted.

Lee tried bearing down, shouting "All right" in a stern voice. When that didn't work, he again changed leaders. It didn't help.

"Well," Lee told himself, "I'll just drag them up."

Shedding his heavy coat and gloves, Lee picked up his snow hook, figuring he could use the line to drag the sled upward, easing the team's load. The team advanced several steps. Encouraged, Lee tried it again, with the same results. He developed a system: dragging his sled about eight feet, setting the hook backwards to hold it in place, then guiding his leaders forward until the slack was taken up.

I'm going to get soaking wet here, the musher realized after a time.

Stripping to his undershirt and pants, Lee considered giving the dogs a breather where they stood. Quest history argued against it. *A lot of teams have tried resting here and never got going again.*

He recalled passing Jerry Riley, the 1976 Iditarod champion, not far from where his own team was now stalled. Riley, who had finished the Quest in second place only the year before, had been leading the race when his team crashed on the mountain and the musher called it quits.

You not only may not win *this race,* Lee realized. *YOU MAY NOT FINISH.*

He squatted by his dogs, petting them as he assessed the situation. *This is the point you've got to take everything you've learned in twenty years of dogs, and figure out what it takes to get them over. What do they need? What can I do?*

He'd heard that climbers on the upper reaches of Denali pause to catch a breath between each step. The sled-pulling routine struck him as similar. "I'm not going to sit here and lose this race," Lee vowed. "If it's eight feet at a time, I'll take it eight feet at a time."

He resumed hauling his sled by hand. After a while, Lee took the heaviest items out of his sled, two armloads' worth, and piled it all some sixteen feet ahead. The musher walked back to young Clovis, who was again in lead by default, prepared to coax him. Before he knew it, the dog was hauling his teammates straight for the pile.

It gives him a target!

Lee moved the pile higher up the slope. The result was the same. The musher didn't even have to pull his sled at all. He merely gave the word and walked alongside Clovis, who made a beeline to the next cache.

Cresting the first of the summit's two pitches, Lee threw everything inside his sled bag and mushed into the bowl, which was cloaked in thick fog. The wind kicked up as Lee's team neared the base of the final wall. Clouds parted revealing markers leading straight up.

Lee saw his front four dogs staring at those markers. *They know where we're headed.* He saw their heads turn back down the mountain. Again, he read their minds: *No way are we going up there!*

Lee stopped the team before his spooked leaders did any damage. He had ten strong dogs—more than enough to cruise over this summit. The barrier here was psychological. Clovis, Canvas, and his other young leaders had never faced a challenge of this magnitude. *This is where I could use Miles.* His old leader would have stormed over the ridge or died trying. Once more, Lee found himself cursing that hole in the ice approaching McCabe Creek, the bad-luck mishap that had knocked Miles out of the game.

"OK," Lee whispered, regaining control. "We'll do this one the same way."

The musher unloaded his sled and, with several trips, carried the gear about a third of the way up the slope. Returning to the sled, he ordered Clovis and Canvas forward. The leaders went right up the mountain, continuing on past Lee's pile. Pushing his sled from below,

Lee's lungs burned. He wanted to hurl. *They're NOT going to stop because of me.*

Nearing the top of the rise, the musher cried: "OK!" The team dashed up onto the summit's exposed crest.

Fierce winds buffeted dogs and man. Lee's face stung from bombardment with course chunks of ice and sand. He was soaking wet and stripped to his inner clothes—his parka and mitts both heaped with the gear stashed near the bottom of the last slope. Flipping the sled on its side, Lee stomped his snow hook into the hard pack, praying the combination might anchor his scared puppies. Soaking wet and gasping, he staggered back down the slope.

By the time he reached the pile, Lee's nose felt solid; both nostrils were plugged with ice. *My face is freezing!* Scooping up gear in his stiffening hands, he flung himself at the climb.

Regaining the summit, Bruce Lee felt the wind sucking his life away. The threat was no abstraction. He'd been with Jeff King the night his neighbor from Denali Park froze a hand on Rosebud, forcing him to scratch from the 1988 Quest.

Lee knew that his own nose was probably frozen, along with parts of his ears and who knows what other body parts. *You've got to do something right, like right now.*

He was tempted to flee; a wild charge would put him at the bottom of the valley in a matter of minutes. But his hands were barely functional now. *If you wait, you may not even be able to get your mittens on.*

Deal with it now, Lee told himself. *Right now, in these few minutes, even if everything gets soaking wet. At least you'll be warm enough to get out of here.*

Ignoring the cruel wind, Bruce Lee methodically redressed himself. It was an act of faith in the power of reason, because the frosty gear initially chilled him further.

The descent was rough. Then Clovis and Canvas kept losing the trail down in the valley. The musher repeatedly scouted the Quest markers on foot, then dragged his team back to them across ice and gravel. The frontrunner was spent and hugely relieved when he finally mushed into the Quest's Mile 101 Steese camp.

Accommodations were sparse at the closed gas station, which now functioned as a storage yard for trucks and industrial equipment. Quest volunteers had opened the bunkhouse cabin for mushers, and the handful of officials, handlers, reporters, and others motivated to make the four-hour drive from Fairbanks. Lee made short work of his dog chores and headed inside, where he hung his wet gear over the stove and began gulping water.

The latest timesheet showed Nadeau out of Central two hours behind him. *At least I knew where I was going,* Lee thought, reflecting on his summit ordeal. He did some quick calculations, then turned to an official. "If Andre isn't here in four or five hours," he said, "I'd think about taking a look to see if he's OK."

With that, the battered race leader sought the bunkroom.

Wanting to keep it handy, I left the guide rope dangling from my waist. Nearing the last wall I saw it was futile. Given the sheer angle, I was needed pushing the sled from below. Kahn and Hobbes had to handle this. "Go ahead. Go ahead," I cried, offering the command like a prayer.

Though this climb was far steeper than the last, nobody showed even a hint of quitting. Though the trail was soft, the snow cover was deep enough to provide Khan and Hobbes with a defined groove, which made all the difference.

We climbed and climbed, attaining what I reckoned to be the quarter mark, then the halfway point. Ever onward and upward.

I noticed a bright red shape ahead on the right. A Fulda parka. The coat was dangling from what I took to be a marker, roughly two-thirds of the way up the mountain. The flare of color on the blue-white landscape struck me as funny.

For all I knew, some poor bastard was missing that coat right now. Or, and this was even better: Had somebody tackled the climb wearing it, sweated up a storm, and simply cast the parka off rather than risk stopping on this infernal hill. *I can see that happening. Oh yeah.*

The parka came alive, revealing a bearded man clutching what appeared to be a large-format camera. The discovery excited Khan and

Hobbes, who suddenly dashed off on a soft diagonal path toward the photographer.

"No. No. No!"

Hesitant to offend me, Hobbes and Khan froze. The two leaders looked up at the summit ridge, still distant. Then they looked down.

Once, in the process of colliding with a station wagon while riding a motorcycle, I reached out in what felt like slow motion and grabbed the lip of a half-open side window, snatching myself clear as the bike crumpled under me. Seconds stretched as I stared through the window at a screaming young passenger. "He's hanging on!" the kid cried. "He's hanging on!"

The wagon traveled at least another block before the driver finally pulled over. "Please, don't tell my Dad," the kid whimpered afterward. His license showed he was sixteen years old.

On another occasion, flying through the air for what seemed like an eternity, I turned my shoulder and neatly caught the impact with a backpack, saving my hide. I'm not bragging. These weren't thought-out escapes. I'd compare them to a bug's mad scramble when a rock is over-turned.

Roughly forty feet of gang line separated the sled from my lead dogs. Time slowed as Hobbes rose on her hind legs and twisted downward, drawing Khan with her. I found my hand on a snow hook, saw myself leaping, incredibly slowly, mind you, and stabbing the hill above the sled.

Life resumed its frantic pace as the entire team gleefully joined the leaders' rebellion. All nine of my dogs cascaded through the deep powdery snow, passing in a disorganized rabble on the far side of my sled. Below me, the group sorted themselves out under the pressure of the tightening gang line, which abruptly snapped the sled around.

Perched atop the hook, I braced, gripping the anchor line with both gloves. Everything rested on what happened next.

The line sprung taught.

The hook held, arresting the team's plunge.

Now what? The dogs and sled faced straight down the Quest's steepest goddamn mountain. I was scared to move. *If this hook pops . . .*

A motion from the photographer converted my paralysis into

rage. *He's responsible for this*, I decided, forgetting our troubles on the lower slope.

Feeling righteous, I screamed at him: "THE CAPTION ON THAT PHOTO OUGHT TO READ 'PHOTOGRAPHER FUCKS UP ASCENT.'"

He came rushing over. "Can I do anytink?" the German asked.

"Just stay the hell out of the way," I snapped.

I was already feeling embarrassed by my outburst. "Listen," I said, "I'm a photographer myself. I admire your hustle reaching this spot, but that's NOT the place to be standing. The dogs are distracted, you understand? Take photos from above. Understand?"

He didn't argue.

I rose, stomped the hook more firmly into the snow, and then boldly strode/slipped down the mountain, leaving the German cowering by my sled. Taking Khan and Hobbes by the neck line, I turned the leaders around and, scrambling to stay ahead, guided them back up the hillside until the gang line again stretched taught.

The brief climb left me gasping. Far above us I could see the first evening stars peeking over the summit's black rim. *Still got a nasty hill to climb here.*

I hauled on the gang line behind Khan and Hobbes until their comrades pulled the sled back around, facing uphill. All of this was done with artificial confidence owing to the silent witness and his camera. In truth, I remained wary. Disaster had been averted, but barely.

I retrieved the snow hook and shoved the sled forward. "All right, Khan. All right," I barked, giving my best imitation of a Marine drill sergeant. The dogs cooperated. We resumed the climb, but haltingly this time.

Pausing was dangerous, but I couldn't help it. I'd push for three steps, then I had to gather myself for another faint charge. Three steps, then stop. Three steps, then stop. *The Mowth would enjoy this*, I thought, smiling at Mowry's likely reaction to my miserable physical state. I could hear him crowing: "The Machine isn't just red-lining, it's shot, O'Donoghue—sucking valves, blowing oil. Face it, you're getting old!"

I couldn't let Mowry have the last word. "Go ahead, go ahead," I gasped. My voice was hardly authoritative at this point, but the dogs needed to know I was still watching them, still driving this outfit, fragile though I might feel. And I was scrutinizing Khan and Hobbes every step. My eyes never left their heels.

Our goal, the top tripod, was within reach when the trail vanished under the sand-blasting effects of the winds. The little snow that did remain here was crosshatched with snowmachine tracks. Khan and Hobbes battled each other, pulling us right, then left, then right. "Straight ahead! Straight ahead!" I shouted, reinvigorated by terror.

Onward the dogs came. Charging back down the mountain we'd so nearly conquered.

Between the big, frosty parka and his icy mustache, Nadeau towered over his dogs like a weathered statue of Joseph Stalin, at 9:30 P.M. on February 18, when his sled glided to a stop, just past the frontrunner's resting team.

The statue sprung to life, revealing a snow-caked rookie, who had been far more worried about his team's condition than he let on. That was the reason he called off the chase in Central, all but conceding the race. But Andre Nadeau's seasoned soldiers proved even tougher than their master dared hope, marching straight up and over Eagle Summit. He'd reached Mile 101 only two and a half hours behind Lee.

Nadeau's arrival caused a furor, of course, but the penetrating wind, combined with the musher's reluctance to speak English, soon tempered the excitement of the media and other race spectators. They retreated to the cabin, leaving the second-place musher huddled over his cooker. Lee awoke from his nap parched; he remained a bit dehydrated from his ordeal atop the summit. Emerging from the bunkroom in search of something to drink, he was hit with a question: "So, is Andre sleeping in there with you?"

"I didn't even know he was here," the veteran blurted. His was more surprise to learn that Nadeau had pulled in more than an hour ago. "Is he still here?"

"Oh, he's out fooling with his dogs," responded one of Nadeau's handlers.

An alarm wailed inside Bruce Lee's brain.

He got in and I didn't know it. It doesn't make sense that he's still out fooling with his dogs in this windy place. There's no way this adds up.

The musher slipped on his boots and went to see for himself.

Outside the trailer a single dog team was resting under the glaring yard lights.

You dropped your guard! He hasn't given up. He saw a window of hope and stepped right into it, Lee realized. *This won't be over until you cross the finish line.*

Nadeau's stealth put him back on the trail roughly seventy-five minutes ahead of Lee. There was an inch of fresh snow on the ground. The rookie's dogs were working hard—even before they hit Rosebud, the Quest's last mountain.

Trailing the Ghost out of Mile 101, Lee had a hunch Nadeau's move might actually backfire; those Siberians were putting down a scent for his own leaders to follow and that couldn't hurt mushing across Rosebud's long, bare ridge. But his better-rested team overtook Nadeau's near the top of the first rolling hill. The veteran ordered his leaders on by and reclaimed the Quest lead.

The other team quickly fell behind. But one of Lee's leaders balked climbing the next rise. "Oh no," he gasped. "Not again."

He was changing leaders when Nadeau mushed up from behind. The rookie executed a neat pass and continued up the mountain, giving Lee's excitable dogs something to chase. As soon the ridge leveled off, Lee's team shot ahead, reaffirming the musher's belief that fatigue wasn't the issue. *It's just a mental thing,* he observed. *You don't have that hardened leader.*

At the base of the next pitch, Lee's young leaders staged another strike. This time Nadeau hung back, electing to snack his dogs.

He's waiting to see if I can get them over, Lee realized, reading the implied challenge. *He's not going to give me a free ride.*

Lee walked forward and petted his leaders. "C'mon, guys, let's go," he said, walking on ahead. Showing off their lessons from Eagle Summit, his dogs picked themselves right up and paced their master up the slope.

It was dead calm and clear at 2:30 A.M. on February 19, when the Quest veteran mushed onto Rosebud's top ridge. The moon, entering its last quarter, cast its silvery glow across a grand expanse of surrounding valleys. But Lee's eyes were glued to his lead dogs. They were the weak point. He coaxed and praised them, using every trick, every cue he could think of to instill confidence.

Descending the mountain, Lee felt a lightness of being, an abrupt easing after nine hundred miles of mounting tension. And why not? His swift dogs had only to pad their lead on this downhill dash through the woods, then it was clear sailing to Fairbanks.

No one had briefed mushers on the glaciation unleashed by several days of wild temperature swings. Patches of ice and overflow turned the woodsy, winding trail into a careening nightmare. Small willows and alders repeatedly smacked the sides of his sled, flipping it once, twice, six times.

Picking himself off the ground after one of the latter crashes, the leader of the Quest found himself laughing at the cumulative pain. "This just isn't going to be easy, is it?"

While Lee sensed his young dogs were mentally fragile, their speed remained supreme. He hadn't even seen Nadeau since coming off the summit.

Spreading straw for his dogs behind Angel Creek Lodge, where the rules of the race mandated an eight-hour stay, the veteran ticked off the passing minutes with barely suppressed joy. *I'd like to have an hour on him*, Lee thought, reckoning that a lead of that magnitude would him the liberty of giving his dogs a break or two during the final hundred-and-ten-mile sprint for the finish.

But Nadeau dashed that hope, trailing him into the checkpoint by twenty-nine minutes.

"Well, that's probably enough," Lee said. "But we won't be stopping on the way in."

❖ ❖ ❖

Again, I flung down the hook. Stomped on it. Squatted on the twin blades. And watched the dice roll.

The bottom of the summit basin was no longer even visible. *If this breakaway succeeds*, I thought, staring into the darkness, *if we have to do this over—even if no dogs are crippled, even if this weather holds, I won't make it.*

"I flat won't make it," I repeated out loud, suddenly as tired as I was energized a moment earlier.

Dumbly, I realized the hook was holding.

The German was at my side. "Can I halp?"

My anger was exhausted, along with all pride. "Yes," I said, "you could stand on this hook. Understand? Put your foot here."

"Yes, I know," he said, "I, too, am a musher."

The comment revived my fury. *If you're a musher*, I thought, *what the hell were you doing distracting dogs halfway up a mountain?* I let it go. Leaving him by the sled, I trudged down to fetch the dogs.

This time I guided Khan and Hobbes all the way to the tripod, where we took a delicious pause. It was about 8:00 P.M. It had taken us more than five hours to go, perhaps, twenty-five miles. But I didn't care if they were slowest on the trail, my dogs stood on top of a world populated by stars dancing over a wavy black horizon. Scratching Khan behind the ears I reveled in a breeze sweeping this narrow plateau, ruffling fur on Danger and my other long-haired dogs. To my eye, they all had the bearing of champions. "All hail, the conquerors of Eagle Summit!" I shouted.

It was too dark to make out the distant valley floor, but the descent to it appeared alarmingly steep. I considered rough-locking my runners, the equivalent of putting chains on tires for traction, to slow our upcoming descent. But I hadn't seen the chain Freshwaters helped me make since Dawson, and didn't want to waste time looking for it. *Don't sweat it. These dogs are as tired as you are.*

My headlamp caught a distant marker. Pulling Khan to a likely connecting trail, I took position behind the sled and ordered the team over the edge.

The thin snow was peppered with loose rocks and patches of dirt churned by the brakes of prior teams, making for a thrilling ride. I restrained the dogs as best I could, but I had to keep laying off the brake or risk tearing it off on the rocks. Khan and Hobbes took advantage of the freedom and soon had the whole team loping down the slope.

Several lights were creeping along on a distant ridge. *Folks must be following us on the highway.* One light, particularly bright was aimed in my direction. I waved, wondering if it was a video crew. Had Fulda's army stuck around for the finish? "Nah," I said, amused at my own apparent craving for coverage.

Kate was wearing that shining light. Her doubts remained strong when the second headlamp first peeked over the ridge. "It's probably a snowmachine," she whined to Erica, who had remained behind to share Kate's lonely vigil. But the time for gloom was past. "Of course, it's Brian," Gwen's mom said, laughing and hugging my wife.

The light was certainly dimmer than the first. And the musher's decent was much, much slower this time. Then Kate actually heard my voice: "Go ahead. Go ahead, Khan," carrying across the canyon.

"Oh, Babe," she yelled. "Babe, I'm here."

The canyon acoustics didn't offer two-way communications. I saw the light tracking the team's progress from afar. That was comfort enough.

As it was, controlling the sled demanded full attention. With the runners skipping between high sides of hard-packed snow and the deep powdery trough cut by earlier teams, it wobbled crazily. I found myself gingerly straddling those runners, using my weight to counterbalance the sled's ever-changing plane of descent. It was strenuous task. My arms soon turned to lead. On the verge of losing control, I intentionally rolled the sled, then dragged, belly down, for about ten feet while it plowed a new trench.

"Whooa!" I grunted stupidly late, as if my dogs were likely to rip loose the anchor provided by the overturned sled. "I am seriously freaking thrashed," I muttered, grinning like an imbecile as I lay there in the snow.

Watching from the highway, Kate saw what she now accepted as my light blink out. She combed the dark hillside through Jim Crabb's binoculars, but couldn't penetrate the darkness. *Brian must be having trouble with his headlamp,* she decided.

The dogs, refreshed by the pause, took off the instant I righted the sled. My dance on the runners began anew. "Rock and roll," I said, enjoying the dipping, tipping ride.

My control, tenuous from the start of our descent, steadily worsened. I wasn't the least bit sleepy, but the events of the previous hours left me utterly drained. Just before the slope flattened out the sled again rolled, slamming me down hard on the icy turf.

Glancing up, I saw Search watching me with concern. "Don't worry, girl," I said, dusting myself off. "Takes more than that to kill the boss."

Nearing the valley floor, the trail became icy fast and fragmented into a broad band of parallel side-hill threads. Judging from the paw prints and runner tracks, there was no single preferred route. A sweep of my headlamp beam turned up markers affixed to nearly every scrub tree. Some were left from years past. I took comfort in the confusion: Mile 101 was definitely straight ahead.

A glare of ice stretched before us. Khan and Hobbes trotted straight across, making for the double-lined funnel ablaze with reflective markers heralding the entrance to Mile 101. Gwen's team was parked just beyond a long trailer. I stopped my dogs alongside the rusty unit, hoping it might cut down on the wind whipping through the camp.

Kate greeted me with a dazzling smile.

"How did it go?" she asked, brightly.

"Babe, I was at my limit. My absolute limit," I blurted, feeling my knees sag under weight of the passage. "Dogs turned around on me *twice* up there. I had serious doubts about making it."

My wife looked perplexed. "Gwen said it wasn't that bad."

❖ ❖ ❖

The end game had begun.

Lee, for the second time in his life, led the Yukon Quest approaching Valley Center.

He had been thirty-five years old in 1991, a man in his prime, mushing dogs that appeared unstoppable as early as Dawson. Neither Lee, nor Schandelmeier, who was then thirty-seven, regarded the third member of the Quest's front pack as a serious threat. In his patched parka and graying pig tails, Charlie Boulding looked so much older and frailer than his forty-eight years.

Coming off his eleventh- and then tenth-place finishes in the two previous Quests, the cackling trapper with the Carolina drawl had joked that he was racing because he "enjoyed pain." His dogs were so thin they looked played out from the start, particularly Lilly Mae, the lead dog named for Boulding's first wife. "She's so ugly, I was looking forward to shooting her," he'd say, a gleam in his eye. "But Lilly Mae ended up being the best dog I ever owned—because I was so hard on it, wanting it to fail."

Ol' Charlie was good company, but a threat to win? Yeah, right.

Moving up the Yukon River that year, though he possessed the fastest-trotting team, Lee played conservative. He thought he was being so crafty letting Schandelmeier's powerful young crew set the pace. As for Boulding's raggedy outfit, well, it was amazing they even managed to keep up.

Schandelmeier remained in first place leaving Angel Creek, then the last checkpoint before the finish. Lee trailed him out, reasonably confident the young dogs ahead were overdue for a fall. He was right about that. Schandelmeier was never a factor. The real adversary rose up from behind on that night already electrified by the Aurora. Ol' Charlie had set him up: He'd trained that mangy Lilly Mae and her companion Charlotte to lope.

They couldn't rock and roll the entire seventy-five miles. No dog team could sustain such abandon that close to the end of a thousand-mile race. But dropping his artful concealment of the team's true forte, Boulding called them up for short bursts, repeatedly chasing down Lee's team, then melting back into the night as he gave those hell-hounds another break. All the while, edging ever closer to the finish. Stalking the prey.

Boulding bided his time until they were past Valley Center. On the next surge, he sent Lilly Mae and Charlotte charging ahead. Bruce Lee retained hope, even then. Twenty miles from the finish line, only forty-five seconds separated the pair. But then spectators spooked Lee's leaders at a road crossing and the cackling trapper stole away for good.

Of course, Boulding's legend was just getting started. He went on to become the Quest's first two-time winner and a top contender in that richer race to Nome. None of which sweetened the taste of Bruce Lee's crushing five-minute loss. *I should have been racing Charlie way back on the Yukon*, he reminded himself yet again.

His present lead over Nadeau provided no assurance. The race route had changed in the seven years since Lee's last Quest. Instead of the straight shot from Angel Creek, the trail now dipped into North Pole, paying homage to a refinery serving as a major Quest sponsor. The detour added some thirty-five miles to the home stretch, a fearsome development for a competitor nursing Lee's memories.

As far back as Circle, Nadeau had worn a confident smile talking about his plans for the punishing final run. "I will march straight through, because I can do one hundred miles."

Lee, on the other hand, knew that was farther in one shot than his young dogs had ever been in their entire lives. On two occasions during training, he had trucked his team to North Pole and run them through to the finish line. He was hoping the memory would kick in when his dogs reached the same stretch tonight.

Many sled dogs possess a remarkable ability for recalling trails. But Lee's young leaders were unproven in that regard. Fatigue and stress might overshadow those fleeting training experiences. In addition, the musher knew, none of his dogs were going to be pleased at North Pole, where he intended to blow through an apparent checkpoint, ignoring the rituals practiced over the past thousand miles.

The trail didn't enter the actual city of North Pole. The new route took Quest teams over a dam and past a park pavilion on the outskirts of town, where mushers were expected to don their numbered bibs before continuing to the finish line in Fairbanks.

"Who's got my bib?" Lee shouted, nearing the pavilion.

A woman stepped forward from the crowd.

Lee spied the bib in her hand. He paused only long enough to grab it. "Let's go," he cried, leaving race officials and cameramen staring at his back.

A few hundred yards past the pavilion, Lee noticed his leaders were glancing backward, acting puzzled. *That's not good.*

Approaching a marked turn, Lee delayed giving the usual command, testing to see if his leaders remembered the trail. They nearly missed the turn before the musher broke his silence. *That tells me you guys don't really know where you are.*

The team's attitude seemed to improve after the trail dropped back onto the Chena River. Passing the first houses outside town, however, his leaders were distracted by the residential lights, the bonfires and the shouts from spectators on the riverbank. Suddenly, Lee's leaders left the trail, hauling for one of those exciting houses.

The musher had to stop and pull his dogs back to the trail. The incident was repeated several times, causing Lee to change and re-change his leaders. The musher tried nearly every dog in the team before he noticed that Tiger, a young female, far from discouraged, was impatiently hitting her line, pulling toward the trail. Lee had seldom used Tiger in lead, but her behavior suggested the move was overdue: *She's the one who remembers where we are.*

With young Tiger paired in lead with Hawk, a four-year-old male, Lee's team took off, flying down the river toward Fairbanks. The Ghost's threat faded with each joyous ripple in the chain stretching ahead of the musher's sled.

"No one can take this from us now. We're going to win," whispered Lee, uttering the forbidden words at last.

Another musher approaching his first-ever victory might have looked ahead, reveling in to the celebration to come. Lee's state of mind was closer to reluctance. Any minute now, he knew, all hell was going to explode.

Bruce Lee switched off his headlamp and focused on the present—willing himself to remember this moonlit moment on the frozen Chena, shared with these fine dogs, his pups all, bounding forward as one.

You'll never be here with these dogs in this place again.

By North Pole, Nadeau knew the game was up. Lee had expanded his lead to three hours. The musher from Quebec rested his dogs twenty minutes, then leisurely mushed into Fairbanks. The big prize, the Quest's $30,000 winner's check, had slipped away. But Andre Nadeau knew the satisfaction of proving critics, indeed the cream of Alaska's mushing community, wrong: His beautiful dogs hadn't folded. The

Ghost's team had risen to meet every challenge, conquered every mountain, on the Yukon Quest Trail.

The team's arrival, at 3:13 A.M. on February 20, earned Nadeau the Quest's $24,000 second-place paycheck, plus coveted honors as rookie of the year. His finish, a mere three hours, forty-six minutes, behind Lee, also more than fulfilled the goal Nadeau decreed on his pre-race questionnaire: "To finish five hours after the first musher or five minutes before the second..."

Brenda's dad, defending champ Rick Mackey, finished a distant third, nearly ten hours off Lee's pace but comfortably ahead of Schandelmeier and Turner. Paddy Santucci was next, winning new respect by finishing sixth despite being down to eight dogs as far back as Dawson. All of them were pulling as Paddy's sled crossed the finish line.

As Gwen and I greedily scarfed lukewarm plates of Chef Boy-R-Dee spaghetti at Mile 101, those top drivers and eleven other proud 1998 Quest finishers were gathered in Fairbanks eating chicken and listening to The Mowth deliver what was, by all accounts, a speech even more rambling than his usual banquet fare.

Veterinarians finally tripped up Louis Nelson in Central, holding him there until the coast was clear. Alf had come through in the clutch, marching over Eagle Summit like Rin-Tin-Tin, or maybe Lassie, on steroids. Afterward, Mowry somehow held off Carroll's eleventh-hour charge, despite favoring ribs bruised, if not busted, from the worst sled-crash in his career.

At $1,800, the paycheck was thinner than he hoped entering the race, but gratifying for a guy recently feeling bankrupt. The outcome wasn't merely fortunate, it was practically historic, or so seemed to Tim "The Mowth" Mowry, pondering his unblemished personal record as a sled-dog racer.

"This makes two Iditarods and seven Quests without a single scratch," declared the driver of the fourteenth-place team in the 1998 Quest, pounding the podium with a beer for emphasis.

No one could take that from *him*, either.

A DOG NAMED NIGEL

15

KHAN IN LEAD

Entering the Quest, Bill Steyer felt his dogs were capable of placing in the top half of the field, possibly one of the top fifteen paying spots. By the evening of February 21, however, those goals were beyond reach. Bragging rights were all that remained for Bill and the eight other mushers holding positions eighteen through twenty-six at the tail end of the 1998 Quest field.

Bill, showing the drive that propelled him to a ninth-place finish in Fairbanks' grueling Equinox Marathon the previous fall, aimed to mush the eighteenth dog team across the finish line.

He faced a major disadvantage. His team's layover at Angel Creek was to be an hour longer owing to the time penalty assessed for leaving Bunko at Stepping Stone, some five hundred miles back. To reduce that penalty's bite, Bill rested just four hours before striking out alone for Rosebud.

It galled Brenda Mackey to watch Bill pack, but fatigue had dampened the teen's competitive fire. She stumbled through her chores, returned to the trailer, and promptly fell asleep on the floor.

Amy Wright was already sprawled on a mattress. She awoke to find Brenda shivering on the floor nearby. "I'm so cold. I'm so cold," the young musher chattered in her sleep, reminding Amy of a motherless puppy. She hauled Brenda onto the mattress beside her and both women fell back asleep.

Thus Bill gained a two-hour lead over Brenda, Rusty, Tetz, Keith, and Amy. But the group subsequently shaved an hour off his team's time crossing Rosebud, which placed all six on roughly even footing at the checkpoint one hundred and ten miles from the finish line.

Walter lingered at Mile 101. He was smarting from Rusty's outburst and rude comments from other members of the so-called "Party Pack." At this point, he didn't care if he beat them. He felt nothing for those people but distaste. His wife Nancy, the team handler, and the dogs provided all the company Walter Palkovitch needed or wanted.

Unaware of the seething resentments, the press dubbed Rusty's group the Magnificent Seven. At Angel Creek, lodge owner Annette kept using the nickname and it rubbed Brenda the wrong way. That math was all wrong: Bill and Walter weren't part of anything, and Gwen and I were too far behind.

As the eight-hour clock expired, mid-afternoon on February 22, Rusty led the back pack's charge toward Fairbanks. Streaking away from Angel Creek, he left Brenda with nothing to chase but runner tracks. She plugged along just ahead of Tetz, while Bill killed the last minutes of his penalty hour.

Bill overtook the pair about five miles out of Angel Creek. Passing them both, he set his sights on catching Rusty.

Watching Bill disappear into the thick forest, Brenda again

swallowed disappointment. *Whatever.* She'd been around dog racing long enough to know there's always another day to settle scores.

Only a few miles down the trail, however, Brenda glimpsed her quarry. By nightfall, her leaders were dogging Bill's heels. She had to ride her brake to keep from passing him, which Brenda now realized she ought not to do. The youngest of the Mushing Mackeys finally had Bill Steyer's team figured out.

Rusty beat the others in and out of North Pole. Tetz was next, followed by Brenda. A miscue in a parking lot some twenty miles before had again dropped Bill behind, but only seconds separated all three.

While veterinarians inspected the trio's dogs at North Pole, other Quest volunteers helped mushers don their numbered race bibs.

"One of those dogs ate the other's fish," a woman told Brenda, pointing to Bill's team.

"Well, I don't care," the teen snapped. "It's not my dog."

What she cared about was beating Bill into town.

Brenda took Tetz aside to share her insight. "Bill's got chase leaders. If we're ahead of him on the river and get our dogs really going on the turns," she explained," he won't have a chance to keep up."

Less than fifteen minutes elapsed before the three were ready to go.

Bill had seen Brenda and Tetz whispering. "Would you mind if I fell in behind Thomas?" he casually asked Brenda.

Like hell, she thought, but kept that to herself.

Leaving North Pole, Tetz's dogs tangled. Brenda shot in front. She was poised to lead all three teams onto the river when Sky, eager for another piece of ass, nudged Camaro off course and up a bank. Tetz surged back ahead, tailed by Bill. That was the order when Brenda rolled up from behind.

"Bill," she shouted. "Trail!"

"What did you say?" blurted Bill, who hadn't heard a formal demand to pass since the early days of the race. He couldn't believe he was hearing it now from Brenda. *Doesn't she know my team is faster?*

"Trail," she repeated firmly.

Quest Rule No. 7, concerning "Standard Race Courtesy," states that a team caught from behind must relinquish the trail upon request at any point outside "no-man's land," as the final mile of a sled dog race is traditionally known.

More irritated than anything, Bill stopped his team. He'd be re-passing the girl soon enough.

The instant she was clear, Brenda called up those seven dogs of hers and sprinted away from Bill's nine.

Where'd she get that speed? Bill wondered, giving chase.

Tetz remained in front but his leaders were faltering. So Brenda passed him, too. All three teams were loping as she led the boys onto the Chena River. Bill was enjoying himself, reveling in this competition down the stretch, when Lemon suddenly squatted to take a crap.

"We'll never catch them now," the musher groaned, watching the headlights vanish around the bend.

Rosebud's lofty ridge terrified Gwen. The expansive view awakened her fear of heights, kindling incipient dread that grew with each new rolling rise, because Gwen had heard that Rosebud's descent came without warning. Her twelve dogs remained so wildly powerful the musher feared she was racing toward disaster.

Call it a sixth sense, but Gwen *knew* the killer hill when she came upon it. She halted Taco and Hootch well back from the edge. Ignoring the team's "Rah! Rah! Rah!" barking frenzy, Gwen ran to scout the slope.

"Holy shit," she said, surveying the water bottles, snack baggies, and other debris strewn from tumbling sleds. "I am NOT going down there with twelve dogs. I'm just not doing it."

Gwen turned four of her most loyal dogs loose—rules be damned—and unhooked tugs from several others. At first, the freed dogs looked uncertain, even panicky. But they were soon sniffing busily and, tails wagging, followed their mates off the mountain. For once driving a team she could actually control, Gwen found the fearsome descent positively enjoyable.

The success of her "big naughty move," as Gwen cheerfully labeled it, was confirmed when those loose dogs rejoined their mates at the bottom of the hill.

Now entering familiar country, Taco and Hootch were smoking in lead. Gwen's team flew through the icy sections and everything else, putting her on pace to record one of the fastest times from Mile 101.

The pair's confidence showed as they boldly swung the team to the right at a junction of several well-traveled trails. Gwen wondered at their choice—seeing no Quest markers any direction—but then she spied a metal reflective sign. "Angel Creek Cabins," it proclaimed, "6 miles."

The distance was a bit farther than Gwen expected, but wasn't that a Quest trademark? Counting down the miles, Gwen found the lack of familiar markers annoying, but then who could get lost with permanent reflectors gleaming from what seemed to be every third tree. "Those guys must have figured we didn't need any help," she decided.

The reflectors guided her to a cluster of empty state park cabins. "Oh, no," Gwen said, realizing she'd just made a twelve-mile error.

Gwen stayed calm, determined to think matters through. Her dogs had come a long way this morning and the weather was heating up fast. Hootch and Taco wouldn't be happy about a quick turn around. She resolved to stay thirty minutes, tossing out snacks, pretending life was grand.

It occurred to Gwen that her untimely detour held a potential benefit.

"Maybe Brian will get far enough ahead of me that I'll get the Red Lantern."

The more Gwen rolled that one over, the better it felt.

Neither Gwen nor I knew it, but we had unexpected competition in the sorry scramble for the Quest booby prize. The new contender for the Red Lantern had already toured the finish line that morning, but couldn't officially cross it.

Bill had rebounded from Lemon's untimely dump to overtake Tetz. But both mushers were having leader troubles. They leapfrogged toward town in a series of messy passes.

Around midnight, Tetz noticed a disturbing wobble in one of his dogs. Not wanting to take any chances, he stopped and loaded Nigel, the faltering pooch. Not long afterward, Tetz again caught and re-passed Bill, then he slammed to a sudden halt.

"My God," he cried, peering inside his sled bag. "My dog's run off!"

"I've lost a dog," Tetz repeated, looking stricken in the glare of Bill's headlamp. "What should I do?"

"That's not good, Thomas. Not good," Bill said. "I guess you should wait here, or go back and find your dog."

Bill continued down the river mushing on auto-pilot; the beauty of his own finish shattered by passing what felt like a horrible roadside accident.

Thomas Tetz didn't kid himself. Nigel wasn't coming back. The dog had been a late addition and remained skittish. He, too, continued toward the finish line. He didn't know where else to go.

Rusty lived just off the river in North Pole. His leaders weren't happy about passing up familiar side trails, any one of which, they knew, would have taken them straight to their beloved houses at T.L.C. Kennel. With each missed shortcut, Rusty's team slowed another notch. He was barely moving when Brenda's team closed from behind.

"Why don't you go ahead of me," Rusty said, turning to face the approaching driver.

"No," Brenda said, "you led most of the way from Angel Creek. I'm just going to stay behind you."

"That's not fair," said Rusty, flashing his toothy grin. "You've obviously got the faster team. Doesn't make any difference to me."

So it was that Brenda Mackey become first among the last, crossing the Quest finish line shortly before 2:00 A.M., fourteen days, thirteen hours and forty-seven minutes after leaving Whitehorse.

Brenda stood by and welcomed Rusty with a hug. Afterward, she tossed out liver snacks to every dog in both of their teams. She hung around the chute, rooting for Tetz to appear next on the river. She was disappointed, a half-hour later, when Bill mushed the twentieth team across the Quest finish line.

Bill didn't mention the dilemma confronting Tetz. He had given that a lot of thought and finally decided that he didn't want to be the one to call attention to a problem that might result in another musher's disqualification.

Thus Brenda and Rusty were shocked, along with everyone else, when the stalwart German showed up, twenty minutes later, mushing one dog too few.

The rules left race officials no discretion: Tetz couldn't check into Fairbanks unless he had all ten of the dogs he took out of North Pole. The stunned musher parked his team alongside the finish-line chute.

"Jeez," whispered Brenda, who couldn't believe the sudden shadow falling across their glorious, long-anticipated, at times seemingly impossible Quest finish. *Thomas looks crushed and who wouldn't be?*

Rusty, ever practical, gathered his spare dog food and presented it to Tetz. He presumed, and rightly, the group's Ironman wouldn't just give up. Tetz had to find his dog, that's all.

I had planned to cap training with a run over Rosebud to Mile 101. Mowry argued against it. "You don't want to traumatize your team O'D," he said. "Believe me, Rosebud isn't something your dogs are going to want to see a second time."

Describing the trail, he grinned evilly: "You keep thinking this has got to be the top, but you're wrong. You'll see another ridge in the distance and think: '*No way* can the trail go *up there*.' But it always does. Over and over and over."

Recalling The Mowth's dire predictions, I changed my mind about dropping Cinder and Scrim. Neither was looking strong, but they had made it over Eagle Summit and the incident with Luther left me paranoid about freak injuries.

The actual climb wasn't terribly steep, but Mowry was right: It went on forever. Cinder and Scrim, meanwhile, not only weren't pulling, they were limping. *You'll be loading them next and it serves you right.*

Khan was in single lead as we chugged past the last trees, beyond the low brush, out onto a long rolling ridge towering over neighboring peaks and valleys. The low morning sun rained burning arrows, igniting countless twinkling crystals in the surrounding hills. Parking the team on the crest, I dug out my last bag of whitefish and snacked the crew. *What a day!*

Throwing my arms wide, I slowly twirled in place, opening myself to the balmy wind and stretching my fingers over the vast world below. "Tim, my man," I shouted, recalling my old roommate's sourpuss description of this passage. "Did you ever happen to catch the view!"

The drop off Rosebud was thrilling, but I kept the sled upright and somehow avoided overrunning Hobbes and Feets in wheel. Descending through the woods, I whistled Khan up and he broke into a lope. That didn't last, of course, and it was just as well. Patches of glacial overflow made for treacherous footing and I couldn't afford to additional injuries. Scrim and Cinder, though they looked stronger with the mountain behind us, were definitely headed home as soon as we hit the lodge. That meant I was down to seven dogs for the finish-line drive. *Gwen only has, what, twelve dogs still? Thank God, it's downhill all the way to town. No, that's not true. But it's mostly flat anyway.*

Near the bottom of the valley, the trail broadened, showing signs of heavy snowmachine traffic. The day was heating up fast. Too fast for my liking. These trails were made for speed. Figuring there was nothing to lose, I moved Danger into lead with Khan.

"Let's go home," I cried.

Danger yanked Khan into a seldom-seen higher gear. I saw the looming form of Angel Rocks, landmark site of Kate's first kiss from her favorite musher, and a stone's throw from the namesake lodge.

Before I knew it, lodge owner Steve Verbanac, a familiar cranky face, was chiding me about parking the team in an undisturbed section of snow, a practice beneficial for the dogs, which he construed as unnecessarily spreading Angel Creek's burgeoning Quest mess. A small voice came to the rescue.

"MY Daddy!" Rory cried from his perch in a backpack kiddie carrier shouldered by my bodacious wife, who'd just received word we were in.

My heart soared hearing his cheerful voice. I plucked him out of Kate's backpack, feeling stronger than I had in days. "Who's this?" I asked, pointing to the closest dog.

"Feets!" Rory shouted.

"And this?"

"Hobbes!"

"Where's Daddy?" Kate asked, joining in the fun.

"On the trail," Rory Patrick declared triumphantly.

Later, inside the lodge, Kate drew my attention to our usually bold toddler shyly cozying up to Gwen, who was encamped with her family in a nearby booth.

"He definitely has a thing for blondes," I said, between bites of a cheeseburger.

"Like his father?"

"Only the one in front of me."

His own race completed, Bill Steyer's considerate nature reasserted itself. He called the lodge to give Gwen a pep talk.

"Don't drag it out," he said, urging Gwen to scrap her usual rest schedule and run the team straight into town. "You can do it. Your team is stronger than mine. And it's worth it."

Gwen appreciated the advice, which matched what she'd heard from Schandelmeier before the race. The notion of running dogs one hundred miles straight still frightened her, but the end *was* in sight. After all, she was in the Quest to learn, to experiment.

Kate and Rory left for home. I headed off for a nap. When I awakened Mowry was hovering over the team. My old friend and coach, now filling in as handler, had been studying my packing job, with an eye to shedding weight.

"Get rid of that cooker, O'Donoghue. And what are you doing carrying two snow hooks? You're done camping. This is a race, or have you forgotten that?"

Actually, the spirit of competition among the last teams on the trail had never been keener.

The search for the dog Nigel, which expanded into the air with the assistance of army helicopters, had raged most of the day. A harnessed sled dog couldn't remain at large for long in Fairbanks. But the fugitive might freeze Tetz in place until that Red Lantern had his name on it.

I was in the bar with Mowry, sipping a good luck beer when Annette got a call from Quest headquarters.

"I guess they returned the dog to that poor musher," the bartender said afterward. "But they say he's so worn from it all—he's out there camping on the river tonight. They don't expect him to cross the finish line until tomorrow."

"You gotta be kidding?"

"No, no, that's what they're saying."

"So Tetz is camping on the river," I said, "within miles of the finish line."

"Something like fifteen miles out," the bartender said.

It defied belief, but there it was: Tetz was sleeping, in a near coma of fatigue for all we knew, an hour or two shy of victory in the last race left, the race to avoid the damn lantern. *A gift from the gods? Or is he taunting us?*

I didn't care. I pictured Peter O'Toole playing blue-eyed Lawrence—urging Bedouins to take on the Turks. *What was it he said? "Nothing is written!"*

Despite her detour, Gwen had beaten me into Angel Creek by twenty minutes. She was free to leave at 10:20 P.M.

As the hour approached, Steve, in his official capacity as Angel Creek's checker, roared off on a snowmachine to inspect a troublesome river crossing close by. He found the trail awash in knee-deep water, a hazard that might yet worsen, raising the possibility both teams would be soaked in the first mile. While Steve and Annette, not to mention the lodge's regular patrons, wouldn't have minded watching rough, tough Quest mushers take a dunk, protecting the dogs took priority. Taking everything into consideration, Steve decreed that Gwen and I should leave together at 11:00 P.M. and follow the road out, crossing the river on a bridge before rejoining the Quest Trail. The Mowth and a handful of able-bodied, albeit intoxicated, volunteers were recruited to stop traffic while the last Quest teams commenced their duel.

The plan suited Gwen, who wouldn't have made it out on time anyway.

As the appointed hour approached, Khan was growling and pawing the snow behind the lodge.

"You got your money's worth in that dog," Mowry said, impressed to see such fire in a leader nine hundred miles into the race.

"Oh yeah, he's everything Plettner promised," I said, referring to the

Iditarod friend who leased me Khan for $500. "But you know, I have a hunch I might have done better if he got hurt early on, forcing me to use the other leaders. Khan's slower than dirt."

"Shoot, he got you this far."

He had me there.

Hootch's happy trill carried above the raucous barking of his friends. Gwen was leaving two dogs behind: sore-wristed Ruffian and Frost, who'd gotten so fat over the trip he was having trouble keeping up. She was fooling with her sled when the digital dial read 11:00:00 and I pulled the hook.

"We've got the lead," I shouted to Mowry. "For five minutes, anyway."

A few cheers rang out as the Savage One stormed past the lodge. I was now down to seven dogs, having finally bid good-bye to Scrim and Cinder, but the team felt strong coming off the eight-hour break. The moment we hit the pavement, however, Khan dropped into a meandering plod. Gwen rolled past before we even reached the bridge.

I stopped the team after we gained the woods. *Here goes nothing,* I figured, shifting Cyclone and Danger into lead. Khan, stung by the demotion, whined pitifully. "Sorry, my friend," I said, rubbing the black hackles rising from his thick neck. "I've gotta give it a shot."

In the second half of the Two Rivers 200, Danger and Cyclone put the team into overdrive on this same trail, passing four or five teams as we burned through the first thirty-five miles. Danger lost it at that point, diving between trees. But a good thirty-mile dash might make the difference tonight. We were bound for Two Rivers, my backyard, where Gwen faced a hundred chances to peel off on another side trail, perchance going far enough astray for me to skate through.

On cue, Danger surged like champion. We soared ten feet in what felt like a single maniacal bound. Then Cyclone landed on his heels, skidding forward on his butt. I stopped and petted both leaders, rubbed their bellies and tried again. But the little guy with the sore toes remained mutinous.

"Aw, damn, Cyke, you want her to get away?"

He slunk in the snow, eyeing me warily.

I don't need this. Cyclone occasionally responds to persuasion. I dropped to my knees and bit the little bastard on the ear. He yelped and shied away. I took him by the collar and forced him to look at me. "No more bullshit. When I say go, we go. Right!"

Danger was bouncing in place, restrained only by the gang line.

"Good dog," I said, petting him. I petted Cyclone too. Both leaders were wagging their tails as I returned to the sled.

"All right!"

Cyclone sat down again. "You win," I said wearily.

The gang line stretched rigid as steel from Danger. He looked like an honest-to-God lead dog. *Why not take a chance?*

I shifted Cyclone inside the team, leaving Doc May's Psycho holding the point on his own. "You've been waiting for this, haven't you?" Danger was panting happily, his wide mouth gaping like a wolf ready to feed. *I should have tried this to start with.*

Gripping the handlebar tightly in one hand, I reached for the snow hook with the other. The team shot forward. My sled floated, maybe, one hundred yards, before Danger streaked off into the woods, entwining teammates in a half-dozen trees before I managed to stop.

"You son of a bitch," I cried, stomping up to untangle the mess.

A couple I knew from the newspaper were parked overlooking a lonely road crossing at 2:00 A.M. Rod and Julie couldn't hear it over the pickup's engine, which was running to provide heat, but a jingling, panting sound was gaining strength in the snow-blanketed forest. Suddenly, a tiny headlamp came floating from the trees. Jumping out of the pickup, the pair watched Mighty Khan march his diminished band across the pavement.

"Hey, Gwen come thorough yet?"

"About forty-five minutes ago," said Julie.

"You're kidding," I said. "Forty-five minutes?"

"At least."

We've come about thirty-five miles, meaning we still have twice that far to go.

"Looking grim, boys and girls," I said. "Git up Khan, git up."

The Mowth had talked me into dumping extra booties, batteries, tools, the second snow hook, the cooker and most of my dog food at Angel Creek. We left packing virtually nothing but a few meal pans and snacks for this final sprint to the finish. Mowry's strategy called for grabbing some hot water at Valley Center, something only locals and longtime Quest racers realized was available, to brew a homestretch drink for the dogs.

Four days after Lee's victory, however, the store had abandoned its announced twenty-four-hour Quest schedule. *Where do I get water now?* I wondered as I paused across from Valley Center's darkened windows, doling out snacks. I couldn't melt snow, not without that pot sitting back at Angel Creek. *How about chopping a hole in the ice? That might work when I get to the river,* I decided, making rough calculations on how to best stretch those juicy whitefish chunks.

Rod and Julie had raced ahead to intercept us. "So how'd Gwen look?" I asked, giving the dogs another few minutes to finish their snacks.

"We didn't get a good look because she never stopped," Julie said. "But her team seemed pretty strong to me."

"That's not what I wanted to hear."

We all laughed.

"Brian should be here within the hour," some fool affiliated with the local visitors center informed listeners of KFAR, the Fairbanks talk radio station.

"What drugs is he eating?" I blurted. "Jesus. Does he think I've been saving my real leaders? Holding back for some lightning sprint to the finish?"

The rants drew curious looks from Danger and Feets. "Good dogs," I said soothingly. "Good dogs, go ahead."

I'd been listening to the station's coverage on the Walkman with a sinking feeling.

Tetz had roused himself and cruised into town, finishing the race at 8:00 A.M. on February 24.

Gwen hadn't gotten lost. She hadn't run into a vicious moose, or fallen into the river, or any of the other possibilities to which I'd been clinging these last few hours. Taco, Hootch, and their seven rowdy friends never faltered. At 9:35 A.M., after fifteen days, twenty-one hours on the trail, Gwen Holdman had earned her Quest finisher's patch, a feat I was then twenty miles shy of matching. *Good for you, girl.*

Our race was, in fact, over by North Pole, where I trailed Gwen by nearly an hour. Like most everyone else, she was in and out of the pavilion in about ten minutes, stopping only long enough to wolf down a pair of hot dogs. After running sixty-five miles on hardly any rest, I pulled into the pavilion's glaring lights riddled with doubts.

Searchlight looked shaky and flopped the instant the team halted. I remained worried until her ears perked at the rustling of the snack bag. She was still game.

"They all look fine," the vet pronounced.

"I'm the one who's hurting. You guys wouldn't have any coffee, would you?"

They led me inside. I was tempted to ask if they had water for the dogs. But a demand for the same resulted in a musher's disqualification the year before. *Only 35 miles to go.* Again I mentally counted the whitefish. *Got at least three chunks apiece.*

Thirty minutes later, my dogs had transformed themselves into tight balls, which pulsed with each breath. I slid a thermos of fresh java into the sled's rear pocket, then adjusted my headlamp and gloves. The dogs would have usually been watching by now, but none stirred. *You may have screwed up stopping here.*

"On your feet," I said, uncertain what might happen.

The dogs uncurled and began stretching. They were all standing before I even called "ready," the signal to snap the gang line tight. At the head of the line, Khan's hackles bristled and he glanced back, anxious as always.

"How do you like that dog in front?" I asked the vet.

He smiled.

Winding along the Chena River toward town reminded me of traveling on an Amtrak train between Washington, D.C., and New York: a long voyeuristic ride overlooking backyards and the dirtiest parts of every city. The Fairbanks I glimpsed above the banks of the river looked dingy, and oddly foreign.

At the moment predicted for my arrival, I was dragging the curs away from Tetz's overnight camp, which Khan had gleefully invaded, sniffing for leftovers. The owner of the nearest house, another musher, observed my troubles and came down to the river.

"How far is it to the finish line anyway?"

"A good fifteen miles from here."

"You could do me a big favor," I said, already astride the sled. "Call those idiots at the radio station and tell them where we're at. I hate the thought of people waiting around. Tell them I'm doing, like, five miles an hour here, not twenty."

"Yeah, we heard them talking about it," the musher said, grinning at the sight of Khan's lumbering gait.

We were losing the race with the sun. Hour by hour I watched the fireball inching higher, feeling the temperature on the river climb as it nibbling away at the protective shadows. *These dogs could really use a drink,* I realized, watching Hobbesey gobbling snow. The ice on this river appeared several feet thick—unless I chanced upon the perfect spot chopping a hole would take forever.

Passing out the last of our whitefish, about 11:00 A.M., I eyed houses overlooking the river, wondering how someone might react to a musher knocking at the door with an empty cooler in hand. *So much for self-sufficiency, eh? Quest musher shows his ability to survive against all odds.*

Luther and Search, the youngest dogs left in my team, were too dumb to eat snow. Each time we stopped, I pulled on their fur, making sure it snapped back, demonstrating they were still hydrated. I was thinking I might have to shut down for the afternoon when a breeze picked up, cooling things down considerably. The draft soon had me digging for better gloves and slipping on the parka I'd thought was packed for the duration. I've never been so glad to be cold, deliciously cold; Khan and the crew were again prancing.

Passing under the first of the bridges downtown, Danger, whom I had paired with Hobbes in wheel, began pulling furiously. May's **Quest** veteran *knew.*

As the finish-line banners came into view, Danger's attitude spread, challenging Khan's supremacy. I had to ride the brake hard to keep the surging upstarts from overtaking my plodding hero. Cyclone, contrary as ever, ducked under the gang line and crowded Feets, adding an asymmetrical bulge to my short string.

Kate was waiting at the end of the chute.

"I made it," I cried, stopping the team short.

"Cross the finish line," someone shouted.

I lifted my toe, releasing the brake, and Khan led the twenty-sixth dog team into the Quest finish chute, exactly sixteen days, nine minutes after leaving Whitehorse. I reached up and slapped the banner, as I once slapped a burl arch in Nome. That was another life—lacking the golden rewards of hugging Kate and Rory in the shadow of the Cushman Street bridge.

A Native woman slipped through the crowd and presented me with a satiny black, four-foot-long, piece of whale's baleen, something appropriate for a museum, or diced into tiny pieces of jewelry. Hand painted in yellow on one side were the words: "Yukon Quest 1998."

"I thought there should be something for the last musher," said the woman, rendering me speechless with her generosity. She disappeared before I could get her name.

The completion of the journey, so long in coming, felt surreal: I was watching as someone else petted my dogs, accepted the congratulations from my friends, then held my son bouncing in his arms answering questions from reporters and cameramen. Familiar faces blurred past: Jack, Rattles, Crabb, Race Marshal Dave Rich, and Judge Joe May, all of them hooting and clapping, along with fellow mushers Rusty Hagan, Dave Dalton, Mowry.

Gwen was standing in her trademark green parka on the far side of the chute, looking a bit lost without her dogs.

Kate, finally freed from the burdensome race rules, entrusted Rory to friends and danced between the dogs, cooing and stroking her original babies. My wife knew the way to win a tough sled dog's heart: She threw each of them a thick raw steak. Hobbesey choked hers down in about three bites.

Eel Man pulled me back to earth, or to the frozen Chena, anyway. "This is for you," the Alaska's Quest president said, handing me a shiny new red lantern.

Iditarod's booby prize is topped by a golden dog whose paint would sizzle if the lantern were ever lit. And that would take a major overhaul, because a plastic logo from a sponsoring bank sits where the wick ought rightly be. This new lantern, manufactured by Fairbanks' own Wilbur Brothers Sheet Metal, consisted of a boxy, glass-faced reflector, powered by a single candle. Less fancy, perhaps, but a working lantern—making it a fitting memento of the Yukon Quest.

"It's cool," I said, hoisting the lantern so folks could see it.

"Someone else was supposed to get it though," I told Eel Man. "I'm pretty sure this is some kind of mistake."

EPILOGUE

Being a former sportswriter, The Mowth is a self-proclaimed statistical authority. "You better get your ass moving," he told me early in the race, "because it's already been done, O'Donoghue. I can't remember the guy's name, but you're not setting any records with another red lantern. It's been done."

As far as I was concerned, that settled it.

So when reporters at the finish line lined up to ask how it felt to make history by finishing last in both of the mushing world's premiere events, I smiled and said, "You better check your facts, some other guy already did it."

Calls were made to the headquarters of each race organization. The names of last-place finishers in twenty-six Iditarods and fifteen Quests were faxed and compared. The result was headlined in the February 25 issue of the *News-Miner:* "He stands alone with second red lantern."

Thus my ineptitude took on historic proportions.

And I never saw it coming—which serves me right for relying upon a Mowry fact.

❖ ❖ ❖

I took one last run with Khan. Refreshed by a week off, the old leader was at his rip-roaring finest, pushing ten miles an hour as he romped down the old training trail, executing turns with undreamed precision.

Driving an empty sled, something I hadn't attempted in more than a thousand miles, added a thrilling edge. Dropping onto a lake, I caromed off a berm and took flight, overturning the sled as I crashed upon the ice. Khan and his eight Quest-hardened companions gleefully dragged the boss some three hundred yards.

"How's this for a last-place Quest team?" I shouted, belly surfing past an open-mouthed skier.

The next day I sent Khan home to Lynda Plettner's with a friend bound for the start of Iditarod.

Not long afterward, I loaded Martin and Luther in the dog truck and returned them to Dave Dalton, the Quest's eleventh-place finisher, who was already making plans for 1999. Cyclone and Topher remained within petting distance across the road at the McKee's.

With the exception of big Toph, whom I would've gladly hauled to a glue factory, each parting was like losing a member of the family.

❖ ❖ ❖

A trophy is a trophy. I brought the Quest's Red Lantern to Award Maker, a local trophy shop, and had my name and trail time inscribed on it.

When I returned for my hard-won prize, an Athabascan Indian couple was at the counter, picking up awards for the spring carnival dog races in Galena.

"You got that red lantern in the Quest? The Yukon Quest?"

"That's right," I said.

We admired the lantern together. Then Carl Huntington introduced himself and I found myself embarrassed. A Red Lantern, no matter how nicely dressed up, holds no luster in the presence of Huntington, past champion of the Iditarod, the Fur Rendezvous, and the Open North American.

"I bet you don't have any of these at home," I said.

"Oh, I won the red lantern the first time I raced in the North American," Huntington said. He paused while I digested that, then he smiled and added: "But you know the next year I won that race."

"So there is hope?"

We laughed.

Before we parted, I told Galena's old champion driver about Danger's subsequent adventure.

When several younger dogs faltered on longer training runs, Doc May began having second thoughts about Danger's banishment. Though he'd vowed to never give him the chance to screw up another race, May missed that darn dog.

One of his handlers met me at the Quest finish line and snatched Danger for possible inclusion in Doc's Iditarod team. It'd been done before. Charlie Boulding, for one, took four dogs from his third-place Quest team in 1992 and finished the Iditarod with them a few weeks later. It's not common, however, and in this age of animal-rights scrutiny, subjecting dogs to back-to-back thousand-mile races invites trouble from race veterinarians.

But Mark May, a three-time Quest finisher making his first bid at the race won by his father in 1980, was a renowned sled-dog vet. And he knew that Danger, for all his misadventures, was a supreme athlete.

Danger came off the Quest Trail with a cut pad and looked disturbingly thin for an athlete about to embark upon a thousand-mile race. With round-the-clock feedings, Doc packed another eleven pounds back on Psycho Dog's frame before the Iditarod started on March 7.

Less than two weeks after crossing the Quest finish line, Danger was Nome-bound.

Wary of Danger's past antics, Doc May ran him mostly in the middle ranks of the team. Trailing another team out of Shaktoolik, where the Iditarod Trail stretched across the sea ice of Norton Sound, May couldn't resist. He put Danger in lead with Marsh, a full-blood brother from another litter. Nothing crazy happened. So, when another leader developed a sore shoulder, May again turned to Danger, this time on the gradual, grinding climb up Topkok. It was like giving the team a turbo boost.

May's dogs screamed up the coast, propelling their driver into Iditarod's coveted top twenty, as well as earning him the 1998 Rookie of the Year Award. Standing under the burl arch in Nome, Doc said his dogs deserved the glory, particularly that Quest-hardened "iron dog."

Huntington's mirth faded as he listened. Then he spoke with the reverence all players share for the immortals of their game.

"There should be a *special* award for a dog like that."

Indeed.

I was proud of Danger. But his terrific run with May thrust me into a funk. *I got, what, forty miles out of Danger in lead? What if I'd used him more?*

Such is the curse of long-distance mushing. A guy is lucky to even cross the finish line before the little voice inside begins rehashing those poorly chosen camps, untimely naps, mistakes made packing—all the numerous ways you, the coach, failed those fine friends up front.

The voice is relentless and seductive, whispering things you might try differently—next time.

—Two Rivers, Alaska
February 1999

1998 Yukon Quest International Sled Dog Race Standings

Position Musher	Total Time-days, hours, minutes	Prize	Scratched:	At:
1 Bruce Lee	11:11:27	$30,000	Cor Guimond	Fortymile
2 Andre Nadeau*	11:15:13	24,000	Tony Blanford	Stewart River
3 Rick Mackey	11:21:09	18,000	Dieter M. Dolif	Stewart River
4 John Schandelmeier	11:22:19	12,000	John F. Nash	Stepping Stone
5 Frank Turner	12:01:25	8,000	Terry McMullin	Stepping Stone
6 Paddy Santucci	12:03:08	6,000	Dan Turner	Pelly Crossing
7 William Kleedehn	12:03:40	5,000	Jim Hendrick	Pelly Crossing
8 Keizo Funatsu	12:04:53	4,200	Stan Njootli	Pelly Crossing
9 Brian MacDougall	12:05:44	3,700	Mike King	Pelly Crossing
10 Doug Harris	12:06:33	3,300	Kurt Smith	McCabe Creek
11 Dave Dalton	12:06:41	2,900	Ned Cathers	Pelly Crossing
12 Jerry Louden	12:08:48	2,500	Michael Hyslop	Carmacks
13 Dave Olesen*	12:09:36	2,100		
14 Tim Mowry	12:23:10	1,800		
15 Larry Carroll	13:00:11	1,500		
16 Louis Nelson, Sr.*	13:03:45			
17 Aliy Zirkle*	13:21:40			
18 Brenda Mackey*	14:13:47			
19 Rusty Hagan*	14:13:48			
20 Bill Steyer*	14:14:39			
21 Keith Kirkvold*	14:15:13			
22 Walter Palkovitch*	14:15:41			
23 Amy Wright*	14:17:04			
24 Thomas Tetz*	15:20:09			
25 Gwen Holdman*	15:21:35			
26 Brian O'Donoghue*	16:00:04	Red Lantern		

* Yukon Quest Rookie

INDEX